assau

WIEN

Lambach

Gmunden

Bad Ischl

Mariazell

Wiener Neustadt

Bruck a. d. Mur

Leoben

Judenburg

Graz

Spielfeld

Villach

Klagenfurt

Austria

McGRAW-HILL POCKET TRAVEL GUIDES

AUSTRIA ★ THE BRITISH ISLES ★ FRANCE
SPAIN ★ ITALY ★ WESTERN GERMANY

In preparation
PARIS

★ THE WORLD IN COLOUR SERIES ★
ITALY ★ THE PARIS WE LOVE
THE PROVINCES OF FRANCE ★ SCANDINAVIA
SPAIN AND PORTUGAL
SOUTH AND CENTRAL AFRICA
NORTH AFRICA

In preparation
GREECE ★ SWITZERLAND ★ GERMANY

Austria

EDITED BY
DORÉ OGRIZEK

McGRAW-HILL PUBLISHING COMPANY LIMITED

NEW YORK LONDON TORONTO

AUSTRIA
Copyright 1955

Text prepared under the direction of
DOMINIQUE LE BOURG *and* JEAN DESTERNES

Illustrations by
BEN ★ J.-A. CARLOTTI ★ PIERRE NOEL
JACQUES POIRIER

Maps by
AUBRY ★ ANDRÉ JUNG ★ JACQUES LIOZU
JACQUEMOT

Statistics by
HERVE MAISTER

Translated by
WALTER LONGHURST

*We should like to acknowledge with thanks the assistance given by
Dr W. Bauer of the Austrian State Tourist Department*

Printed in the Netherlands

CONTENTS

BY READING ACROSS, THE APPROXIMATE EQUIVALENTS OF CURRENCIES LISTED CAN BE COMPARED

U.S.A. Dollars Cents	U.K. £ sh. d.	DENMARK Kroner Øre	NORWAY Kroner Øre	SWEDEN Kronor Øre	AUSTRIA Schillings Groschen	BELGIUM Francs Centimes	FRANCE Francs	GERMANY West-marks Pfennig	ITALY Lire	NETHERLANDS Florins cents	PORTUGAL Escudos Centav.	SPAIN Pesetas Centesimos	SWITZERLAND Francs Centimes
0.01	0-0-1	0.07	0.07	0.05	0.25	0.50	3	0.04	6	0.04	0.29	0.41	0.04
0.07	0-0-6	0.48	0.50	0.36	1.80	3.50	24	0.29	44	0.27	2.00	2.87	0.30
0.14	0-1-0	1.00	1.00	0.73	3.60	7.00	49	0.59	88	0.53	4.00	5.74	0.60
0.15	0-1-1	1.04	1.07	0.78	3.90	7.50	52	0.63	100	0.57	4.29	6.15	0.65
0.19	0-1-4	1.31	1.36	1.00	4.90	9.50	66	0.80	119	0.72	5.43	7.79	0.82
0.20	0-1-5	1.38	1.43	1.04	5.20	10.00	70	0.84	125	0.76	5.71	8.20	0.86
0.21	0-1-6	1.45	1.50	1.09	5.40	10.50	73	0.88	131	0.80	6.00	8.61	0.91
0.23	0-1-8	1.59	1.64	1.19	6.00	11.50	80	0.97	144	0.88	6.57	9.43	1.00
0.24	0-1-9	1.66	1.72	1.24	6.20	12.00	84	1.00	150	0.91	6.86	10.00	1.04
0.26	0-1-10	1.80	1.86	1.35	6.70	13.00	91	1.09	163	1.00	7.43	10.66	1.12
0.29	0-2-1	2.01	2.07	1.50	7.50	14.50	100	1.22	181	1.10	8.29	11.89	1.25
0.30	0-2-2	2.08	2.14	1.55	7.80	15.00	104	1.26	188	1.14	8.57	12.30	1.30
0.35	0-2-6	2.42	2.50	1.81	9.00	17.50	122	1.47	219	1.33	10.00	14.35	1.51
0.41	0-2-11	2.84	2.93	2.12	10.00	20.50	143	1.72	256	1.56	11.71	16.81	1.77
0.43	0-3-1	2.98	3.07	2.23	11.10	21.50	150	1.81	269	1.64	12.29	17.63	1.86
0.46	0-3-3	3.18	3.29	2.38	11.90	23.00	160	1.93	288	1.75	13.14	18.86	1.99
0.53	0-3-9	3.67	3.79	2.75	13.70	26.50	185	2.23	331	2.02	15.14	21.73	2.29
0.95	0-6-10	6.57	6.79	4.92	24.60	47.50	331	3.99	594	3.61	27.14	38.95	4.10
1.00	0-7-2	6.92	7.15	5.18	26.00	50.00	350	4.20	625	3.80	28.57	41.00	4.32
2.80	1-0-0	19.36	20.02	14.50	72.50	140.00	975	11.75	1750	10.65	80.00	114.80	12.12

PREFACE

To our way of thinking, nothing can be more precious than the time people spend at work — nothing, that is, except the time that these same people spend on their holidays from work. This series of guide books, therefore, has been planned specially to meet the needs of the holiday-makers of today, who may be described as follows:

they are in a hurry, for their annual holidays last only three or four weeks;

they love new things and, every year, this thirst for novelty drives them in ever-increasing numbers along the roads of all countries;

they are "motorized" and they all, from riders of power-assisted bicycles and scooters up to drivers of big cars, show the same craving for independence and freedom of action.

That is why this book, above all things, is a road-book; its form, however, and the diverse information that it holds, make it valuable for all — even for those not possessing their own means of transport.

The road-book takes the form of a series of separate itineraries, dividing up the area into large touring regions; the roads are carefully numbered and exact distances are given (a kilometres-miles conversion table is included on page 9). The motorist is thus left free to combine various routes, according to his whim and the extent of his holiday. We are thus dealing with travel that is "organized", but organized to suit the individual taste.

The itineraries take in towns and places that one "has to see" before one can claim to know a country. Here lies the main interest of this guide book; it does not say everything, but what it does say merits your attention. It chooses for you. It chooses the best road, the most picturesque scenery, the most interesting buildings in the town where it invites you to break your journey. It goes even further. In this church or that art gallery, it will take you to just *the* reredos or *the* statue that it considers to be worthy of your admiration, omitting details and objects of only secondary interest. The authors well appreciate that, just because you are a tourist, you won't suddenly turn into an archaeologist.

It may also be pointed out that the driver is helped to get through places by very clear diagrams showing entrance and exit routes, together with direction indications, and that the routes to

be followed around big towns are shown on the plans in red . . .
You have only to follow the guide.

But these road maps are only a part of the whole work. The
chapter of practical information contains all kinds of detailed
explanations and advice about daily life, currency, transport
systems, places for winter sports, health resorts, shopping, etc. . . .

So that you may complete your understanding of the land by
having access to positive facts, we have included—for the first
time in a work of this nature—a chapter of technical information
about the country's economic and social life, under the heading
of "Austria in Figures". From information given therein can be
traced, without need of any commentary, the evolution of the
country by comparison with pre-war conditions. This chapter
will be found repeated, with similar illustrations and headings, in
the other volumes of this series, so that instructive comparisons
between the leading countries may be drawn.

Figures alone are of course powerless to express the soul of a
country. That is why we offer you a series of portraits of national
celebrities, bringing together many of those who, past or present,
have in some way contributed to the greatness and the cultural
wealth of their native land: here are great names of History, the
Arts, and Letters, and outstanding figures of the present age.

It will thus be seen that the novel plan of these guide books
owes nothing to set forms and everything to experiment. The
ideas of our readers will be just as valuable as our own; and we
shall be happy to receive their suggestions, their comments and
their final corrections. The series, planned to be of practical
assistance, forms the complement to those books of the WORLD
IN COLOUR series, which are still the most irresistible invitation
to travel and the most vivid souvenir of countries visited. It is our
hope that this present series will enjoy the same approval and the
same popularity among an even wider public.

MILES CONVERTED INTO KILOMETRES

Miles	0	1	2	3	4	5	6	7	8	9
0		1.60	3.21	4.82	6.43	8.04	9.65	11.26	12.87	14.48
10	16	17.7	19.3	20.9	22.5	24.1	25.7	27.3	28.9	30.5
20	32.1	33.7	35.4	37.	38.6	40.2	41.8	43.4	45.	46.6
30	48.2	49.8	51.4	53.1	54.7	56.3	57.9	59.5	61.1	62.7
40	64.3	65.9	67.5	69.2	70.8	72.4	74.	75.6	77.2	78.8
50	80.4	82.	83.6	85.2	86.9	88.5	90.1	91.7	93.3	94.9
60	96.5	98.1	99.7	101.3	103.	104.6	106.2	107.8	109.4	111.
70	112.6	114.2	115.8	117.4	119.	120.7	122.3	123.9	125.5	127.1
80	128.7	130.3	131.9	133.5	135.1	136.7	138.4	140.	141.6	143.2
90	144.8	146.4	148.	149.6	151.2	152.8	154.4	156.1	157.7	159.3
100	160.9									

Example: To express 96 miles in kilometres, find 90 in the first vertical column at the left, then follow the horizontal line as far as the figure shown in the column under "6"; at the junction of the two columns, read 154.4

PRACTICAL INFORMATION

Austria has no set holiday season. In winter and summer it is a paradise for the holiday-maker.

The Tyrol, the Arlberg, and Vorarlberg, world-renowned ski centres, are blessed with magnificent snow-covered slopes from November to June. Vienna, Salzburg with its Festival, Badgastein, the green setting of the Salzkammergut, the warm lakes of Carinthia will hold you in their spell from spring to autumn. To its picturesque countryside and gay folklore, Austria has the additional attraction of being a hospitable country for the foreigner, well organized for the tourist and the sportsman. Last but not least, the rate of exchange is favourable and the cost of living advantageous.

AUSTRIAN TOURIST OFFICES

LONDON, W.1, 49 Dover Street. Tel. GROsvenor 1662.

NEW YORK, 17, N.Y. 48 East 48th Street. Tel. MUrrayhill 8-0355.

VIENNA. Österreichische Verkehrswerbung, Vienna 1, Hohenstaufengasse 3-5.

Diplomatic and Consular Representatives
IN AUSTRIA

U.K. British Embassy, VIENNA. Consulates: VIENNA 1, Wallnerstrasse 8 (Tel. U 26491 and U 26359); and Innsbruck (Tel. 5620).

U.S.A. American Embassy, VIENNA. American Consulate, Salzburg.

AUSTRIAN REPRESENTATION ABROAD

LONDON, S.W.1. Austrian Embassy, 18 Belgrave Square. Tel. SLOane 5153. Consulate, 18 West Belgrave Mews. Others at Birmingham, Manchester, and Edinburgh.

WASHINGTON, 8, D.C. Austrian Embassy, 2144 Wyoming Avenue N.W. Consulate-General at New York; consulates at Atlanta, Chicago, Cleveland, Detroit, Dallas, Los Angeles, New Orleans, Portland, and San Francisco.

OTTAWA. Austrian Legation, 136 Queen Street. Consulate at Vancouver.

FORMALITIES

Passport and Entry Visa. British and American citizens, for the British, American, and French zones, require up-to-date passport (no visa). For Vienna: passport and special permit known as the "Grey Card". Application should be made to local consular or Passport office (for U.K., the Passport Office, Clive House, Petty France, London, S.W.1, where also special permits for the Russian Zone outside Vienna, and for the Danube steamers are obtainable).

Customs. The following can be imported duty-free: Personal belongings (clothing, jewellery, etc.), 1 camera with 12 plates or two rolls of film, 1 film-camera of 8mm, 9mm, or 16mm with 1 film; binoculars, 1 musical instrument, 1 gramophone, 1 radio-set, 1 typewriter, 1 tent with equipment, 1 perambulator, 1 sports outfit for personal use, including skis, tennis rackets, guns, and cartridges.

Tobacco, alcohol: 200 cigarettes, or 40 cigars, or 200gr of tobacco; 1 bottle of wine, opened, normal size; 1 bottle of spirits, opened, $\frac{1}{4}$ litre; toilet water, $\frac{1}{4}$ litre, and small quantities of perfume for personal use. (For frontier traffic, the quotas are 25 cigarettes, or 5 cigars, or 25 gr of tobacco duty-free.)

Dogs: No formalities. Muzzles required.

Currency. Importation of Austrian schillings and foreign currency (in cash or traveller's cheques) is unlimited. Each traveller can export up to 10,000 schillings in Austrian notes, and unlimited quantities of foreign currency.

Foreign visitors can obtain Austrian money for foreign exchange at banks, tourist agencies and Exchange Offices of the Österreichische Verkehrsbureau, at the stations in Vienna (West), Linz, Salzburg, Innsbruck, Villach, and Kufstein. These Exchange Offices are open for business on the arrival and departure of all big international trains.

In addition, some hotels are authorized Exchange Offices in smaller places where there are no banks or tourist agencies.

For foreign currency regulations, a child is considered as a person and is able to take advantage of the privileges noted above.

Austrian Currency. Austrian schilling = 100 groschen. Coins of 1, 2, 5, 10, 50 groschen and of 1, 2, 5 schillings. Notes of 10, 20, 50, 100, 500, 1,000 schillings.

Exchange Rates (approximate). 100 schillings are worth:

1 Municipal Police.   2 State Police.   3 Frontier Guard.   4 Railway Official.
5 Customs Officer.   6 Fireman.   7 Postman.

£1 7s. 6d.; $3.60; 1,345 French francs; 184 Belgian francs;
17 Swiss francs; 2,025 lire.

ADVICE TO MOTORISTS

The Austrian Automobile Club is the *Österreichischer Automobil
Motorrad und Touring Club* (ÖAMTC), Vienna I, Schubertring 7;
Tel. U 13.5.80. Numerous branches in the main towns.
The motorist is helped by the road-map issued by the ÖAMTC
(10 miles to the inch, approx), and one for different areas issued
by Hölzl Strassenkarten (2¾ miles to the inch, approx). The state
of roads is indicated on the ÖAMTC map; the major roads are
good, but because of snow it is necessary to carry chains in winter.
Roads are numbered in accordance with those given in this
book, but you should be warned that these numbers are not

shown on signposts and are seldom indicated on road maps. **Documents required by the owner-driver.** *Custom certificate:* triptych or Customs clearance sheet. In lieu, motorists can obtain a pass or permit at the offices of the ÖAMTC, at frontier crossings or the Customs post, for a charge of 30 schillings for 10 days, 40 S for 20 days, and 60 S for 30 days. The 10-days pass can be extended for two further periods of 10 days on payment of 30 S each time. *Driving papers:* international certificate for cars, international driving licence. Rear right wing of car must carry nationality plate (black letters on white background).

Motor fuel and oil are unrationed. The quality of petrol is average; motorists are therefore recommended to ask for super-fuel. Ordinary petrol costs 3.90 S a litre, and the super-fuel 4.35 S a litre. Gas-oil varies from 2.16 to 2.55 S a litre, according to the district. The price of lubricating oil varies from 8 S to 16 S a litre, according to quality.

Service stations remain open all night in the towns, and qualified mechanics are readily found. Garage charge for the night ranges from 7 S to 10 S, puncture repair 15 S, draining oil, and greasing, 100 S plus a tip of 10 %. For petrol, a tip of 1 or 2 S.

Highway Code. Driving and priority on right, except on the priority roads, even in towns ("Stopstrassen"). In the towns, obligatory halt before a crossing. Traffic signs conform to the international code.

Some roads in Lower Austria, Carinthia, and Styria are subject to a small toll-charge.

Passage of Cars through Mountain Tunnels. The Austrian State Railways have instituted a railway ferry service for cars and trailers through the tunnels of the Arlberg (St Anton-am-Arlberg—Langen-am-Arlberg, 11 km), and from Tauern (Böckstein—Mallnitz, 12 km). The charges are: cars, trailers, motorcycles, 0.05 S per km for each 10 kg, with a minimum charge of 75 S for cars up to six-seaters and 87.50 S for those with 7 or 8 seats. Travellers take their seats in the passenger coaches or service coaches. (Fares: St-Anton-am-Arlberg—Langen, 2.80 S; Böckstein—Mallnitz, 3 S, 3rd class.)

HINTS FOR CAMPERS

The principal Associations are: the ÖAMTC (see earlier). —

Österreichischer Camping-Club, Vienna III, Reisnerstrasse 2. Tel.: U. 19-2-38.

Österreichischer Camping-Verband, Vienna IX, Türkenstrasse 3, Tel.: A. 12-0-06.

Permits and Sites. — Camping is free in Austria, subject to securing the prior permission of the Town Hall, the village authorities, or the owner of the land. Austrian Camping Clubs, newly founded, have undertaken to increase the number of camping sites already in existence. A guidebook is now being prepared.

TRANSPORT

Entry Routes. *By Road:* Frontier posts on tourists roads are open day and night.

By Air: The international lines (including British European Airways and Pan American Airways) serve one or other of the six Austrian airports: Vienna, Graz, Innsbruck, Linz, Salzburg, and Klagenfurt. (B.E.A. addresses: LONDON, S.W.1, Dorland Hall, 14-20 Regent Street. Tel. GERrard 9833. VIENNA, Wiener Flugzentrum, Kärntnerring 10. Tel. U 45.5.30-3). There is no national internal air company.

By Train: The great European expresses run to Austria—the Orient, Arlberg, Ostende, Austria, Brenner, Tauern, Tirol, and Steiermark, all of which have through carriages from the Channel port; and also the Rome-Vienna express.

Internal Transport. *Railways.* Three classes. Fares: the charge per km in 3rd class is the same in all trains, local, fast, or expresses, on the basis of 0.25 S per km for a journey between 1 and 100 km, with a sliding scale of reductions for longer journeys. In local trains, the 2nd class fare is 50% higher than the 3rd class; the 1st class fare is 2½ times the 3rd class rate. Railway tickets obtained abroad are payable in local currency. If the traveller wishes to take his retrun ticket in Austria, he must, under the present monetary regulations, pay in cash for tye non-Austrian section of his journey and in schillings for the Austrian section. The name of the traveller and number of his passport are put on the ticket. *Reductions,* for parties up to 20 persons, 20%; above 20 persons, 25% to 30%. For a round trip in Austrian territory of not less than 400 km and returning to the original departure point, reduction of about 12% for individual travellers; of 800 km minimum, roughly 20% (validity of these tickets is 2 months). For return tickets, reduction of 25% in cases of *(a)* visits to international fairs, *(b)* journey of less than 250 km in each direction: in the region of the Ausserfern (Ehrwald, Zugspitzbahn, Reutte, Vils line)—from Vienna, provincial capitals and 60 other stations (validity 6 days)—Sundays, and public holidays.

Motor-coaches: charge per km: 0.25 S to 0.30 S.

Taxi-cabs: About 4 S per km (where the meter has not been modified, and indicates the fare in the old Reichsmarks, multiply the sum by 8 for small journeys and by 5 for longer journeys).

Tramcars in Vienna: Stopping places are indicated by "H" or "Haltestelle". Flat-rate fare of 1.30 S. for any journey.

DAILY LIFE

Hotels. The Austrian tourist industry grows in importance daily; the hotels are all very clean, comfortable, but generally simple, although some spas have palatial establishments.

Charges are not very high. A room for one person in an ordinary hotel costs from 10 to 20 S, in a middle-class hotel from 30 to 60 S, and from 100 to 170 S in a luxury hotel. To these charges, which vary according to the district, must be added a residence tax of from 0.50 to 2 S, and even 6.50 S at some thermal resorts (Badgastein). Service charge is from 10 to 15% according to category. Full board costs 40, or 50 S per day in a small town or isolated village, and 70 S to 200 S in larger towns for a stay of at least three days. Reductions are made for children if they do not have a separate room.

Hotels listed in the Itineraries are classified according to International usage: **** luxury, *** 1st class, ** good, and * moderate standard, but clean and well run.

Restaurant charges are low. A simple meal costs 15 S, an average meal 25 S, and in luxury restaurants 40, 50 S and even more. Breakfast costs from 6 to 10 S, a beer 1.50 to 3 S, tea 2.50 to 4.50 S, and an ice-cream 2 to 3 S.

Tipping.—Remember always to give a tip for a service rendered, even a small one, to the porter, hotel page-boy, or car-park attendant. The tip can vary between 1 to 5 S according to the service rendered. Taxi-cab drivers and hairdressers' tips should be from 10 to 15%. (It must be remembered that salaries are

1,000 Schillings

100 Schillings

50 Schillings

500 Schillings

20 Schillings

5 Schillings

10 Schillings

2 Schillings

1 Schilling

50 groschen

10 groschen

5 groschen

2 groschen

small.) Tips are not expected by the usherettes in cinemas, concerts, and theatres.

The shops are open from 8 to 1, and from 3 to 7. Closed on Sundays and one week-day, varying from one province to another.

Banks are open from 8 to 1, and some from 3 to 4 also.

Post offices are open from 8 to 12 and from 2 to 6.

Tobacconists. — Tobacco and cigarettes are obtainable only in the "Tabak-Trafik", open at the same time as other shops. Cigarettes can however be obtained from a restaurant or café waiter, so long as a drink is ordered. Ordinary cigarettes are sold singly, as well as by the packet.

Holidays — In addition to the religious fêtes, there are holidays on 1st May and 26th December, St Stephen's Day.

CALENDAR OF FESTIVALS AND DISPLAYS

March: International Spring Fair (Vienna).
April–May: Spring Fair (Graz).
May–June: Festival Weeks (Vienna).
June: International Ski Racing (Grossglockner).
July: Festival Weeks (Graz).
July–August: Festival (Bregenz). — Summer International Academy of the Mozarteum (Salzburg).
July 26–August 31: Festival (Salzburg).
July–August: International Export and Sample Fair (Dornbirn); Water Sports Festival (Lake Wörth).
August: Export and Sample Fair (Innsbruck).
August–September: European Forum — International University Weeks (Alpbach).
September: International Autumn Fair (Vienna).
September–October: Autumn Fair (Graz).

SPORT

Associations and Federations to be noted:
Ski-ing: Österreichischer Skiverband, Rathaus, Innsbruck.
Climbing: (1) Österreichischer Alpenverein, Innsbruck, Gilmstrasse 6-3; (2) Österreichischer Gebirgsverein, Vienna III, Lerchenfelder Strasse 28.

Austria is a paradise for the mountaineer: 409 huts and numerous mountain hostelries extremely well equipped, allow the tourist to make long excursions, ascents, and difficult climbs. There are numerous accredited guides and porters.

Golf: Österreichischer Golfverband, Vienna IV, Mommsengasse 5.

Riding: (1) Österreichischer Campagnereiter Gesellschaft, Vienna I, Josefplatz 5; (2) Wiener Trabrennverein, Vienna I, Nibelungengasse 3.

Rowing: Österreichischer Ruderverband, Vienna III, Stalinplatz 5.

Yachting: Österreichischer Segelverband, Vienna I, Dominikanerbastei 24.

Fishing: Austrian National Tourist Office in Vienna (address above). Streams and lakes, reserves of the Danube, provide anglers with extremely varied sport.

Shooting: Foreigners are allowed to bring in their shotguns and cartridges to the French, British, and American occupied zones, if they first obtain a certificate issued by an Austrian Consulate abroad indicating the type and calibre of the gun, and the amount of ammunition carried. This certificate will be stamped on arrival and departure by the Austrian Customs authorities. To use the gun, the foreigner should seek a short-term shooting licence from the responsible authorities at his place of stay, such as the Bezirksverwaltungsbehörde, or the Federal Police. He must also obtain a permit from the owner of the shoot, and a shooting permit issued by the responsible authorities of the shooting district (Bezirkshauptmannschaft).

PURCHASES

Good value for money:

Articles of leatherwork, interesting both in quality and price (cases, ladies' handbags, brief-cases, etc.). The best place to buy them is in Vienna, in the famous Kaerntner Strasse, or in the big towns.

Sports equipment and accessories: ski-ing and mountaineering equipment in particular (boots, skis, coloured shirts, hand-made sweaters). All (or mainly) products of the local craftsmen: material and embroidery (sheets and table napkins decorated with lace, blouses and fine lingerie, peasant skirts (hand-woven), Tyrolean embroidered braid, called *Borten*, etc.), carved wood-

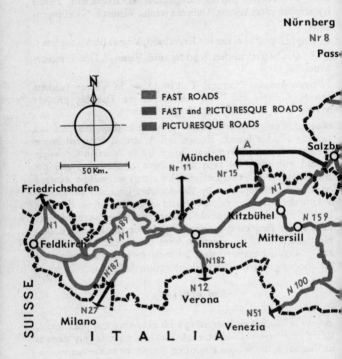

FAST ROADS
FAST and PICTURESQUE ROADS
PICTURESQUE ROADS

N

50 Km.

DEUTSCHLAND

Nürnberg
Nr 8
Pass

Friedrichshafen

München
Nr 11

Nr 15

A

Salzb

N1

Kitzbühel

N 159

Mittersill

N1

N 189

N1

Feldkirch

Innsbruck

N182

N 100

M87

N 12

Verona

N27

N51

Milano

Venezia

SUISSE

ITALIA

MAP OF THE PRINCIPAL

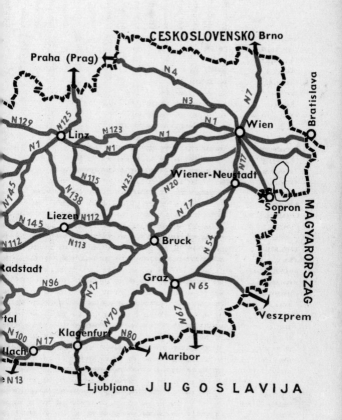

HIGHWAYS OF AUSTRIA

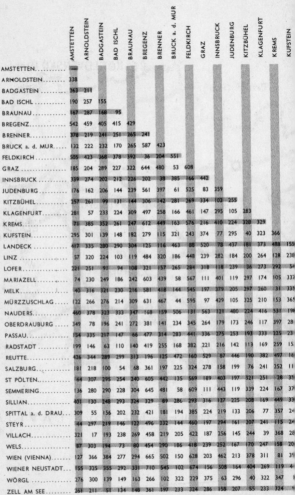

	AMSTETTEN	ARNOLDSTEIN	BADGASTEIN	BAD ISCHL	BRAUNAU	BREGENZ	BRENNER	BRUCK a. d. MUR	FELDKIRCH	GRAZ	INNSBRUCK	JUDENBURG	KITZBÜHEL	KLAGENFURT	K REMS	KUFSTEIN
AMSTETTEN	—															
ARNOLDSTEIN	338															
BADGASTEIN	263	211														
BAD ISCHL	190	257	155													
BRAUNAU	167	287	168	95												
BREGENZ	542	459	405	415	429											
BRENNER	378	219	241	251	265	241										
BRUCK a. d. MUR	132	222	232	170	265	587	423									
FELDKIRCH	505	423	368	378	392	36	204	551								
GRAZ	185	204	289	227	322	644	480	53	608							
INNSBRUCK	339	274	202	212	226	202	38	385	166	442						
JUDENBURG	176	162	206	144	239	561	397	61	525	83	359					
KITZBÜHEL	257	261	99	131	144	306	142	289	269	334	103	255				
KLAGENFURT	281	57	233	224	309	497	258	166	461	147	295	105	283			
KREMS	71	385	352	261	247	612	449	163	576	216	410	224	328	329		
KUFSTEIN	295	301	139	148	182	279	115	321	243	374	77	295	40	323	366	
LANDECK	417	335	280	290	304	125	116	463	88	520	78	437	181	373	488	155
LINZ	57	320	224	103	119	484	320	186	448	239	282	184	200	264	128	238
LOFER	221	251	91	94	108	321	157	265	284	318	118	239	36	273	292	54
MARIAZELL	74	230	249	186	242	603	439	58	567	111	401	119	297	174	105	337
MELK	40	316	321	230	216	581	418	144	545	197	379	205	297	260	31	335
MÜRZZUSCHLAG	122	266	276	214	309	631	467	44	595	97	429	105	325	210	153	365
NAUDERS	460	378	323	333	347	168	159	506	131	563	121	480	224	416	531	198
OBERDRAUBURG	349	78	196	241	272	381	141	234	345	264	179	173	246	117	397	28
PASSAU	154	335	217	147	66	477	314	283	441	336	275	253	193	333	225	23
RADSTADT	199	146	63	110	140	419	255	168	382	221	216	142	113	169	259	15
REUTTE	426	344	289	299	313	196	125	472	160	529	87	446	190	382	497	16
SALZBURG	181	218	100	54	68	361	197	225	324	278	158	199	76	241	252	11
ST PÖLTEN	64	307	295	254	240	605	442	135	569	189	403	197	321	251	28	35
SEMMERING	136	280	290	228	304	645	481	58	609	111	443	119	339	224	167	37
SILLIAN	401	130	248	293	324	329	89	286	293	316	127	225	208	169	449	33
SPITTAL a. d. DRAU	309	55	156	202	232	421	181	194	385	224	219	133	206	77	357	24
STEYR	44	297	219	146	122	496	332	144	460	197	294	161	207	241	115	24
VILLACH	321	17	193	238	269	458	219	205	422	187	256	145	244	39	368	28
WELS	87	303	194	73	80	454	290	186	418	239	252	167	170	247	158	20
WIEN (VIENNA)	127	366	384	277	294	665	502	150	628	203	462	213	378	311	81	35
WIENER NEUSTADT	155	325	355	292	331	710	545	102	674	156	508	164	404	269	119	4
WÖRGL	276	300	139	149	163	266	102	322	229	375	63	296	40	322	347	1
ZELL AM SEE	261	211	51	134	148	361	197	233	324	286	158	207	56	233	324	

TABLE OF DISTANCES BETWEEN

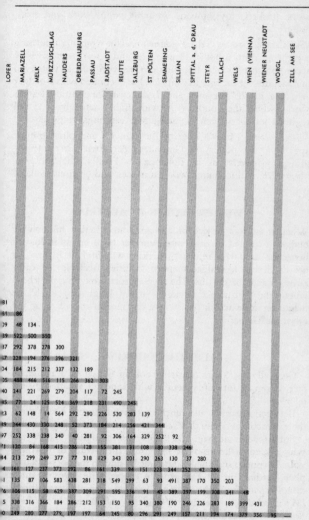

THE PRINCIPAL TOWNS

work (caskets, toys, pipes), wrought copperwork and iron pottery, etc.

The National Costumes: the *Trachtendirndel* for women, comprising a gathered skirt, a bodice, a pinafore, and a scarf (models vary according to province, but they can be worn just as well even in town during the fine season); felt hat decorated with a badger "shaving brush" for men and *Lederhosen* (long-lasting leather shorts, which the youths wear with embroidered braces); old regional jewellery such as medallions, ear-rings, rings, etc.

Miscellaneous: Make a note of the cameras and photographic apparatus; the pottery of Gmunden; Augarten porcelain; engraved glassware, as in Bohemia ... Finally, the antiques: silverware, multicoloured wooden statues, and precious trinkets.

WINTER SPORTS IN AUSTRIA

Whether he is a novice or a champion, whether his holiday budget is limited or otherwise, whether he is happy in luxury hotels or mountain refuges, the skier will find in Austria his heart's desire. Magnificent sports facilities available: 26 cable railways and 202 ski-lifts. The tiniest resort provides a ski-school where the instructors (speaking many languages) teach the Schneider style which has won seven medals out of 18 at the Olympic Games.

AUSTRIAN COOKING

Generally speaking, Austrian cooking is that of a mountain race, designed for hardy people with appetites whetted by the open-air life.

Between breakfast and luncheon, served around one o'clock, there sometimes comes the *Gabelfrühstück*, a light stop-gap repast.

Soup appears more often at midday than at night. It is thickened with a kind of home-made macaroni, meat-balls, or raw egg-yolk. Do not be surprised to find side by side on the hors-d'oeuvre plate, sardines in oil and gruyère cheese. The favourite meat dishes, apart from the national veal escallop in breadcrumbs (*Wienerschnitzel*), are stews (*Goulash*) and boiled beef (*Rindfleisch*). Sour cream sauces and horseradish sauce are characteristic. At all meals appear potatoes or the substantial flour quenelles

PRINCIPAL WINTER SPORTS RESORTS	Altitude (metres)	Cable railways	Ski-lifts	Ski schools	Jumping platforms	Ski-joring	Skating rinks	Competitions	Sports equipment shops
LOWER AUSTRIA									
Annaberg	973		1	x	x	x			x	x
Mönichkirchen	1,000		1	x	x				x	x
Puchberg	580	1	1	x	x	x		x	x	x
Reichenau-Hirschwang..	486	1		x	x			x	x	x
Semmering	1,000		2	x	x			x	x	x
CARINTHIA									
Kanzelhöhe- Gerlitzen	1,910	1	4	x	x				x	x
Mallnitz	1,185		2	x	x	x	x	x	x	x
Turracher Höhe	1,763		2	x					x	x
UPPER AUSTRIA									
Feuerkogel-Ebensee	1,625	1	3	x	x				x	x
Hinterstoder	650		1	x	x	x			x	x
Spital am Pyhrn	647		2	x	x	x			x	x
SALZBURG									
Badgastein	1,013	1	4	x	x	x	x	x	x	x
Bad Hofgastein	860		3	x	x	x	x		x	x
Gerlosplatte	1,695		1	x	x				x	x
Loferer Alpe	1,570		1	x	x				x	x
Mitterbergalpe	1,600		1	x	x				x	x
Mühlbach	854		1	x	x				x	x
Radstädter Tauern...	1,738		5	x	x				x	x
Saalbach	1,003		7	x					x	x
Saalfelden	744		1	x	x				x	x
Salzburg-Stadt	424	2		x	x	x	x	x	x	x
Salzburg-Gaisberg	1,286		3	x	x				x	x
St Johann/Pongau	610		2	x	x				x	x
Zell am See	758	1	3	x	x	x	x	x	x	x
STYRIA									
Hohentauern	1,250		1	x						
Klachau-Tauplitz	891		3	x				x		
Mariazell	862	1	2	x	x	x	x	x	x	
Mitterndorf im Salzkammergut	797		1	x	x					
Prebichl	1,227		2	x					x	
Schladming	740		1	x	x	x	x	x	x	x
Spital/Semmering	769		1	x					x	x
TYROL									
Berwang	1,336		1	x				x	x	x
Ehrwald	996	1	1	x		x	x	x	x	x
Fieberbrunn	788		1	x	x	x			x	x
Fulpmes	835			x	x					x
Galtür	1,583		1	x	x				x	x

PRINCIPAL WINTER SPORTS RESORTS	Altitude (metres)	Cable railways	Ski-lifts	Ski schools	Jumping platforms	Ski-joring	Skating rinks	Competitions	Sports equipment shop
Gerlos	1,241		1	x	x	x		x	x
Gries am Brenner	1,255		1	x				x	x
Hintertux	1,494		1	x				x	x
Hochsölden	2,070		3	x				x	x
Igls/Innsbruck	900	1	3	x	x	x	x	x	x
Innsbruck	574	3	2	x	x	x	x	x	x
Ischgl	1,377		2	x		x		x	x
Iselsberg/Osttirol	1,118		1	x			x		x
Jochberg	922		1	x	x	x	x		
Kirchberg/Tyrol	838		1	x	x	x	x		x
Kitzbühel	763	3	7	x	x	x	x	x	x
Kössen	588		2	x	x	x	x	x	x
Kufstein	503		1	x	x	x	x	x	x
Kühtai	1,960		1	x					x
Lermoos	995		2	x	x		x	x	x
Lienz/Osttirol	673		3	x	x	x	x	x	x
Matrei am Brenner	993			x	x			x	x
Mayrhofen	630	1	1	x	x	x	x	x	x
Nauders	1,365		1	x				x	x
Obergurgl	1,927		2	x				x	x
Reutte	854		1	x	x		x	x	x
St Anton/Arlberg	1,304	2	3	x	x		x	x	x
St Christoph/Arlberg	1,768	1	1	x					x
St Johann/Tyrol	649		1	x	x	x	x	x	x
Seefeld	1,180		4	x	x	x	x	x	x
Serfaus	1,427	1	1	x					x
Sölden	1,377		3	x		x	x	x	x
Steinach/Brenner	1,048		1	x	x		x	x	x
Vent	1,893		1	x				x	x
Westendorf	785		2	x			x	x	x
VORARLBERG									
Au/Bregenzerwald	796		1	x				x	x
Bludenz	585		1	x	x		x	x	x
Brand	1,047	1	1	x				x	x
Bregenz	398	1	1	x	x		x	x	x
Bürserberg	870	1	1	x					
Damüls	1,428		2	x				x	x
Dornbirn/Bödele	429	1	1	x	x		x	x	x
Faschina	1,500		1	x					x
Gargellen	1,424		3	x				x	x
Gaschurn	986		3	x			x	x	x
Langen am Arlberg	1,218		1	x					x
Lech am Arlberg/ Oberlech	1,447	1	4	x		x		x	x
Parthenen	1,021			x					x
Schröcken	1,260		1	x				x	x
Schruns	689		3	x			x	x	x
Stuben	1,409		1	x				x	x
Tschagguns	684		3	x	x			x	x
Warth am Arlberg	1,499		1	x					x
Zürs am Arlberg	1,720		3	x	x	x	x	x	x

PRINCIPAL THERMAL STATIONS	Respiratory	Nervous system	Metabolism	Urinary disorders	Skin	Circulatory system	Infantile maladies	Rheumatism, articulation	Gynaecology	Digestive disorders	Bone diseases
Althofen		x	x			x		x	x		x
Bad Aussee	x					x	x	x	x		
Bad Deutsch-Altenburg		x		x	x			x			
Baden (near Vienna)		x		x	x			x		x	x
Bad Fischau			x					x			x
Badgastein		x	x	x		x		x			
Bad Gleichenberg	x			x		x				x	
Bad Hall	x	x			x	x			x		x
Bad Hofgastein		x	x	x		x		x			
Bad Iselsberg		x	x						x		
Bad Ischl	x		x			x		x	x	x	x
Bad Kleinkirchhelm		x	x	x				x			
Bad Neydharting								x	x	x	x
Bad Schallerbach	x	x			x			x		x	x
Bad Vöslau			x					x			x
Bad Weinberg			x		x					x	
Goisern					x	x		x		x	
Hintertux		x						x			x
Hohenems								x		x	x
Kitzbühel								x	x		x
Lägenfeld		x	x		x			x			x
Mattsee		x						x			x
Obladis	x		x					x		x	
Salzburg		x						x	x		x
Schruns		x	x			x		x		x	
Solbad Hall in Tirol	x		x			x		x	x		
Vienna	x				x			x		x	x
Volderwildbad		x	x							x	
Warmbad Villach			x					x			x
Wildbad Einöd			x	x		x					

known as *Nockerln* or *Knödeln*. Game is often accompanied by jam or stewed fruit.

To conclude, there come the entremets *(Mehlspeisen:* floury dishes): pancakes, sugared omelettes, puddings, etc. Viennese pastry includes some masterpieces. The *Torte*, which is not a tart but a giant cake with seductive layers. If you still have an appetite, ask for whipped cream to top your excellent coffee or some good frothy chocolate *(Schlagobers).*

Drink white wine (some famous types), beer, or fruit-juice: apple or raspberry *(Apfelsaft* or *Himbeersaft).*

ITINERARIES

With the mountain range of the Eastern Alps running practically right through the country from East to West, Austria received from Nature the most enduring heritage possible: a magnificent and incomparable variety of scenery. From the green or blue lakes set among the rocks, tumble the noisy streams, full of fish. Austria's mountains and forests are a paradise for shooting and fishing, climbing and ski-ing. Its eastern situation ensures long periods of snow: from early December the slopes are snow-clad from 700m up; the snow remains until March at 1,400m and until the end of April at 1,800m.

The road network follows the geographical configuration of the country. One main highway runs through the Vorarlberg and the Tyrol, while secondary roads link up the valleys.

Our first itinerary ends at Innsbruck. This city, the turn-table of Austria, is worthy of an itinerary on its own (No. 2), which takes you through the Tyrol up to the Italian frontier.

The following itinerary (No. 3) links Innsbruck to Salzburg. Two routes are available for the motorist: the national No. 1 which runs by the Bavarian Retreat; the other allows him to visit the great winter-sports centre of Kitzbühel and to rejoin the alpine road of the Grossglockner (Itinerary No. 4).

Salzburg, birthplace of Mozart, Festival City, and the Salzkammergut form a natural circuit of excursions which follow the necklace of mountain lakes (Itinerary No. 5). Itinerary No. 6 has been planned partly for the tourist who wishes to go directly to Carinthia or to Graz without touching Vienna, and partly for visitors who are obliged to return from Vienna by the road taken for the outward journey. The next itinerary leads directly, down the Danube Valley, to Vienna which, of course, is the subject of a complete chapter. From Vienna, Itinerary No. 9 runs first across the south of Lower Austria, then the south of Styria, and ends at Klagenfurt, starting point for trips to the Lake District of Carinthia, which form the tenth itinerary. Finally, the last itinerary provides a picturesque change for the return to Salzburg or to rejoin the great west-east artery described in the first chapters.

Passages in italics indicate secondary excursions or deviations off the main itinerary route.

GENERAL MAP OF THE ITINERARIES:

TOPOGRAPHICAL DICTIONARY

Alt: Old.
Bad: Bath.
Bach: River, stream.
Bahnhof: Station.
Berg: Peak,
  Mountain.
Brücke: Bridge.
Burg: Fortress.

Dom: Cathedral.
Dorf: Village.
Garten: Garden.
Gasse (Gas.): Lane.
Gasthof: Inn.
Haupt: Principal.
Hauptstrasse: Road.
Haus: House.

Heim: Land, home.
Höhe: Height,
  eminence.
Hof: Court.
Hofburg: Palace.
Kirche: Church.
Kloster: Cloister.
Kunst: Art.

Small numbers beside Itinerary No. indicate pages where itinerary will be found.

Kurhaus: Casino.	Platz: Square.	Stift: Monastery.
Land: Country.	Rathaus: Town Hall.	Strasse (Str.): Street.
Landhaus: Local	Reich: Empire,	Tal: Valley.
Government House.	Kingdom.	Tor (Tür): Door,
Landstrasse: Road.	Sankt: Saint.	Gateway.
Markt: Market.	Schloss: Castle.	Turm: Tower.
Münster: Cathedral.	See: Lake.	Volk: People.
Museum: Museum.	Spital: Hospital.	Wald: Woods.
Neu: New.	Stadt: Town, City.	Weg: Path, footpath.
Pass: Pass (mountain).	Stadtturm: City Tower.	Weinstube: Tavern.
Pfarre: Parish.		

BREGENZ-INNSBRUCK

PRINCIPAL ITINERARY: VIA FELDKIRCH AND LANDECK: 206 KM.

The No. 1 motor-road which runs from one end of Austria to the other was, until 1952, the only one available for the motorist driving from the western frontier of Austria to Innsbruck. From Lake Konstanz *(Bodensee)*, which is shared by

Switzerland, Germany, and Austria, it runs south at first to
Dornbirn and Feldkirch, then turns east along the Ill, going
through Bludenz, the last of the four towns of the Vorarlberg
into which open the lateral valleys of the Ill. The Montafon
valley henceforth will allow the tourist who prefers scenic
beauty to speed, to make an interesting detour by way of the
Silvretta glaciers and to rejoin the main itinerary between St
Anton and Landeck. The direct road crosses the Arlberg, enters

the Tyrol and follows the valley of the Inn, from which run off the Paznaun, the greater Inn, Kauns, Pitz, and the Ötz, as far as Innsbruck, capital of the Tyrol. The Vorarlberg is a small region (pop. 188,000). Its towns and industries are not very important (only three undertakings employ more than 500 hands). Apart from the tourist trade, its principal resources are the manufacture of cloth and lace, and the harnessing of water-power which forms its wealth. Since the opening of the road linking the Bregenz forest and Warth, in the Arlberg, a second itinerary is available to the tourist: it runs through the forest of Bregenz and follows the valley of the Lech, through the Ausserfern region with Reutte and the Zugspitze, and reaches Innsbruck from the north-west. A complete tour of the Vorarlberg and the Western Tyrol can therefore be made by taking one itinerary for the outward journey and the other on the return.

The forest of Bregenz extends from Lake Konstanz to the foot of the Arlberg. Its inhabitants are the only shepherds in Austria who, in May, leave the village and move to a farm half-way up the alpine pastures, the *Maisess* (May residence). With the arrival of summer, the peasant leads his flocks up the mountain while his wife and children go back to the village. In September, everyone gathers again at the *Maisess* to return to the village for the winter. All the forest, as well as the valley of the Lech and the Ausserfern, is dotted with lakes and streams in which trout abound.

The two itineraries are set among the mountains, a real paradise for the mountaineer and skier, where almost every resort has its ski-lift or cable-seat track which enable the visitor to explore all the beauties of this perfect holiday country.

Gastronomy: The cooking in the Vorarlberg, land of shepherds, is the plainest in Austria and strongly influenced by Swiss cooking. The hotels and pensions, naturally, serve all Austrian dishes such as the Wienerschnitzel and countless pastries. Thanks to the cattle-breeders of the Montafon, the beef is excellent. Potatoes appear at all meals; the *sauerkraut* is very good and often served raw, as a salad. Two notable specialities: the Lake Konstanz mackerel and the cheese fritters. Trout abound in the forest of Bregenz and the Lech valley. Beer is usually served with meals (as it is throughout Austria), light in colour and usually very strong, or else cider. There are, however, two good Austrian wines: *Goldgelb* (white) and *Blutrot* (red).

PRINCIPAL SIGHTS

CHURCHES: Parish churches of Bregenz and Kaltenbrunnen; St Nicolas at Feldkirch. MUSEUMS: Bregenz and Bludenz. CASTLES: Alt-Ems and Neu-Ems at Hohenems; Schattenburg at Feldkirch; Gaienhofen at Bludenz; Wiesberg at Pians; Naudersberg. ABBEYS: Stams. VIEWS: Waterfalls of Stuiben; hydroelectric centres of Parthenen and Wald; bridge over the Trisanna; S.O.S. children's town at Imst; the Pfänder at Bregenz.

LOCHAU ★

Near the frontier, on left of road. Holiday resort with beach. The Hotel Schloss Hofen, former castle, is transformed into an hotel and, in winter, into an hotel school. Bar, dancing, restaurant with superb view over lake. The road follows the curve of the eastern bay to Bregenz.

A Recommended Hotel

Lochau: ★★ Hotel Schloss Hofen.

BREGENZ ★

(pop. 22,000 - 398m), capital of the Vorarlberg. Scene of an annual festival *(mid-July to mid-August)* at which the main attraction is "The Lake Theatre": a giant raft anchored in the bay opposite stands tiered like an amphitheatre, forms the stage for operettas.

Enter by the Reichsstrasse. The **Provincial Museum** *(March-Sept.: 8-12 and 2-6; Oct.-Feb.: 8-12, 2-5)*: of particular note are the altar of Hohenems (1580) and the Roman frescoes (5th century). This part is the New Town, known as the Lower Town, the business and communications centre. After the Town Hall we reach the gate of the Old Town ("Upper Town") which backs on to the Gebhardsberg. The town wall dating from the 13th century is preserved in part. Visit the *St Martin's Chapel*, built in 1362, with its residential tower containing very beautiful frescoes. Also see the cycle of Gothic frescoes in the *parish church*. Behind the stadium are the stands for the "Lake Theatre", the beach and the **Seeanlagen** (lake promenade). On right, the music pavilion where the local brass bands and the Vorarlberg Broadcasting orchestra give concerts throughout the summer. Bregenz has numerous hotels, cafés, restaurants, and dance-halls.

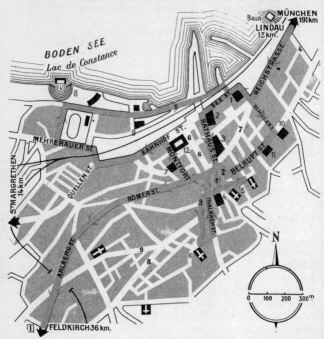

1 Main Post Office.   2 Provincial Museum.   3 Town Hall.   4 Gate to Old City.   5 St Martin's Chapel and Tower.   6 Parish Church.   7 Tourist Information Bureau.   8 Lake Theatre Stands.   9 Music Pavilion.   10 Cable Railway for the Pfänder.   11 Youth Hostel.   12 Station.
1 Maurachgasse.   2 Deuringstrasse.   3 Kirchstrasse.   4 Am Tannenbach. 5 Seeanlagen.   6 Kaiserstrasse.   7 Anton-Schneider-Strasse.   8 Gallusstrasse.   9 Riedergasse.

For fishing, apply for card at J. Reiner's stores, Schulgasse 3. Inquiries concerning shooting: Bez. Obm. Jussel Kunibert, Reichstrasse 6.

Bregenz is dominated by the Pfänder, a 1,056m mountain, from which there is a breathtaking view over Lake Konstanz and the forest of Bregenz. The cable-railway cars leave every half-hour from June to September; hourly from October to May; every ten minutes if traffic is heavy. The trip lasts eight minutes. There is a restaurant on the Pfänder. Youth hostel near starting-point of cable-railway.

There is an equally beautiful view from the summit of the Gebhardsberg (600m) on which are found the ruins of the castle of the Montforts and a pilgrim church. Restaurant at summit of mountain. The Bundestrasse (national highway No. 1) runs via the Bregenzer Ache and the hamlet of Lauterach. On left, the wooded mountains of the forest of Bregenz; on right, the Rhine and Lustenau.

N. — 10 km

Some Recommended Hotels

Bregenz am Bodensee: ** Hotel Weisses Kreuz. * Hotel Post.

DORNBIRN ★

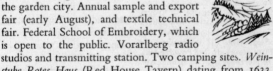

(pop. 22,500 - 429m), industrial town (textiles), the most densely populated in the Vorarlberg; it is known, however, as the garden city. Annual sample and export fair (early August), and textile technical fair. Federal School of Embroidery, which is open to the public. Vorarlberg radio studios and transmitting station. Two camping sites. *Weinstube Rotes Haus* (Red House Tavern) dating from 1633. In the immediate neighbourhood are the romantic gorges of Rappenlochschlucht and Alpenlochschlucht, and the winter-sports resort of **Bödele** (1,148 m).

N. — 7 km

Some Recommended Hotels

Bödele: * Bödelehotel.
Dornbirn: * Hotel Weisses Kreuz.

HOHENEMS ★

N. — 19 km

Holiday resort and thermal spa *Bad Ems* (rheumatism, gout, skin diseases) radio-active sulphur spring, radiological institute. Dominated by ruins of the Alt-Ems castle and the Neu-Ems castle (14th-15th century).

On the road, to left, is the Kummenberg. The district

stretching at the foot of this region is called "the garden of the Vorarlberg" and produces excellent wine: *Goldgelb* (Golden Yellow) and *Blutrubin* (ruddy ruby). After Götzis, comes Feldkirch.

A Recommended Hotel

Hohenems: ★ Gasthof-Pension Schwefelbad.

★ FELDKIRCH

1 Schattenburg. 2 Town Hall. 3 St Nicolas Church. 4 Cats Tower. 5 Coire Gate. 6 Schiller-Str. 7 Montfortgasse. 8 Kreuzgasse. 9 Volkshalle. 10 Robbers Tower. 11 Zeughausgasse. 12 Walgau-Str. 13 Burggasse. 14 Platz Neustadt. 15 Powder-Mill. 16 Herrengasse. 17 Bahnhofstr. 18 Reich-Str.

(pop. 15,000). Western gateway to Austria (tourists coming from Zürich, after crossing Liechtenstein, here rejoin road No. 1; Customs and Exchange Bureau at Tisis). Small medieval market-town by the Rhine and the Ill. Its name first appears in MSS dating from 830 A.D. Dominating the town is the **Schattenburg** Castle (10th century), from which there is a splendid view over Feldkirch, Switzerland, and Liechtenstein. Picturesque and very ancient Castle Tavern. The **Town Hall** houses some beautiful wood carvings. **St Nicolas Church** (1478): the pulpit is the finest example of Gothic cast-iron in the whole of Austria (1521). In centre of town are numerous arcaded streets; the Cats Tower (1491) of which the bell weighs nearly 8 tons; the Robbers Tower; the Coire and Mill gateways; the powder-mill and fountain. Business quarter: Marktgasse, Schmiedgasse, Montfortgasse, Kreuzgasse. Famous boarding-school for boys run by the Jesuit Fathers: *Stella Matutina*. Open-air concerts by the municipal band in the costumes of Old Feldkirch, folklore recitals in the evenings at the **Volkshalle** which holds 2,000 people. *Andreas Hofer Weinstube*, Tyrolean tavern, music, dancing, folklore evenings, native wines, Gymnasiumstrasse. Stadium,

swimming pool, tennis courts, camping sites. *Information
Bureau, Travel Agency and Exchange Office:* Kirchplatz 1.

A Recommended Hotel

Feldkirch: ✶ Hotel Hecht, 10 Neustadt.

FRASTANZ ★

from which there is a beautiful view over a mountain
range (2,055m), on right of road, **the Three Sisters.** They
are, according to legend, three sisters of Frastanz who were
turned into stone because one Sunday they went to pick
raspberries on the slopes of the Garsella instead of attending
Mass.

A Recommended Hotel

Frastanz im Walgau: ✶ Gasthof Stern.

NENZING ★

(sanatorium, camping site). On left, view over the Grosswalsertal and, further on, the mountains of Bludenz. Then,
on left, the Hängende Stein (Hanging Rock) and the Hoher
Frassen. To right, the Scesaplana.

BLUDENZ ★

We approach through the
Werdenberger Strasse. The
town is dominated by the
Gaienhofen Castle and the
parish church, approached
by a covered stairway of
100 steps. Narrow alleys,
medieval arcades. On the
Upper Gate is a fresco
representing Duke Frede-
rick of the Empty Pocket,
who sought refuge at
Bludenz when he was
banished from the Empire
soon after 1400. **Regional
Museum** (*Wed. and Sat.:
2-4; Sun. and holidays:*

1 Town Hall. 2 Museum and
Stadttor. 3 Pfarrkirche. 4 Station.
5 Wichner-Strasse. 6 St Peterstr.
7 Alte Landstr. 8 Bahnhofstr.
9 Spitalgasse.

10-12) with impressive relief of the Vorarlberg to scale
of 1/25,000.

Bludenz has been named the Gateway of the Alps, because five alpine valleys meet here: the Walgau, by which one arrives coming from Feldkirch, the Klostertal which leads to the Arlberg, the Grosswalsertal which leads by a narrow road of 29 km (1 : 12) through the resorts of Sonntag and Buchboden to Fontanella (1,152m) and to Faschina (1,500m), small holiday and winter-sports resort (open-air swimming pool, fishing), and finally the Brandnertal and the Montafon.

Some Recommended Hotels

Bludenz: ★ Hotel Post. ★ Hoher Frassen.

The **Brandnertal** (*Bludenz-Brand, 13 km, maximum gradient 1 : 12). Follow the Wichnerstrasse, cross the railway and the Ill (heading south-west). After 2 km: Bürs, 568 m. The road climbs* *with several bends past the St Wolfgang Chapel to Bürserberg a small winter-sports and holiday resort (870m). Cable railway on the Tschengla (1,227m). 6 km after Bürserberg:* **Brand** *(1,100m) health resort \ and winter-sports station at the foot of the Scesaplana (2,967m). To the east rises the* **Zimba** *(2,645m). Cable railway up the Niggenkopf (1,750m). Fishing. Good hotels, including the up-to-date Scesaplana.*

The **Montafon** (*Bludenz-Parthenen, 30 km). One of the loveliest Alpine valleys in Austria. Leave Bludenz by the St Peterstrasse. Instead of turning left into N. 1, continue straight on cross the Ill and the Montafon railway track. This valley, first settled by the Celts, then the Romans, the Alemannians, and finally the Valaisians, still keeps the beautiful national costumes decorated with embroidery and worn by the peasants on fête days. The road runs through St Anton-im-Montafon (652m) to* **Schruns** *(689m), chief town of the Montafon. Holiday and winter-sports resort. Very long ski-lift on the Kapellalpe (1,857m). Intermediate station at 1,355m. Local museum with folklore exhibits. In September, annual cattle fair (Montafon cattle). Bank and post office in church square in centre of Schruns. Montafon tourist inquiry office in station. On road leading to Tschagguns (two minutes from Schruns) along a canal, the swimming pool (on left) and, on right, the* **Kuranstalt Montafon**, *a very modern cure centre with fine hotel. Ultra-short-wave treatment, underwater massage, etc.; obesity, liver troubles, arthritis. Kneipp cures. Sauna open to public.*

Tschagguns *(684m) is an old site of pilgrimage, now a winter-sports and summer resort, very popular. Ski-lift up the Grabsalpe (1,500m; 15 min trip); from there a ski-lift climbs to 1,780m. Ski-jumping platform lit up at night. Folklore evenings and weekly concerts; bar, tea-room and dancing at the Hotel Sonne (good cellar), youth hostel on the heights. From Schruns, the road continues along the Ill. After 6 km, a narrow road turns off on right to* **Gargellen** *(1,424m) (8 km, 1 : 7), health resort and winter sports. Evening dances. Starting point for climbs in the Rhätikon and the Silvretta. Remarkable Alpine flora. Continuing along the main road, St Gallenkirch is reached before* **Gaschurn** *(951m), summer and winter-sports resort in a charming setting. Climbing in the Ferwall and the Silvretta. Guides. A little further on is* **Parthenen** *(1,021m), and the giant hydroelectric power installations of the Ill, which have earned Montafon the name "Valley of white coal". A funicular runs up beside the giant pipes through which the water runs, to Tromenir (1,700m), hauled by a single cable up a slope which at times reaches 4 : 5. The tip-truck used*

for transporting material weighing many tons can quite safely accommodate passengers. To counter the slope, the seats of the truck are slung right back. From Tromenir, a small railway runs to the **Fermunt Dam**, *also at 1,700m. This trip can be made on foot, but warm clothing is recommended because of the icy tunnels. Another funicular climbs from this barrage to 1,950m, then a second light railway runs to the Ober-Fermunt Dam at the foot of the glaciers, behind which rises the* **Piz Buin** *(3,312m), the grandest mountain in "The Blue Silvretta". The Ober-Fermunt dam is 80m high, with a 432m wall and a capacity of 430,000 cubic metres. The Ill power plant output is 600 million kwh annually, exploiting only half of its capacity. In 1954, annual production reached a milliard, and will eventually reach 2 milliard kwh when all the installations have been completed. This plant provides current for the whole province and exports the surplus abroad. Magnificent* *alpine excursions from Ober-Fermunt. Trips into the Tyrol and Switzerland through the Silvretta Mountains. Guides at Parthenen. The Ill hydroelectric company has now built a motor-road from Parthenen to the lakes of the Fermunt Dam which links the Montafon valley to the Paznauntal in the Tyrol, over the Silvretta Mountains.*

Some Recommended Hotels

Brand: * Hotel Scesaplana.
Gargellen: * Hotel Madrisa.
Parthenen: * Gasthof Silvretta.
Schruns: * Kurhotel Montafon.
Tschagguns: * Sporthotel Adler.

★ BLUDENZ

N. I 20 km

Leave Bludenz by the St Peterstrasse, past St Peterskirche (St Peter's) and turn left after crossing the railway. Go through Innerbraz. On left, waterfalls surrounded by the staging of a new hydroelectric plant which will supply additional power to the Arlberg Federal railway, now supplied by the Spullersee Dam, north-west of:

★ WALD

N. I 7 km

The natural lake of Spuller, 1,825m up, forms a reservoir of 13,500,000 cubic metres, thanks to two dam walls of 20m and 30m. The water runs through a 1,800m long underground gallery to the falls below the **Grafenspitze** (1,870m), clearly visible above and on left of road, and then gushes through two compression pipes into the turbines of the hydroelectric station of **Danöfen** beside the road running from Wald to **Klösterle** (1,069m), a small summer and winter-sports resort (camping sites).

★ LANGEN AM ARLBERG

N. I 9 km

The road runs below the railway track just before the station which stands at the entrance to the **Arlberg Tunnel**, 10,270m long. Langen is the starting-point for the whole Arlberg region. Many garages are found here, for, although the authorities make strenuous efforts to keep the Arlberg and Flexen passes clear, they are always liable to be closed by an exceptionally heavy snowfall. Motorists can then leave their cars at Langen and go on to Zürs and Lech by horse-drawn sleigh. Motorists making for the Tyrol who do not wish to pass through the Arlberg by road—which is very good and whose gradient never exceeds 1 : 8 on the western slope and 1 : 6 on the eastern—can have their cars trans-shipped by railway through the Arlberg Tunnel to St Anton *(10 services daily in the two directions when the pass is closed; six services daily in normal weather, and in summer. Fares: S 75 per car, plus S 2.80 per passenger).* The road runs up past **Stuben** (1,409m), holiday and winter-sports resort, towards the Rauzalpe.

A little before this, 1.3 km after Stuben, turn left; this is the **Flexenstrasse,** *renowned for its tunnels, galleries, and protective roofs against avalanches and landslides. Marvellous view over Stuben and the mountains. After the Flexen Pass (1,784m), the road runs gently down to* **Zürs am Arlberg** *(1,720m), one of the best-known and most fashionable winter-sports resorts in Austria. First-class hotels with all modern comforts, but still retaining the typical Austrian character. Bars, dances, fêtes, ski-carnival. Three ski-lifts, one of 1,470m in length leading to the* **Zürsersee** *(2,245m), and another of 1,550m up the* **Hexenboden** *(2,230m) which saves two hours of climbing. Zürs has snow from November to May, and this long period, plus its long slopes bare of trees, make it an ideal ski-ing centre. Among the competitions held there, the most famous is the giant slalom of the Zürsersee, held around mid-April. Owing to the absence of trees, Zürs is not an ideal spot for a lengthy summer stay. But, with its ample hotel accommodation, it is recommended as a stopping-place for motorists, who can break their journey and be certain of finding a room in a very good hotel at the height of the season.*

Lech am Arlberg *(1,447m). Very sunny alpine health resort and winter-sports centre, as renowned, but less fashionable than Zürs. Two ski-lifts. An automatic cable railway, the first to be built in Europe, links the hotels of Lech and Oberlech (1,705m). Evening dances, balls. Numerous ski competitions, including* *the* Westencup, *held during January. Every summer, at the end of August, Arlberg car and motor-cycle rally. Swimming pool, tennis courts. Beautiful fresco dating from the 13th century on outside wall of town hall.*

Continuing along the road, Warth *is reached (see secondary itinerary later), from which the Tyrol can be entered either through the forest of Bregenz (road No. 200) or by the Lechtal.* The Arlberg Pass forms the frontier between the Vorarlberg and the Tyrol.

Some Recommended Hotels

Langen am Arlberg: ★ Hotel Arlbergerhof.
Lech am Arlberg: ★ Sporthotel Schneider.
Oberlech am Arlberg: ★ Hotel Sonnenburg.
Stuben: ★ Hotel Post.

★ ST CHRISTOPH AM ARLBERG

(1,803m), winter-sports station where all Austrian ski-teachers must take a course before being granted a licence by the Government. Cable-railway up the Galzig (2,080 m), built in 1952 for the 25th jubilee of the famous ski-race "Arlberg-Kandahar" to serve the track reserved for the ladies championship. The St Christoph Hotel is a former convent built in 1386. Youth hostel. The road then runs down towards St Anton-am-Arlberg.

A Recommended Hotel

St Christoph am Arlberg: ★ Gasthof Hospiz.

★ ST ANTON-AM-ARLBERG

(1,304m), one of the best-known winter-sports resorts in the world, cradle of the Alpine ski technique (Hannes Schneider school). Very good hotels (the Dutch Royal Family come here every year). Fashionable atmosphere. Tennis courts, shooting, fishing, camping sites, swimming in the Moorsee, a lake 20 minutes from St Anton. Cable railway up the Galzig. Eastern exit of the Arlberg Tunnel. Drivers who have had their cars transported by rail through the tunnel pick up the road at St Anton. This runs gently

N. 1 - 6 km

N. 1 - 22 km

down following the Stanzertal, through the village of Pettneu to Pians.

Some Recommended Hotels

St Anton-am-Arlberg: ** Hotel Post. * Hotel Schwarzer Adler.

(913m). Recommended visits: the Castle of Wiesberg, the ruins of several fortresses and the waterfalls, as well as the impressive **Trisanna Bridge**, 225m long and 88m high. Starting point for **visits to the Paznauntal** *(from Pians to Galtür, 40 km). Follow the Trisanna (waterfalls). Climb of 1 : 10 to Kappl (1,258m), base for climbs in the Ferwall Mountains, and to Ischgl (1,377m), at the mouth of the Fimbertal. Health resort. Swimming pool. Evening dances. Excursions in the Ferwall Mountains, the Samnaun, and the Silvretta. Through Paznaun, which gave its name to the valley, to Galtür (1,583m). Health resort surrounded by giant mountain peaks: the Fluchthorn, Ballunspitze, Piz Buin, Dreiländerspitze, etc. Peasant theatre, café-dances, open-air concerts. Swimming pool. Winter sports. From Galtür, excursions can be made to the Silvretta (tour of the Montafon valley). The Ill hydroelectric company has undertaken construction of a road running from Galtür to the Madlener-Hütte (1,986 m) in the Silvretta Mountains and to the lakes of Fermunt.*

(pop. 5,000 - 816m). The biggest town in the higher Inn valley. Regional museum, small church built to commemorate the plague which ravaged the district in the 18th century. 12 castles (fortresses sometimes in ruins) in the neighbourhood. The town is dominated by **Landeck Castle.** Folklore displays, open-air concerts, theatrical shows. Swimming pool, tennis courts, stadium, camping sites. Near Landeck is the **Pontlatz Bridge**, around which were fought the battles for the freedom of the Tyrol in 1809. Landeck is the starting point for a visit to the Kaunsertal and the higher Inn valley, which leads via Nauders to Switzerland and Italy.

N. I 5 km

N. I 20 km

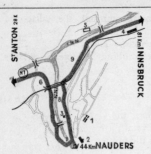

1 Church. **2** Castle. **3** Post Office. **4** Station. **5** Swimming Pool. **6** Innstrasse. **7** Gerber-Brücke. **8** Malser-Strasse. **9** Jubiläumsstrasse.

Kaunsertal and Higher Inn Valley tour (*Landeck–Nauders: 40 km*). *By the Pontlatz Bridge to Prutz (861m), holiday place with an acidulated mineral spring. Nearby is found* **Ladis** *and* **Obladis** *(take right fork), summer resorts specially recommended for rest. Alpine rest home for children, hotel, cure establishment (sulphur spring and acidulated spring). Hochserfaus Observatory and fortress of Laudeck. Houses of a very special style: the Rhaeto-Roman style which is found only in this area. At Prutz, leave the Inn, take the road which follows the Faggenbach and runs into the Kaunsertal (42 km from Landeck). By Kaltenbrunnen (1,098m) see the remarkable pilgrim church in the forest, to Feuchten, last village in this valley (1,273m), and to the Gepatschhaus refuge on the edge of a huge glacier. Continuing*

from Prutz towards the south-west by the road along the right bank of the Inn, we come through Hochfinstermünz to **Nauders** *(1,365m). To be visited: the Naudersberg Castle, the ruins of the Hochfinstermünz. Café-bar, open-air concerts. Swimming pool. Exit towards Italy over the Reschen-Scheideck pass (1,490m): 5 km. The Reschensee. Exit towards Switzerland, towards Schuls and the Engadine, via Martinsbruck: 8 km.*

From Landeck, by Zams, to Imst.

Some Recommended Hotels

Ladis: ★ Hotel Bad Ladis.
Landeck: ★ Hotel Schwarzer Adler.
Nauders: ★ Hotel Margarethe Maultasch.
Obladis: ★ Kurhotel Obladis.

★ **IMST**

(828m). Health resort in a very beautiful setting, the *Oppidum Humiste* of the Romans. In the Middle Ages,

Imst was an important communications centre with a flourishing mining industry and big trade. Imst was then famous particularly for its bird dealing. The bird-fanciers of Imst, often grouped in big companies, exported canaries as far away as Russia, England, Turkey, and Egypt. The town was destroyed by fire in 1822. Today, its main industries are textiles and tiles. Recommended visits: the regional museum and the *Zur Post* inn, former lordly mansion, as well as the **S.O.S. children's village** run by the Societas Socialis, a village of orphans and children removed from unworthy parents. In the neighbourhood is the Rosengartlschlucht Gorge and the Pitztal, a valley running down to the south. Imst has a peasant theatre, a beach and swimming pool. Famous folklore fête during Carnival-time: *Imster Schemenlaufen*. This is a procession of hideous masks, carved in wood and crowned with vast artistic head-dresses representing scenes of village life, decorated with numerous large and small bells. The ugly masks and the noise of the bells are supposed to frighten and chase away the evil spirits of winter.

Imst has the first "motel" (motorist hotel) in Austria, to the west of the station, on left of the road arriving from Landeck, where drivers can rent bungalows and do their own cooking, or take their meals in the "motel" hotel.

A Recommended Hotel

Imst: ⋆ Hotel-Pension Hohe Warte.

9 km from Imst, a road branches to the south, in the Ötztal. **Visit to the Ötztal** *(from national highway to Obergurgl: 40 km). The Ötztal is one of the favourite valleys of mountaineers and skiers. The resorts in this valley are all health centres, winter-sports resorts and bases for trips in the Ötztal Alps.* **Ötz (820m),** *at the foot of the Acher-kogel. To be visited: collection of regional art, mural paintings in the Stern inn. Holiday courses for foreigners. Water sports on the Pieburger See, a few minutes from Ötz. Tennis courts. By Umhausen and the Stulben water-falls, one fall of 150m can be seen on left of*

road, to Längenfeld, 1,179m. Sulphur spring, Kurhotel (cures by taking waters, and baths). Fine Gothic church with baroque-style interior.

Sölden *(1,377m), very popular resort. Tennis, horse-riding, folklore displays. Linked to* **Hochsölden** *(2,077m) by cable seat railway, the second longest in Austria. The trip takes 23 minutes, and is the only means of communication with the hotels of Hochsölden. The cable carries both passengers and their luggage, as well as supplies for the hotels. By the Kühtreien-schlucht (gorge) to Zwieselstein (1,472m), where the valley splits up: to left, the Gurgltal; to right, the Ventertal. Vent lies 13 km from Längenfeld (1,893m), opposite the Wildspitze (3,774m). The Längenfeld-Vent road is very bad, and can be used in winter only by motor-sleigh or caterpillar tractor.*

Obergurgl *(1,927m) is reached via Angern (Untergurgl) (gradient 1 : 10). Obergurgl is the highest parish in Austria. Vent and Obergurgl are dream resorts for alpine-skiers, for they are surrounded by peaks of over 3,000m, on the slopes and glaciers of which one can ski even in summer. Professor Piccard landed on the Obergurgl Glacier after his first ascent into the stratosphere. The priest of Obergurgl parish, Franz Senn, was the first to undertake climbs of the Ötztal Alps. He founded the Austrian Alpine Club towards the end of the 19th century. Today, a great number of refuge huts, well-marked paths admirably maintained, and guides at all centres in the Ötztal allow novice climbers, and even non-climbing tourists, to ascend some of the Ötztal Alps.*

Some Recommended Hotels

Hochsölden: ★ Hotel Enzian.
Obergurgl: ★ Hotel Edelweiss und Gurgl.
Ötz: ★ Hotel Drei Mohren.
Sölden: ★ Hotel Bergland.

The road runs in front of the Petersburg Castle (on right) and a little to the north of **Stams** (671m), of which the magnificent Cistercian **Abbey**, founded in 1284, can be seen. It houses the famous *Rose Grill* by Bachnetzer (1716). Noteworthy parish church built in 1318 by King Henry of Bohemia. By **Telfs** (carnival procession like that of Imst)

to Pettnau, where the old Tyrolean inn, the Öttl inn, merits
a halt as much for its interior as for the Tyrolean cooking
and excellent cellar. After **Zirl** (622m), the road runs along
the *Martinswand* (St Martin's Wall), in which a cross
commemorates the fact that Emperor Maximilian I was
lost here in 1113, while hunting chamois, and was rescued,
according to legend, in a miraculous way. By the village
of Kranebitten to

INNSBRUCK ★

SECONDARY ITINERARY: BY THE FOREST OF BREGENZ, LECH
VALLEY, AND THE AUSSERFERN: 229 KM.

BREGENZ ★

Leave Bregenz by the Arlbergstrasse, turn left behind
the bridge, take the first road on right. After 6 km, again
turn left. By road No. 200 to:

N. 1 — 14 km

ALBERSCHWENDE ★

(721m), very sunny holiday resort near the pilgrimage site
of **Bildstein.** Through the hamlets of Egg and Andelsbuch.
The road and river run round the **Bezegg** (955m), one
time place of popular assemblies which administered
justice. Commemorative monument: the Pillar of Bezegg.

N. 200 21 km

BEZAU ★

(651m), health resort, chief town of the forest of Bregenz.
Concerts, evening dances. 2.5 km to south is **Bad Reuthe**
(ferruginous springs). Visit Reuthe church (13th century).
Then through the villages of Klaus (on right: Fluhbach
waterfalls) and Mellau, dominated by the Hangspitze
(1,748m).

N. 200 13 km

AU ★

(796m), holiday resort at foot of the Kanisfluh (2,047m)
at the head of the Argenbach Valley. Camping site. A
rather poor road climbs up this valley to **Damüls** (1,428m),
health resort and winter sports (10 km, 1 : 9).

N. 200 5 km

A Recommended Hotel

Au: ★ Hotel Krone.

★ **SCHOPPERNAU**

N. 200   9 km

(856m), holiday resort in a wide valley at the foot of the Hochkinzelspitze (2,415m). After Hopfreben, a small health resort, the rather bad road climbs to:

★ **SCHRÖCKEN**

N. 200   9 km

(1,260m). Summer and winter-sports resort in a beautiful setting: excellent ski-slopes, ski-lift. Beach and skating on nearby lake: the **Körbersee**. Camping site near the lake. A road opened to traffic in 1953 links Schröcken with Warth-am-Arlberg.

A Recommended Hotel

Schröcken: ★ Körberseehotel.

★ **WARTH-AM-ARLBERG**

N. 198   53 km

(1,499m), health resort and winter-sports centre. Guides for climbing. Last village of the Vorarlberg before entering the Tyrol down the Lech Valley. To right to reach the Arlberg Pass and National Highway No. 1 (see main itinerary) via Lech, Zürs, and the Flexen Pass.

From Warth the road now runs down to Steeg, in the Lech Valley, one of the longest valleys in the Tyrol. All the villages encountered: Holzgau, between the Parseierspitze (3,038m) on right and the Mädelegabel (2,649m) on left; Elbigenalp, the oldest parish in the valley; Haselgehr, Elmen, and Stanzach have a particular lure for trout-fishing lovers, and those who are content with humble, but clean, inns. Via Forschach to Weissenbach.

A Recommended Hotel

Warth-am-Arlberg: ★ Berghotel Biberkopf.

★ **WEISSENBACH**

N. 198   9 km

(887m). The region north-west of Innsbruck and south of the Bavarian frontier is known as the Ausserfern. It has a wealth of lakes and streams which are well-known to sporting anglers throughout Europe. At Weissenbach, a road forks to the north-west and follows the **Tannheim Valley**. *(Weissenbach - Schattwald: 20 km). The road runs beside, and then crosses, the Weissbach in the gorge of the Gaicht Pass. On right, the Gaicht-Spitze (1,988m). Nesselwängle (1,147m), holiday resort below the Köllenspitze (2,246m),*

tennis courts. Haller am Haldensee (1,124m)
small summer resort on an alpine lake 2 km
long, rich in fish. The road runs along the
north bank of the lake to the village of Halden-
see; then, on right, a small road leads to Grän
(1,114m), holiday resort with humble inns,
particularly popular with youths. Tannheim
(1,097m) chief town of the valley, holiday resort near (4 km)
the Vilsalpsee, a mountain lake 1,135m up in a beautiful setting.
Via Schöblen to Schattwald (1,072m), last holiday resort before
the German frontier which is found at the **Oberjoch,** *2 km from*
Schattwald. Beyond, on this road, lie Sonthofen (19 km) and
Immenstadt (28 km).

From Weissenbach, along the left bank of the Lech, through
Hornberg, Höfen, Platten, and Winkl, to:

REUTTE ★

(854m), chief town of the Ausserfern, very
sunny. Holiday resort with numerous
attractions: tennis, swimming pool, theatre
shows, woodland fêtes, folklore evenings.
The Engel family of musicians, comprising
the father and his seven children, each of
whom play several instruments, well-
known throughout the region for their beautiful interpre-
tation of Tyrolean music, live at Reutte where they give
frequent concerts. Many lakes in the neighbourhood for
water sports.

From Reutte, two roads lead to Germany and link up with the
Frankfurt-Salzburg autobahn: one runs via Vils to Kempten
and Ulm (141 km), the other through Füssen to Augsburg
(120 km). To the east, a road (5 km) runs via Breitenwang
(849m), the oldest hamlet in the valley, to the Plansee, a lake
6 km long. There is no holiday resort by the lake, but there are
two hotels, the Seespitz and the Forelle, on the northern bank.
Between the Plansee and the Heiterwanger See, south of the
Plansee to which it is linked, are extensive camping sites.

From Reutte to the south-east to Heiterwang (992m) on
the Heiterwanger See, and to Bichlbach (1,075m), summer
resort from which a road (5 km) climbs to **Berwang**
(1,336m), well-known holiday and winter-sports resort

N. 189 20 km

and one of the sunniest places in the Tyrol, set on a wide plateau. Health cures. Concerts, dancing, bars, and major ski competitions (Bear of Berwang Medal).

Some Recommended Hotels

Berwang: ★ Hotel Kreuz.
Reutte: ★ Hotel Goldener Hirsch.

★ LERMOOS

N. 189 2 km

(895m), alpine health and winter-sports resort on a plateau. Splendid view over the steep slopes of the Wetterstein. Open-air concerts, folklore fêtes, dancing, tennis courts. Leave the road down to the south here, and take that on the left which runs over the Ehrwald Pass to Garmisch-Partenkirchen (26 km), in Germany. At the first fork, keep right, then once again right.

A Recommended Hotel

Lermoos: ★ Hotel Drei Mohren.

★ EHRWALD

(996m). Holiday and winter-sports resort at the foot of the Zugspitze, surrounded by forests of larches. Swimming pool, tennis courts, woodland festivals, open-air concerts. Starting point for one of the most daring cable-railways in Europe (3,375m long), which, in 18 minutes, climbs from Ehrwald up to 2,805m on the Austrian side of the Zug-spitze. At the terminal is the Zugspitzbahn-Berghotel. A tunnel for pedestrians leads from here, in 25 minutes, to the Schneefernerhaus, an hotel on the German slope of the Zugspitze, from which another cable railway climbs 2,963m to the summit of the mountain in four minutes. From a terrace there is a wonderful panoramic view of the Tyrolean and Bavarian mountains, whose names and altitudes are indicated on the parapet of the terrace. Leave Lermoos by the southerly road which climbs via Biberwier to the Fern Pass (1,209m). On the left can be seen remains of the old Roman road which ran on the floor of the valley, and also above the motor-road a route which was once used by the Celts. On right of the road is the Mittersee; on left, the Weissensee. Then, again on right, far below,

	1	Schleppten	0	
		Bio t	2	
		6.—	42	1
		holce.	15130	—

HOTEL ASTORIA

WIEN I.
KÄRNTNERSTRASSE 32

TISCH NR. 2

2	Tarm fisch	26	40
2	Wiener	46	20
1	Bratkartoffel	7	20
1	Salat	6	60
2	?		

the Blindsee. A few winding turns lead to the Fern Pass.
After the pass the road runs through Fernstein, on the Fern-
steiner See. On an island in this lake are the ruins of the
Sigmundsburg, hunting lodge of the Duke Sigismund,
built in 1460. Overlooking the road, on right, is Fernstein
Castle. The Fernstein lake is full of trout. By **Nassereith**
(843m), summer resort in the Gurgltal, and the beautiful
Mieminger Plateau to **Telfs**, where this itinerary overlaps
the direct Bregenz-Innsbruck itinerary. At Telfs as well as
Nassereith, during carnival time, there are some quaint
processions similar to those of Imst. Instead·of leaving Telfs
by the national highway, take the road to the north-east,
then bear right at the first fork. The road is not good, but
is very picturesque. It affords a magnificent view over the
Inn valley. Then via **Mösern** to Seefeld.

A Recommended Hotel

Ehrwald: ＊ Hotel Maria Regina.

SEEFELD ＊

(1,180m), alpine health resort on a high
plateau between the Wetterstein and Kar-
wendel ranges, and internationally known
winter-sports resort ‚with excellent hotels.
Ski school and training classes run by Toni
Seelos, the world champion. Numerous
attractions. International ski-ing contests,
including the "Silver Ball of Seefeld" at the beginning of
March. Beaches on the Wildsee. Skating rink in front of
the Hotel Wetterstein. Camping sites. Kurhotel in the·
northern periphery of the resort, with one of the most
important radio-active springs in Austria, rich in mineral
salts. The baths are taken at the hotel itself, which belongs
to the ·Chamber of Doctors of the Tyrol. Noteworthy
parish church (1431) and Lake Chapel (Seekapelle) built
in 1628 by Archduke Leopold V to house a miraculous
cross. *From Seefeld, road No. 185 runs north, 33 km, via
Scharnitz (963m), holiday resort on the Scharnitz Pass, Austro-
German frontier, and Mittenwald in Bavaria to Garmisch-
Partenkirchen.*

Some Recommended Hotels

Seefeld: ＊＊ Hotel Eden. ＊ Hotel Berghof.

N. 189   52 km

N. 185 and N. 1   22 km

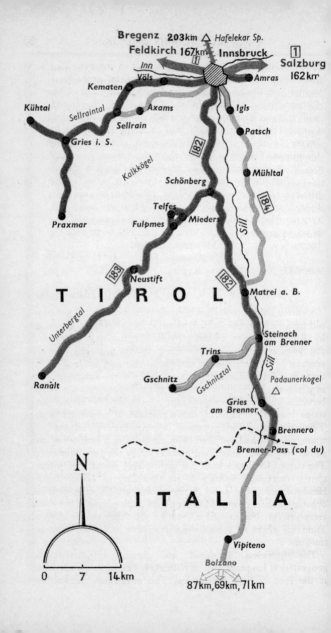

Leave Seefeld to the south. Just before Auland, a road forks right. It serves the big chemical factory where Ichthyol, the internationally known medicament made with the oil extracted from the schist found near Seefeld, is manufactured. Doctors may visit factory on request, guide supplied. The road leading from Seefeld to Innsbruck affords very beautiful views over the Inn Valley, but it should be negotiated with care. Just before Reith (1,130m) begins the famous **Zirlerberg** descent (1,180m) which is used, in the other direction, for hill-climbing trials. Go down in first! Above Zirl is a hairpin bend, with, opposite, a special slope constructed for the cars whose brakes fail. At Zirl, the itinerary rejoins the national highway No. 1 which leads direct to:

INNSBRUCK ★

INNSBRUCK AND ENVIRONS

Centre of the Tyrol, land of mountains where thousand-year-old traditions are maintained, to the great delight of the tourists. In all holiday resorts of this province, on fine days throughout the year, there are country fêtes, processions, and open-air concerts by the local band in traditional costume, while in winter there are Tyrolean evenings. The *Schuhplattler*, Tyrolean dance in which the feet hammer the ground (and sometimes the leather breeches of a rival) in waltz-time, alternate with the yodelling songs known throughout the whole world under the name Tyrolean. On all the mountains, where chamois and deer still roam, refuge-huts have been built; they are well maintained and allow visitors to make long excursions in the best conditions. The city of Innsbruck itself is a fine holiday resort, and winter-sports resort well worthy of its title City of Mountaineers. Headquarters of the Tyrol Alpine School which, each summer, organizes alpine courses of one or two weeks through the finest areas of the Western Alps, and of the Institute of Physical Training, where all Austrian ski professors and instructors are trained.

The expression "Innsbruck site" signifies in international geographical language any city situated, like it, in a wide basin at the foot of high mountains. The mountains surrounding

Innsbruck are well equipped with cable railways and cable seat-carriers. A great number of day, or half-day, excursions in the loveliest Alps of the Tyrol are thus available for the tourist. Innsbruck and its surroundings are indisputably the perfect tourist district of the Tyrol.

Gastronomy: Dishes essentially Tyrolean are: the *Gröstl*, beef cut into small pieces and roasted in the oven with potatoes, and the *Tirolerknödeln*, a kind of meat ball made with white bread and pork fat. The Tyrol, like all Austrian provinces, has its own special pastries: the *Hupfauf* and the *Schutzauf*, cream cheese cakes; the *B'soffner Kapuziner*, made with white bread, almonds, and raisins, and the *Lebkuchen*, a kind of gingerbread cut in the shape of a heart, a tree, or people, etc.

The south Tyrol produces good wines, of which the best known are the *Südtiroler Rötel* and the *Kalterer-See*.

PRINCIPAL SIGHTS

CHURCH: Hofkirche. MUSEUMS: Ferdinandeum and Volkskunstmuseum. CASTLE: Amras. MONU-MENTS: Goldenes Dachl; Helblinghaus; Stadt-turm; Triumphal Arch; Mount Isel. VIEWS: Hafele-kar; Patscherkofel.

★ INNSBRUCK

(pop. 95,000 - 574m). Capital of the Tyrol, one of the most beautiful towns in the Alps, with its famous view over the Nordkette (the Northern Chain). Mountaineering centre, transport and trade centre of Western Austria, it is the site at the end of every summer of a great Exhibition and Export Fair, with sections for the tourist industry and mountaineering. Head-quarters of the Government and administrative services of the Tyrol.

The city is growing so rapidly that even the speeded-up rate of building is still inadequate, and there are a number of temporary housing estates. One of these new colonies can be seen beside national highway No. 1, on arriving from the Arlberg, the *Heilig-Jahr-Siedlung* (Holy Year Suburb). The new Pradl district, east of the station and the viaduct which runs through the city, is a fine example of modern Tyrolean architecture. On the cultural plane, Innsbruck also holds first place among the towns of Western Austria: its University, which comprises 4 faculties, has trained and drawn many distinguished men, including Dr

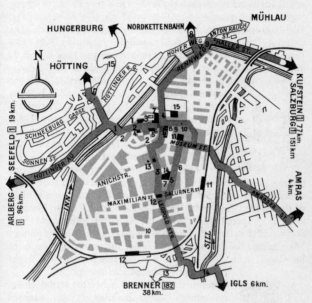

1 Inn Bridge. 2 Herzog-Friedrichstr. 3 Maria-Theresienstr. 4 Rennplatz. 5 Wilhelm-Greil-Str. 6 Bozner Platz. 7 Fuggergasse. 8 Nordkettenbahn. 9 Mühlauer Brücke. 10 Fischer-Str. 11 Hauptbahnhof. 12 Westbahnhof. 13 Brenner-Str. 14 Kloster-Gasse. 15 Höhen-Str.

1 Ottoburg. 2 Memorial to the Dead. 3 Little Golden Roof. 4 Katzung House. 5 City Tower. 6 Burgriese (Giant's House). 7 Hofburg. 8 Hofkirche. 9 Museum of Popular Tyrolean Art. 10 Old University. 11 The Fernandeum. 12 Arch of Triumph. 13 St Anne's Column. 14 The Landhaus. 15 The Hofgarten.

March, physicist, collaborator of Dr Schrödinger, Nobel Prizewinner. A number of young painters and sculptors from Innsbruck and district are also very well-known. The Inn Bridge which

leads into the town from the Arlberg direction, is not the original
bridge built in the Middle Ages to facilitate trade with Germany
and Italy but is a rebuilt version of later date. Before the bridge,
the road runs through the Maria-Hilf and Hötting districts, in
which are found the **Botanical Gardens** in a very beautiful setting
(open: April-September 7-7; October-March 8-5; admission free).
The **Herzog-Friedrich-Strasse** is the heart of old Innsbruck. The
Ottoburg, on left, the city's oldest building, probably dates from
1240, with a medieval dwelling tower erected in 1494 by Maximilian I. There is a very good restaurant in the tower. Nearby
can be seen part of the ancient walls. A little further on is the

Goldenes Dachl (Little Golden Roof), a balcony
sheltered by a pent-roof of gilded tiles. According
to legend, the gilding of this roof cost Duke
Frederick, known as *Empty-Purse*, 30,000 ducats
and he had it built to belie his nickname and
bolster his credit, making believe that the tiles
were of solid gold. In point of fact, this balcony
leaning against the wall of the former Imperial Castle took shape
under Emperor Maximilian I, who wanted to make it a symbol
of the Golden Age which would begin with his reign. He used
it as an Imperial box during the knightly tournaments and
festivals held in the little square. Paintings on the balcony portray
Maximilian, his first and second wife, and many dignitaries of
his Court, with their blazons. The bas-reliefs portray different
games and battles of various epochs.

Opposite the Goldenes Dachl is the **Helblinghaus,**
a beautiful Gothic building (1520), adorned
with rococo-style stuccoes. Many of the city
burgesses, wishing to follow the fashion of their
times, had the marvellous Gothic façades recovered with rich stuccoes. The Katzung House,
however, at No. 16, retains intact its end-Gothic
reliefs. On both sides of the street leading to the Maria-Theresienstrasse are arcades, beneath which are found shops and taverns.
All these houses are still inhabited. On entering by the low gates
and corridors with Gothic vaulting, one has the impression of
returning to the Middle Ages. On left, coming from the Goldenes
Dachl, is the **Stadtturm**, the *City Tower*, which commands a
fine view of the city. In all the lanes of Old Innsbruck, note the
strange form of the roofs in shape of a V, with the angle set in

the middle of the house, giving the impression that the roof has
been put on the wrong way round. At No. 3 Hofgasse is the
House of the German Order built in 1530, and, at No. 12, the
Burgriese, built for his favourite giant, Nikolas Heidls, in 1487,
by Duke Sigismund of the Tyrol, son of Frederick Empty-Purse,
who was as wealthy as his father was poor. On the façade of the
house is a life-size statue of the giant. At the end of the lane, on
left, is the **Hofburg** (entrance in Rennplatz),
former Imperial residence built in 1496 under
Emperor Maximilian I and restored under the
Empress Maria-Theresia in 1770. Visit the "Hall
of the Giants", two storeys high, with its beautiful
rococo-style decorations, frescoes by Maulpertsch, and portraits of Maria-Theresia, Francis I,

etc. by Meytens. One room is devoted to the Tyrolean national
hero Andreas Hofer, who led the struggle for Tyrolean freedom
against Napoleon. Visits with guide *(9-12 and 2-5; Sunday: 9-12)*
include tours of the **Silver Chapel** (Silberkapelle) and the **Hofkirche** (also known as the Franziskanerkirche). Fee: S 3. The
Hofkirche and Silver Chapel can, however, be visited without
a guide. To left on entering is a marble statue of Andreas Hofer,
by Professor Schaller of Vienna. Since 1823 Andreas Hofer's
body has lain beneath this memorial, accompanied by two of
his best comrades-in-arms. Opposite the statue is a memorial
to the dead of the Tyrolean war of liberation of 1809.
On right, a stairway leads to the Silver Chapel (also linked to
the Hofburg), which derives its name from a Virgin and a bas-
relief in silver which adorn the altar. It contains the black and
white marble tomb of Archduke Ferdinand of the Tyrol, founder
of this chapel, who died in 1595, and that of his morganatic wife
Philippine Welser, who died in 1580, decorated with bas-reliefs
by Alexander Colins (1581). The church was built between
1553 and 1563 to carry out the dying wish of Emperor Maximilian I, who died in 1519, to house his **tomb** which is one of
the greatest masterpieces of the German Renaissance. The bronze
statue represents the kneeling Emperor on a tall, white marble
sarcophagus (Maximilian is buried at Wiener Neustadt, his
birthplace). On the sarcophagus are 24 bas-reliefs in Carrara
marble, separated by black marble columns, the work of Alexander Colins who completed it in 1566. A magnificent railing
in wrought-iron and repoussé work, encloses the monument.

A few yards away, on each side of this monumental tomb, stand **28 gigantic bronze statues** which the people of Innsbruck call irreverently, but proudly, "Die Schwarzen Manndln" (The little black fellows). Maximilian I wanted to surround his tomb with all the members of his family and ancestors, even legendary. The statues were ordered by his son Ferdinand I from the greatest sculptor of his day: Peter Vischer of Nuremberg. But as payment of his fees was delayed, Vischer executed only the statues of the legendary King Arthur of England and of Theodoric, King of the Ostrogoths, which are the most beautiful. Ferdinand I entrusted the rest of the work to the Godl brothers, also of Nuremberg, and when they refused to carry on for the same reason as Peter Vischer, to the Tyroleans Hans Lendenstreich and Gregor Löffler. Finally, the grandson of Maximilian had the last statues made by Gilg Sesselschreiber of Augsburg. They include all the great princes and princesses of the houses of Burgundy and Austria.

Beside the Hofkirche is the **Tiroler Volkskunstmuseum** (Museum of Tyrolean popular art) in a building dating from 1560. *(Open 9-12 and 2-5; Sunday: 9-12.)* Ground floor, museum of Tyrolean dress: life-size models carved in wood, wearing the different costumes of all the regions, valleys, and localities of the Tyrol. The sculptor Virgil Rainer (who died in 1948) made faithful reproductions of the people to whom the costumes belonged and who sat as models. The tall bearded person in the last showcase is the sculptor himself. Also on ground floor is a collection of masks and accessories for folklore processions, kitchen and farm utensils, and sleighs of Old Tyrol. Well worth a visit on the upper floors are the old Tyrolean dwellings, faithfully reconstructed, with authentic furniture and utensils. The rooms, common rooms and kitchens (18 in all) from the 15th and 16th century are found on the first floor; those of the 16th and 17th century on the second floor. Other rooms contain very fine furniture: the famous painted wardrobes of Zillertal, wardrobes, cabinets and beds, all painted, of the different districts, and handsome earthenware stoves of all periods; collections of artistic works in wrought iron, crystal, ceramics, wood, and leather, and models of Tyrolean houses. Next to the Museum of Popular Art is the Old University, founded in 1677, and the Jesuit church.

In the Museumstrasse is the **Fernandeum,** the greatest provincial museum in Austria, both for the wealth and variety of exhibits. *(Open 9-12, 2-5; Sunday and holidays: 9-12. July to September: 9-5.)* The museum houses an art collection and historical and natural history exhibits. Make a particular note of the Franz Defregger Hall, a Tyrolean painter (1835-1921), who spent his youth in his native mountains as a shepherd; the room devoted to Dutch masters, and the 7th-century Langobardien tomb. Through the Wilhelm-Greilstrasse, which crosses the Bozner Platz in which stands the provincial travel agency *Tiroler Landesreisebüro,* to the Triumphal Arch, erected by the citizens of Innsbruck in 1765 on the occasion of the wedding of the future Emperor Leopold II, son of Maria-Theresa and Francis I, to the Spanish Infanta Maria Ludovica. As the Emperor died suddenly during the nuptial celebrations, one side of the arch bears mourning symbols.

This is the beginning of the famous **Maria-Theresienstrasse,** a great artery flanked by palaces and great houses, in the centre of which rises the column of St Anne (Annasäule). On left, the church and former monastery of Servites; on right, the Thurn and Taxis Palace (1679), now the seat of the Tyrolean Government, forming the angle of the Maria-Theresienstrasse and the Fuggergasse. In this, beside the palace, is the Neues Landhaus (County Council), which now houses the French Occupation authorities. Adjoining the palace in the Maria-Theresienstrasse, the Altes Landhaus (1728). At 3 Burggraben, is the Innsbruck Tourist Information Offices. Through an arch, beside the Hofkirche, is the Rennweg. On right, the Hofgarten, a fine public garden with a pavilion in which there are always exhibitions by Tyrolean artists. *(Open 10-12, 3-6.)* Follow the Rennweg as far as the Mühlauer Brücke, which is the terminal of the Hungerburg-Nordkettenbahn. By the departure station is a pavilion with gigantic mural paintings of the Battle of Mont Isel in 1809 *(open 7-5 without interruption).* The Hungerburgbahn is a cable railway which runs up to the Hungerburg (863m), departures every half-hour and, at peak periods, every quarter of an hour. There is a beautiful view over the city from the top (trip takes ten minutes). The Hungerburg can also be reached by car along the beautiful Höhenstrasse (4 km) which is a continuation of the Höttingergasse. Every year at the beginning of October a big motor hill-climbing rally is held on the Höhen-strasse. Big car park on the Hungerburg, where there is an hotel and an inn. From there, a 3,600m cable car climbs via the intermediate station of Seegrube (1,905m) to the **Hafelekar** (2,258m) on the Nordkette. *(Ascents from 7 am to 7 pm. Return ticket: S 26.)* About seven minutes on foot to reach the summit at 2,334m. The panorama from the Hafelekar is certainly one of the loveliest in the Alps. Innsbruck has two camping sites: Reichenau on the Inn, and Tivoli on the Sill, near the road leading to Igls. The city is served by several air-lines. The aerodrome lies south-west of the city between Hötting and Kranebitten.

Besides the Tourist Information Office and the Tiroler Landes-reisebüro, there is a branch of Wagons-Lits Cook in the Brixner-strasse, a car-hire service, with or without drivers, in the Wilhelm-Greilstrasse, and a branch of the Tourist Information Office at the station.

The Maria-Theresienstrasse and neighbouring roads form the shopping quarter. Apart from cigarette lighters, ash-trays, purses, etc., decorated with views of the city, the Tyrolean eagle, or an alpine landscape, in more or less good taste, there are fine articles in wrought-iron: ornaments, candlesticks, plate-stands, and ash-trays; ceramics, carved wood figures and animals, printed scarves, dolls in Tyrolean dress, and hand-worked table services.

The Tiroler Heimatwerk, in the Meranerstrasse, displays articles essentially of Tyrolean craftsmanship. There is also some beautiful Loden from the Mühlau textile industry, in the north-east, the only major industry of this business town apart from the new hydroelectric plants. Finally, there are excellent articles of sports-gear, for mountaineers or ski-ers.

For a good meal at Innsbruck, choose a *Stüberl* which serves regional dishes in a typically Tyrolean setting. Excellent beer is found in the numerous *Keller* (cellars). The Stiftskeller, near the Hofkirche, deserves special mention for its fine cooking at reasonable prices. The best "Tyrolean Evenings" are held in the *Breinössl* in the Maria-Theresienstrasse, and at the Hotel Maria-Theresia. Among the taverns which serve good Tyrolean wines, especially the *Südtiroler Rötel*, the best is without doubt the *Goldener Adler*, in the Herzog-Friedrichstrasse, one of the oldest and most famous inns in Innsbruck where many famous men have stayed, notably Goethe. Finally, you must not miss taking coffee and cakes on the terrace of the *Hochhaus*, near the Triumphal Arch, at the corner of the Salurner Strasse and the Leopoldstrasse. This is Innsbruck's skyscraper, and from the café-restaurant on the top floor there is a magnificent view over Innsbruck and the surrounding mountains. Among the spectacles organized in summer (July-August) the most spectacular is without doubt the all-Tyrol band contest, in national costume, which finishes with a giant concert (Monsterkonzert) where the massed bands play under the direction of the conductor of the prize-winning band. The Landesverkehrsamt für Tirol (Tyrol Tourist Office), which has offices in the Altes Landhaus, publishes a Tyrolean Calendar of Events which is found in all tourist inquiry offices.

Some Recommended Hotels

Innsbruck: *** Hotel Tyrol, Südtiroler Platz. ** Hotel Arlbergerhof, 1 Salurnerstrasse. * Hotel Speckbacher, 33 Maximilianstrasse.

Excursions in the Neighbourhood of Innsbruck

1 – **Amras Castle**, 4 km (leave by the Museumstrasse; take the Amraserstrasse which runs through the suburbs of Pradl and Amras). The most famous castle in the Tyrol, standing on the southern slope of the Mittelgebirge. It houses a remarkable collection of arms and the art collection of Archduke Ferdinand II. Open: 15th May to 15th October, 9-12.

2 – **Mount Isel and Igls** (6 km). Follow the Leopoldstrasse which starts at the Triumphal Arch and runs south through the Wilten district, the old Roman colony of Veldidena with its Premonstratensian Abbey. Turn left, cross the Sill, then right. The **Berg Isel**, around which were fought the battles for Tyrolean freedom in 1809, is a Tyrolean national shrine. On its summit stand a monumental bronze statue of Andreas Hofer and a memorial to those who died in the Battle of Mount Isel. A good mountain road through the forest leads to Vill (840m) and **Igls** (900m). International holiday and winter-sports resort at the foot of the Patscherkofel. First-class hotels. All amenities of a fashionable resort. Tennis courts

and beaches on the Lanser See. Three ski-lifts and a cable-railway: Igls-Heiligwasser-Patscherkofel (1,950m). Length 3,760m; ascent: 1,070m; journey takes 20 minutes. Hourly departures from 8.30 to 6.30. In summer, first departure 7.30. Fare for climb: S 14, descent, S 10. Return ticket: S 20.

3 – Sellrain Valley: 25 km. Leave Innsbruck heading south-west by the Innrain and the Völser-Strasse. Through **Völs** (585m) and Kematen, opposite St Martin's Wall, then through the narrow valley of the Melach, almost a gorge, to Sellrain-Rothenbrunn (909m): cure centre with ferruginous spring, and **Gries** im Sellrain (1,238m): holiday and winter-sports resort.

Two little carriage roads ascend from this resort, one to Praxmar (1,693m) in the Lisensertal south of Gries, and the other via the

Kühtaiersattel (2,077m) to the alpine health resort and winter-sports centre of **Kühtai** (1,960m), from which a direct descent can be made in the Ötztal via Wald (1,542m). It is only from this point that the road widens. Although it is used by Austrian motor-coaches, the Gries-Kühtai-Ötztal road is recommended only for motorists who are not afraid of the little Alpine tracks, on which one frequently has to back dozens of yards to let a motor-coach or car coming in the opposite direction get through. A motor-road is, however, now being built. Inquire at the Innsbruck Tourist Bureau.

4 – The Mittelgebirge: 14 km. South-west of Innsbruck by the Innrain to the Peterbrünnl. At the tile-works before Völs, take the beautiful road through the forest which leads to the picturesque villages of the Innsbrucker Mittelgebirge: Götzens (833m), Brigitz (858m), Axams (878m), and Grinzens (900m).

5 – The Stubai Valley: 28 km. Leave Innsbruck to the south.

Follow national highway No. 12, cross the daring bridge of St Steven, 44m high above the Rutzbach. Very beautiful view from this bridge over the Serles, also known as the Waldrastspitze (2,715m). Bear right at the first big fork. Via **Schönberg** (1,026m), view over Stubai glaciers, to **Mieders** (982m) at the foot of the

Serles. On the far side of the valley can be seen Telfes (987m). A fine walk can be made from Mieders, by a woodland path, to the pilgrim shrine of **Maria Waldrast.** Turn right, cross the Rutzbach, to reach **Fulpmes** (940m). Holiday and winter-sports resort. Swimming pool. Visit the forges of the Middle Ages. Fulpmes is renowned for its iron-craft industry: manufacture of climbing-irons, ice-picks, etc. Fine theatre with an all-peasant company. Starting point for excursions in the *Stubaier Gletscherwelt*, the numerous glaciers of Stubai. On the opposite bank are the mineral baths of Medratz with a lime spring. The road continues to the summer resort of Neustift (993m), and the tomb of the priest Franz Senn, founder of the Austrian Alpine Club, then on to Ranalt (1,260m), starting point for climbs between the Pfandlspitze (3,028m) and the Geisschneide (3,025m). The road between Neustift and Ranal is narrow and in bad condition.

Some Recommended Hotels

Igls: ★★★ Grandhotel Iglerhof. ★★ Hotel Maximilian. ★ Berghotel Patscherkofel.

The Wipptal: from Innsbruck to the Brenner Pass and Back: 76 km.

INNSBRUCK ★

Motorists coming from the south of France via Italy will find the Brenner Pass the most convenient entry-point to Austria. Leave Innsbruck by the Leopoldstrasse and the Brennerstrasse. Halt a moment at the Sonnenburgerhof (670m), for the finest view of the Northern Range is obtained here. Then by the Steven Bridge to **Matrei am Brenner** (993m), summer and winter-sports resort, the ancient Roman colony of *Matreium*, with the ruined castle of Trautsohn dating from the 13th century. Peasant theatre, open-air concerts; swimming.

Another road (21 km), not so good or direct but far more picturesque, leads to Matrei via Vills and Igls (see excursion to Igls). Continue from Igls in a southerly direction through the Rosenhügel National Park to Patsch (1,026m), from which there is a beautiful view over the Stubai Alps. After St Peter-Mühltal (1,160m) we follow the old Roman road above the gorge cut by the Sill as far as Matrei.

N. 182   21 km

★ STEINACH AM BRENNER

(1,046m). Alpine health resort and winter-sports centre at the entrance to the Gschnitz-tal. Folklore fêtes, open-air concerts, theatrical and Tyrolean evenings. Tennis courts, swimming pool, shooting. In winter, the *Gasselfahren*, or trotting races for light sleighs. Thermal establishment with the Velper spring, strongly radio-active (66 Mache units). Visit the parish church at Steinach with its altar decorated with a fresco by Knoller, and also the organ workshops. At the approach to Steinach am Brenner, the road forks along the Gschnitz Valley (12 km, 1 : 10). Most direct route to Stubai glaciers. Via Trins (1,240m) to **Gschnitz** (1,242m), starting point for many very difficult races.

Some Recommended Hotels

Gschnitz: ★ Hotel Gschnitzerhof.
Steinach am Brenner: ★ Hotel Steinacherhof.

★ GRIES AM BRENNER

(1,255m). Summer resort and winter-sports centre on the slopes of the Padaunerkogel. Anthracite mine at Nösslach. St Jakob's Chapel, built in 1305, with carved altar of 1480. On leaving Gries, see the small church of Lueg, then, on right of road, the Brenner Lake.

A Recommended Hotel

Gries am Brenner: ★ Hotel Grieserhof.

★ BRENNER PASS

(1,372m). The Brenner is the dividing line of the waters which have their source here and run down on one side to the Black Sea and on the other to the Adriatic. It is also the lowest pass road in the central Alps and the most direct on the north-south route (Berlin-Rome, 1,614 km), known and used by the Romans. Frontier between Italy and Austria since 1918. Customs post at Brennero, in the Pass. From the Brenner, Sterzing (Vipiterno) can be reached, 15 km. From there, three roads lead to **Bolzano**: the right-hand one via Merano (87 km); centre, the least good, follows the Sarntal and crosses the Penser Joch (2,211m), 69 km; and the left-hand one via Brixen (71 km). From

(left margin, vertical:) N. 182   5 km   N. 182   12 km   N. 182   38 km

Brixen, a road runs east via Dobiacco and Sillian to Lienz, in the eastern Tyrol. *(See Itinerary No. 4.)* Return to:

INNSBRUCK ★

INNSBRUCK-SALZBURG

MAIN ITINERARY:
VIA WÖRGL AND THE BAVARIAN REDOUBT: 174 KM.

Only one road leads from Innsbruck to Wörgl, along the river Inn: it is the old "salt road", the salt of Hall, east of Innsbruck, whose mines in the Middle Ages proved a richer source of income than the numerous copper and silver mines of the Tyrol. The small towns encountered on this road: Schwaz, Brixlegg, Rattenberg, have retained their medieval appearance, accentuated by the numerous castles and ruined fortresses in the neighbourhood. Like the veins of an oak-leaf, the lateral valleys run north and south to the Alps of Tux, Kitzbühel, and Zillertal. (Through this valley the motorist who does not fear mountain roads can reach the valley of Krimml which leads to Zell am See.)

Here are the two greatest hydroelectric plants of the Tyrol, the Achensee and the Gerlos, which supply the railways and the two leading industries of the Tyrol: textiles and chemical products, as well as the timber industry which flourishes throughout Austria.

From Wörgl, the motorist can reach Salzburg by two routes. The most direct (main itinerary) runs through Kufstein, Lofer, and the "Bavarian Redoubt". The secondary itinerary allows for visits to the famous resorts of Kitzbühel and Zell am See, by running round the Bavarian Redoubt and following the Salzach between the mountains of the Steinernes Meer and Tennengebirge. The two itineraries are linked by side roads, and visitors can thus follow first one part of an itinerary and then part of the other. The secondary itinerary, via Zell am See, provides opportunities for many excursions in the lateral valleys and runs deep into the Hohe Tauern, where Austria's highest mountain, the Grossglockner, is found. In addition, it is linked with many direct roads: towards Carinthia and East Tyrol via Heiligenblut and Lienz, from Bruck; the Gastein Valley, via Lend, and finally, shortly after Bischofshofen, the road of the Radstädter Tauern which runs to Leoben, in Styria.

Gastronomy: Before crossing into Salzburg, the itinerary runs through another section of the Tyrol. In some localities of this region, inn-keepers stage *Bock-und-Schnitzelfeste* evenings at

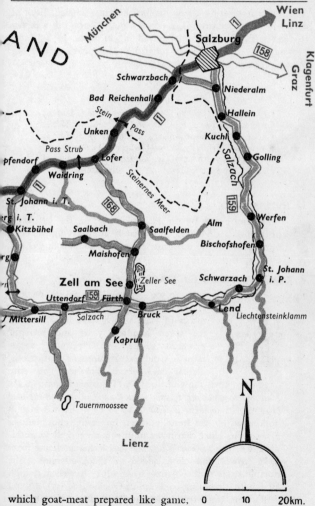

which goat-meat prepared like game,
and escallops, are served. We do not
recommend the goat dish for any but the strongest stomachs.

When you find on the menu "Rehrücken mit Schlag" (back of
deer with whipped cream), it is not a meat course but a pastry
studded with almonds and covered in chocolate. In Salzburg
province, try the "Salzburg tongues". This province is a big
brewing centre of light and dark beer.

PRINCIPAL SIGHTS

CHURCHES: Solbad Hall, Schwaz, and Fügen.
CASTLES: Schwaz, Jenbach, and Kufstein. **ABBEYS:**
Fiecht, and St Georgenberg at Schwaz. **MUSEUMS:**
Kitzbühel. **VIEWS:** Krimml waterfalls; the gorge
of Liechtenstein; the Schwarzsee; the mines of
Hallein, and the Caves of the Eisriesenwelt.

★ **INNSBRUCK**

N. I 10 km

Leave Innsbruck by the Haller Strasse, on the left bank
of the Inn. At Mühlau, immediately after leaving the city,
there is one of the most modern service stations in Central
Europe.

★ **SOLBAD HALL IN TIROL**

(pop. 10,500 - 574m). Thermal station with
salt-water springs coming from the salt
mines of Hall, which have been worked
for seven hundred years and brought
prosperity to the town. Treatments: respiratory troubles, rheumatoid afflictions,
cardiac and nerve illnesses. The cure
establishment is most up to date. (*Visits can be made to the
Hall mines, which are 1,476m up in the mountains, but the road
[19 km] has some steep sections, up to 1 : 3.*) Solbad Hall is
dominated by the Bettelwurf, an impressive mountain of
2,725m. Its chief charm lies in its squares and alleys, remi-
niscent of the Middle Ages. The **parish church,** dating from
1281 (tower and choir added in 1320) contains some
notable stone statues dating from 1494, as well as a high
altar with a painting by Erasmus Quellinus (1657), a pupil
of Rubens, and wrought-iron grills of 1470. Abbey church
and, in the Obere Stadtplatz, the **Stubenhaus,** headquarters
of the Stubengesellschaft founded by the rich burgesses

of Hall in 1508. Interesting mint tower. North of Solbad Hall, *Absam, place of pilgrimage.*

A Recommended Hotel
Solbad Hall in Tirol: ★ Parkhotel.

WATTENS ★
N. 12km

Small industrial town of ever-increasing importance owing to its optical glass industry.

SCHWAZ ★

(pop. 9,500 – 538m). Old mining town at the foot of the Kellerjoch (2,344m). In the Middle Ages, the fame of Schwaz and its silver and copper mines spread across the frontiers of Europe. Nowadays, only mercury is produced here. The parish church, the **Pfarrkirche,** is a notable building dating from 1340. It is the biggest Gothic church and has four naves of the same height, a *Hallenkirche,* possessing two high altars, architecture frequently encountered in Austria and Southern Germany. The roof of this church includes 15,000 copper tiles. The belfry houses the finest bell in the Tyrol, the *Maria Maximiliana,* cast in 1503. Inside the church is the tomb of Hans Dreyling, director of the mines, who died in 1575, designed by Alexander Colin and built by Löffler. In the church of the Franciscans (1507) is a Mater Dolorosa carved in 1520 and a cross by Loy Hering of Eichstädt in 1521. In the cloister behind the church is one of the most important cycle of frescoes of German art, executed between 1519 and 1526. Old mansion of the Fuggers, rich nobles of the region, with beautiful paintings on the façade. Above Schwaz stand the ruins of the **Freundsberg Castle,** pre-11th century, which belonged to the lansquenet leader Georg von Freundsberg. (Camping site at Schwaz.)

Across the valley can be seen the **abbey of the Benedictines of Fiecht,** and, in a romantic gorge, the oldest place of pilgrimage in the Tyrol, the ancient **Benedictine abbey of St Georgenberg.** A little to the west of Fiecht is the Vomperberg, on which is found the "Colony of the Holy Grail", a wealthy sect whose members claim to be the knights and guardians of the Grail.

N. 18 km

Ten km past Schwaz, a road to the north leads to **Jenbach** *(pop. 4,500 - 562m). Summer resort (swimming pool, tennis courts) and industrial town. Parish church built in 1487 by Gilg Mitterhofer. 2.5 km to the west of Jenbach, by a road which skirts the Achensee hydroelectric plant, is the* **Tratzberg Castle,** *16th century, in which can be seen an interesting fresco representing the genealogical tree of the Habsburgs, painted in 1507 in honour of Emperor Maximilian I, and several other valuable pictures.*

Visit to Achensee: national highway 181 to Pertisau: 12 km. *Via Jenbach, by a road which has some slopes of 1 : 3, to the little summer resorts on the southern tip of the Achensee, the biggest lake in the Tyrol, 9 km long: Eben, Maurach, Seespitz, and Buchau (963m). A new road is under construction. At Eben, pilgrim church of the famous Tyrolean saint, St Nothburga (1265-1330), patron saint of maidservants. From Maurach, at the foot of the Ebner Joch (1,954m), a road runs along the east bank of the lake, past the Hotel Seehof and Scholastika, on the northern tip of the lake, then through Achensee and Achenkirch, villages of the Achental. It then links up with the Munich-Salzburg autobahn 25 km south-east of Munich, after crossing the Achen Pass (885m), Austro-Bavarian frontier (climb: 1 : 9, descent: 1: 6). From Jenbach to the Munich-Salzburg autobahn: 81 km.*

Another road from Maurach forks left and leads to **Pertisau** *(929m). Health resort on west bank of the lake. Tennis courts, beach, all water-sports, nine-hole golf course. Lake tours by steamer: Seespitz; Buchau; Pertisau; Gaisalm; Seehof; Scholastika. Lake fêtes and folklore displays. 3 camping sites on lake-side.* 4 km after the fork towards Jenbach, at entrance to the village of Strass, there is a right fork: it is the entrance to the **Zillertal.**

Visits to valleys of Ziller and Tux: 50 km. *Among the Tyrolean valleys, that of Ziller is without doubt the most famous. This is probably due to the companies of singers and dancers of the Zillertal, among the best in the Tyrol, who*

*have made their songs known not only in Austria, but throughout
the world. The houses of the Zillertal are in pure Tyrolean style
and covered with flowers. The painted wardrobes, which are
rated among the finest examples of rustic furniture, are unfortu-
nately rarely found in the valley homes, for they have all been
carried away by art-lovers and antiquaries. In all the Zillertal
resorts, bands in national costume give open-air concerts and
organize forest fêtes, processions of Tyrolean marksmen, Tyrolean
evening galas, etc. Everywhere can be found calvaries, chapels
and pilgrim churches, for the people of the valley are deeply
religious.*

Fügen *(544m), via Schlitters, village whose picturesque wooden
houses, in pure Zillertal style, rise in tiers on the mountain heights,
with a parish church of late-Gothic style which is well worth a
visit. Today, Fügen Castle is an orphanage. The pilgrim church
of St Pankratz is near the village, and then come Uderns,
Kaltenbach, and Aschau.*

Zell am Ziller *(575m). A
holiday resort and winter-
sports centre at the entrance
to the Gerlostal, at the foot
of the Gerloswand. Swimming
pool, peasant theatre. Notable
parish church of 1304, rebuilt
in 1511, with a rococo chapel
added in 1760. Pilgrim church
of Maria Waldrast.*

*On the first Sunday in May,
a quaint folklore fête is staged
at Zell am Ziller, 400 years
old: the Gauderfest. All the
villagers gather in a big field,
to which in procession come*

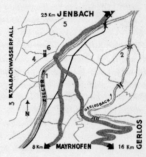

1 Trogerpromenade. 2 Krauss-
weg. 3 Road to Talbach Falls.
4 Eugen-Waldweg. 5 Klöpfl-
Staudach. 6 Herz-Jesu-Kapelle.

*the marksmen, the band and peasants leading the most powerful
of their domestic animals. A big circle is drawn in the centre of
the field, around which are placed enormous barrels of very strong
beer named Gauderbier. Then, one after the other, all the farm
animals meet in single combat. Next, the men of the valley hold
Tyrolean-style wrestling (Ranggeln) contests. The winner of
each contest (man or beast) has the right to a quantity of beer,
commensurate with his size, drawn from the barrels.*

A 15 km road (1 : 12) climbs to **Gerlos** *(1,241m), holiday resort and winter-sports centre at the foot of the Gerlos Pass (1,486m). Swimming pool, riding. The hydroelectric station and the lake which supplies the dam can be visited. Camping site on lake-side. A road runs across the Gerlos Pass to Krimml, in the Salzachtal* (see secondary itinerary below). *This road, used by the Austrian motor-coaches, is not recommended for motorists until the improvement works on the Gerlos Pass, now in hand, have been completed.*

Mayrhofen *(630m). Health resort known throughout the world for the international university holiday courses organized here from July to September by Innsbruck University, in collaboration with UNESCO: Austrian culture, music, and language. It is also a winter-sports resort at the junction of four valleys: Zillertal, Stilluptal, Zemmtal, and Tuxertal. Cable-railway to Penkenberg. Swimming pool. Camping-site. Near the woods, in which are the tennis courts and swimming pool, there is a wooden building which houses an interesting relief map of the Zillertal Alps. In the village there is a wood-carver's studio, which can be visited, and where the visitor can have his bust carved. South of Mayrhofen, by the main road, there are impressive waterfalls in a rugged gorge. Fine car excursion by a picturesque road to Ginzling (999m), in the Zemmtal.*

Via Lannersbach (also known as Vordertux) to **Hintertux** *(1,494m). Alpine health resort and thermal station with an open-air thermal pool whose warm waters, limestone with Glauber salts (72° F.), are radio-active, in a unique setting opposite the Gefrorne Wandspitze glaciers (3,275m). It is also a well-known base for climbing in the Tux Alps. Pay a visit to the Tux waterfalls: the cascades tumble down in three stages under natural bridges formed by the rocks. Then through Strass and Gertrauch.*

Some Recommended Hotels

Hintertux: ★ Hotel Badgasthof.
Jenbach: ★ Hotel Toleranz.

Mayrhofen: ★ Hotel Alte Post.
Pertisau: ★ Hotel Alpenhof.

BRIXLEGG ★

(535m), (18 km from Schwaz), one of the oldest holiday
resorts and winter-sports centres in the lower Inn valley,
surrounded by forests.

*There are numerous fortresses in the neighbourhood, the finest
being the Matzen (1176) and the Kropfsberg (13th century).
A road to the south (9 km) goes through Bad Mehrn, hydro-
mineral station with a gypsum-charged spring.
Treatments: gout, rheumatism. It ends at*
Alpbach *(973m), summer resort and winter-
sports centre in the Alpbachtal. This resort is
the headquarters of the Austrian College which
every summer, in August and September,
organizes international university weeks during
which artists and scientists can meet university*

*youth. The houses of this valley have an individual style and
the painted and carved furniture of the Alpbachtal is considered
the finest in the Tyrol.*

Some Recommended Hotels

Alpbach: ★ Hotel Böglerhof.
Brixlegg: ★ Gasthof Gratlspitz.

RATTENBERG ★

(514m). Charming little medieval town
dominated by the ruins of the fortress built
around 1100 where Chancellor Biehler
was executed in 1651. The town has
completely retained its character of the
Middle Ages. In all the streets a great
number of pretty signs in wrought-iron
can be seen, dating from the Middle Ages. Visit the old
forges and the birthplace of St Nothburga.
Every summer, in August, there is a reconstruction of a
knightly tournament followed by a big folklore festival in
the streets of the town, flood-lighted, torchlight procession,
etc. Several interesting old churches. On the opposite bank
of the Inn: the village of Kramsach (519m), below four
little mountain lakes, with beaches: the *Reintalseen*. Via

Kundl to Mühltal, by the Kundlklamm, an impressive gorge.

★ **WÖRGL**

N. 172   14 km

(pop. 6,000 - 511m). The youngest town in the Tyrol. Industrial town and tourist centre. Swimming pool, tennis courts.
In the neighbourhood, to the south-east, is the bath establishment of Bad Eisenstein. Ferruginous spring slightly radio–active (18 Mache units). Starting point for the road *(15 km)* leading through the Wildschönau to the holiday resorts and winter-sports centres of Niederau, Oberau, and Auffach (from 823 to 936m).

★ **KUFSTEIN**

N. 173, then N. 1   26 km

(pop. 12,000 - 503m). Picturesque town with eight lakes: Hechtsee, Stimmersee Längsee, Pfrillsee, Egelsee, Walchsee, Thiersee, Hintersteiner See, at the foot of the Kaisergebirge. Major summer resort and winter-sports centre, dominated by the **Geroldseck Fortress** (606m) in the tower of which stands the **Heroes Organ** which can be heard for several miles around. It is the biggest open-air organ in the world, built in memory of the dead of the first world war. Organ recitals daily at 12 and 8 pm; in winter, at noon only. Folklore fêtes, historic plays presented in front of the fortress by the peasant theatre company. Water sports on the eight lakes. Gliding school which organizes passenger flights over the Alps. Good taverns and a very interesting inn, the Auracher Löchl. Fine parish church with the tomb of Baumgartner (1493) by Wolfgang Leb. Regional museum. *From Kufstein a road of 32 km in the northerly direction links up with the Munich-Salzburg autobahn (63 km from Munich and 75 km from Salzburg).* Along a lovely road with a continuous view of the Wilder Kaiser (Wild Emperor) mountains to **Ellmau** (812m), summer resort and winter-sports station, and Going.

A Recommended Hotel
Kufstein: ★ Hotel Gisela.

ST JOHANN IN TIROL ★

(pop. 4,300 – 649m). Holiday resort and winter-sports centre at the foot of the Kitzbüheler Horn (1,998m). Tennis courts, swimming pool, shooting. Camping site. Peasant theatre, open-air concerts. Beautiful peasant houses and noteworthy parish church rebuilt in 1725 by Abraham Millauer. A road of 11 km links up to the south, via Kitzbühel, with the secondary itinerary, Wörgl-Salzburg.

Via Erpfendorf and Waidring in the Strubtal, along the Sonnwendwand (1,643m), which is found on the left of the road, towards the Strubb Pass (677m).

A Recommended Hotel

St Johann in Tirol: ★ Hotel Post.

LOFER ★

(639m), at the foot of the Loferer Alp (1,570m). Holiday resort and winter-sports centre. A road 40 km long links Lofer and Zell am See.

Via Unken to the **Stein Pass** (616m), on the Austro-German frontier. The crossing of the "Bavarian Redoubt" does not require a visa. A pass valid for two hours is issued by the Austrian Customs on presentation of passport (fee of S 0.50). Remember to declare currency and notes carried to avoid difficulty on leaving.

A Recommended Hotel

Lofer: ★ Hotel Bräu.

Via Bad Reichenhall and **Schwarzbach**, Austro-German frontier, to:

SALZBURG ★

SECONDARY ITINERARY:
WÖRGL-SALZBURG VIA KITZBÜHEL: 192 KM.

On leaving Wörgl head south-east by the road leading to the Wildschönau. Then take immediately, on left, road No. 170 for the Brixental. The road runs through Mayerhof and Hans.

HOPFGARTEN ★

(pop. 3,700). 11 km from Wörgl, holiday resort and winter-sports centre. Swimming pool, shooting, open-air concerts.

Hopfgarten boasts the longest ski-lift in Europe: 2,870m, climbing from 619m to 1,397m, up the slopes of the Hohe Salve (1,829m). Very beautiful church, and, in the neighbourhood, Itter Castle. The road passes the winter-sports resort of **Westendorf** (785m) with ski-lift for the Alpenrosenhütte (1,600m), then through **Brixen im Thal** (780m), summer and winter-sports resort stretching along both sides of the road. Magnificent parish church of 1789. The fresco of the middle roof is by Schopf (1795). Maria-Louise Bath Institute, with ferruginous spring.

★ KIRCHBERG IN TIROL

(pop. 2,800 - 830m). Summer resort and winter-sports centre at the entrance to the Spertental, into which runs a small road leading to **Aschau**. Pilgrim church in rococo style. On Corpus Christi Day there is a horseback procession (Antlassritt) to the *Schwedenkapelle*, a tiny historic chapel beside the road leading to Kitzbühel, erected on the spot where the Tyrolean cavalry checked the Swedish armies during the Thirty Years' War.

The road runs a little to the east of the **Schwarzsee,** situated 1 km before Kitzbühel, in one of the loveliest settings in the Tyrol, opposite the peaks of the Wilder Kaiser. This lake gets its name (Black Lake) from the colour of the mud which covers its bed. The waters of the lake, which have an average temperature of 75° F., have great curative properties. Treatment for: rheumatism, gynaecological complaints, healing of wounds and inflammation. Mud baths in the actual lake or the establishments on the lakeside, and at Kitzbühel. Two beaches and camping site on lakeside.

A Recommended Hotel

Kirchberg in Tirol: ★ Gasthof Kalswirt.

★ KITZBÜHEL

(763m). One of the most famous health resorts and winter-sports centres in Austria. In the Middle Ages it was a big transit centre which was further enriched by the neighbouring copper and silver mines. Its appearance has changed but little since the 16th century and provides a picturesque setting for the international Society life of the resort, where ultra-modern hotels stand beside old Gothic houses. Kitzbühel gained world renown when the Duke of Windsor, then Prince of Wales, stayed there in 1935. In addition to its first-class hotels, there are many boarding houses and inns. Two of the hotels are installed in former castles: the Lebenberg Castle (1500) and Kaps Castle (1600), typically Tyrolean. Two restaurants must be mentioned: the Chizzo, in which are to be found the finest wines, and the Hinterbräu, former brasserie cellar. Tyrolean evenings are organized during the season almost every day in the hotels, the taverns, or the dance-halls. The best company is the national group of Praxmair singers. The municipal band gives frequent open-air concerts, and magnificent parades mark carnival time. The centre of the town and life in Kitzbühel is the main road, in which are found the Post Office, most of the shops, and the provincial travel agency, as well as the tourist information bureau. A casino, open only in the high-seasons, has now been opened. The insignia of Kitzbühel is the chamois. Attractive souvenirs can be bought in the workshop of a smith in the Hahnenkammstrasse, on the right-hand side coming from the main road. The house is easily recognized, because its façade is buried under a mass of flowers of all colours. The master-smith who receives you in person seems to have stepped from the pages of a tale of the Middle Ages: he is a grand old man in a monk's gown, wearing a beret, with a handsome white beard falling to his waist. He will show you all the articles in wrought iron which are for sale, with a kindliness which also seems to belong to another age.

Since 1952, Kitzbühel has had a gliding school (flights with passengers; launching platform on the Hahnenkamm). Kitzbühel has three cable railways, a cable-seat line and six ski-lifts. These installations give a range of 50 kilometres of downhill runs (22 in all, plus ten in the immediate neighbourhood) in one day alone. Among the races organized each winter, the best known is the *Ehrenbachgasse*.

The **Regional Museum** contains finds from the excavations carried out on the Kelchalpe, south of Kitzbühel, by Professor Pittioni of Vienna, and other interesting relics of prehistoric

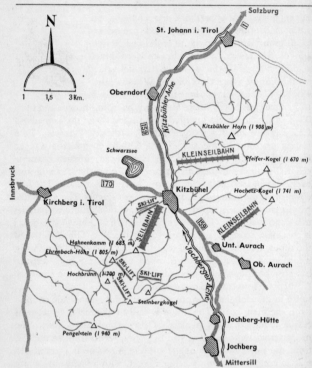

life in the Alps. In the neighbourhood is the Church of St Catherine, whose bells can be heard every hour. The **parish church** is very beautiful. High altar by Benedikt Faistenberger, 1663. Also see the Chapel of the Mount of Olives, with a group sculpted in 1750 and beautiful grills in wrought iron.

From Kitzbühel, a road runs 11 km to the north to St Johann in Tirol, on our main itinerary.

Leave Kitzbühel towards the south. Via **Jochberg** to the Thurn Pass (1,273m). During the run down there is a view over the Hohen Tauern.

N. 159 29 km

Some Recommended Hotels

Kitzbühel: ★★★ Hotel Ehrenbachhöhe. ★★ Grandhotel. ★ Hotel Holzner.

(789m). Summer resort 500m from the
main road, at the entrance to the Felbertal,
national park. In Mittersill Castle, transformed into an hotel, is the Mittersill Club,
an international club which includes in its
membership crowned heads and world-
famous people, and which reopened its
doors in 1948 after a 20-year interval. During the war,
the castle was taken over by a German general who buried
jewels valued at a million dollars in the park. Despite a
meticulous search by the Intelligence Service, the treasure
has not yet been recovered.

The Salzach Valley: Mittersill-Krimml: 29 km. *Through
Hollersbach and Bramberg, passing by the mouth of the Habachtal,
a valley in which emeralds are found in large quantities, following
the Salzach to Neukirchen am Grossvenediger (854m), small
summer resort and winter-sports centre of 1,800 inhabitants, then
via Wald (854m), where the cemetery contains tombstones made
of rare minerals. From Wald, a road (15 km), mentioned in
the description of the Zillertal, climbs to the Gerlos Pass and
drops down to Zell am Ziller. By Krimml, small alpine summer
resort, to the* **Krimml waterfalls,** *the greatest
in the eastern Alps, which tumble in three falls
from a height of 380m. A toll charge of S 0.80
per person is levied on the road leading to the
falls. Take a mackintosh or raincoat. Visitors
climb on foot to the Regenkanzel, then beside
the second falls to the Schönangerlterrasse
(1,306m). Best view of the upper falls from the Berger Blick.
Finally to the Schettbrücke (1,463m), bridge over the upper
falls. Return to Krimml by the Tauernweg. (Restaurant above
the falls.)*

A Recommended Hotel

Mittersill: ★ Gasthof Bräurup.

(778m), at the mouth of the **Stubachtal** which leads to Enzingerboden, 19 km (1,462 m) at the foot of the Kalser Tauern
near the little Grünsee (Green Lake) and the Tauernmoossee
which provides power for the hydroelectric station of the

Austrian Federal Railways, which can be visited. *A cable railway climbs from Enzingerboden to the Weiss See (White Lake) 2,315m up on the slopes of the Kalser Tauern (2,053m), underneath the Sonnblick (3,088m) and the Granatspitze (3,085m). Magnificent panorama of the Hohe Tauern and the Grossglockner.*

★ FÜRTH

By a fork on the right, the old village of **Kaprun**, *with its castle, summer resort with swimming pool, at the entrance to the valley of the same name. Above stands the new Tauern hydroelectric station, one of the biggest in Europe, which draws its hydraulic power from two big man-made lakes between the Kitzsteinhorn (3,202m), the Hoher Tenu (3,368m), and the Grosse Wiesbachhorn (3,570m.)*

A Recommended Hotel

Kaprun: ★ Hotel Kesselfall-Alpenhaus.

★ ZELL AM SEE

(pop. 6,500 - 758m). International holiday and winter-sports resort, one of the most important touring centres in the Alps, on the west bank of the Zeller See, a lake 3.8 km long, 1.5 km wide, and with an average temperature in summer of 73° F. Water festivals, excursions round the lake by boat, with beautiful panorama from the centre. Open-air concerts, society life, tennis courts, beaches, shooting. Gliding — the launching platform is on the Schmittenhöhe (1,968m), which is reached by a cable railway. Excellent ski-runs and international competitions. Harnessed trotting races for light sleighs.

Zell am See has a very beautiful   Roman-style church, of 1230, and a

1 Loferer Bundesstr. 2 Brucker Bundesstr. 3 Bahnhofstr. 4 Franz-Josef-Str. 5 Mozartstr.
1 Church. 2 City Tower. 3 Station. 4 Tourist Information Office. 5 Post Office.

tower of 1250, in the main square. On the east bank is the little summer resort of Thumersbach.

A road to the north links up with the main itinerary. At Mais-hofen, the road forks (15 km) to **Saalbach** *(1,003m) which is called the skiers' village because of its excellent ski-slopes served by five cable-seat lines and ski-lifts. Via Saalfelden (744m), holiday resort and winter-sports centre (pop. 8,000) to the foot of the Steinernes Meer (Sea of Rocks), with the 13th-century Lichtenberg Castle, a hermitage in the rocks, and the Pinzgauer Krippenmuseum (Museum of Mangers of the Pinzgau), to Lofer.*

A Recommended Hotel

Saalbach: ∗ Neues Sporthotel.

BRUCK

(pop. 3,000 - 757m). Summer resort at entrance to the Fusch valley. Swimming pool in lovely setting. Starting-point of the alpine road to the Grossglockner *(See Itinerary No. 4.)*

A Recommended Hotel

Bruck/Glocknerstrasse: ∗ Hotel Lukashansl.

SCHWARZACH

(591m). Summer resort and railway centre. Rail branch line for the Tauern. At the Hotel Post, the **Salzleckertisch** (table of Salt Lickers) around which the Protestants took an oath before their emigration in 1737. In summer, open-air theatre performances.

ST JOHANN IM PONGAU

(610 m). Chief town of the Pongau at the junction of the Wagrainer Tal and Grossarltal Valleys with the Salzachtal, which the road follows. Camping site. Cable-seat line. Visit the **Liechtensteinklamm,** the deepest gorge in the Eastern Alps.

A Recommended Hotel

St Johann im Pongau: ∗ Hotel Prem.

BISCHOFSHOFEN

(547 m). One of the oldest towns in the province. Junction of the Selztal-Graz and Vienna railway. Through Pfarr-werfen, to

★ N. 159 29 km ★ N. 159 6 km ★ N. 159 8 km ★ N. 159 8 km

★ WERFEN

(547m). Summer resort, starting-point for trip to the **Eisriesenwelt Cave,** in the Tennengebirge (3½ hr climb). It is the biggest glacier cave in the world, 40 km long. Visits with guide from April to October at 11 and 2. Sunday, and every day during July and August: 9, 11, 1, and 3. Duration of tour: two hours. The galleries cut in the ice and the vast caves have a fairyland aspect. Above Werfen is the fortress of the Salzburg prince-bishops of Hohenwerfen, built in 1017.

Via **Tenneck,** along the *Salzachöfen,* the Salzach Gorge between the Tennengebirge and the Hagengebirge.

A Recommended Hotel

Werfen: ★ Hotel Eisriesenwelt.

★ GOLLING

(476m). Holiday resort at the foot of the Tennengebirge. *Gollinger Wasserfälle,* falls at the foot of the Hoher Göll. Start of the Dolomites road to Salzburg. The road runs through Kuchl.

A Recommended Hotel

Golling: ★ Hotel Goldener Stern.

★ HALLEIN

(449m). Chief town of the Tennengau. **Salt Mines.** Visits, with guide, from 1st May to 30th September, 12 to 6; Sunday: 8-6. Tour takes about 1½ hrs. Charge: S 11.50. Entrance to the mine is at **Dürnberg,** above Hallein. (Coach road. Cable railway being built.) Visitors don miners' clothing for the tour of these mines. Boat trip on underground salt lake, remains of Ilyrian and Celtic salt mines, underground museum. The visitor slides from gallery to gallery by toboggan, and leaves on a mine truck from the *Wolf Dietrich* gallery, 2,100 metres long with a steep slope, to emerge suddenly into the open-air. Famous custom of Hallein is the Sabre Dance, in which the miners illustrate the dangers of their trade.

THE GROSSGLOCKNER ROAD

AND THE GASTEIN VALLEY: 235 KM.

The alpine road of the Grossglockner provides the motorist with an unforgettable memory both of its boldness and the beauty of the panorama which unfolds as he drives along. Built between 1930 and 1935, it links the Salzburg Country with Carinthia and the Eastern Tyrol. It is a masterpiece of road construction. It rises from 758m to 2,506m and drops down through Heiligenblut to 1,301m in almost a straight line, representing 30 km as the crow flies, as far as Lienz (673m) in the Eastern Tyrol. The gradient never exceeds 1 : 9 and its bends present little difficulty to drivers of great motor-coaches or heavy lorries. The road has an overall width of 6m (5.4 in the tunnels). At the beauty spots, parking places have been constructed where the driver can rest his engine and at the same time admire the grandiose scenery over which stands guard the most impressive Austrian peak: the 3,798m Grossglockner. At the moment, new parking places are being built to cater for the ever-increasing traffic, which had already reached the figure of 1,700 cars per day in 1951. The road is open from early June to early October, dependent on snow conditions. The toll charge is S 20 per head and S 10 for children, who must be less than 1.80m (4 ft 3 ins) to qualify for this charge. At the heighest point of the road is the frontier between Salzburg and Carinthia. From Heiligenblut, the road follows the River Möll up to the northwest of Lienz, capital of the Eastern Tyrol, land of lofty peaks with the Dolomites of Lienz, between the Hohe Tauern and the Carnic Alps. The loss of South Tyrol to Italy completely isloated it before the Grossglockner road was built, and to reach Eastern Tyrol the traveller had to go through Italian territory or go round the Hohe Tauern.

The Eastern Tyrol was the gateway to Austria used by the Romans, who followed the Drave through the Pustertal Gorge north of the high cliffs of the Dolomites, and who founded the

important administrative centre of Aguntum (now Lienz). The itinerary follows the Drave up to Carinthia, just north of Spittal, and then turns north through the Tauern Tunnel, where cars must be shipped by railway, to come out again into Salzburg, in the Gastein Valley, made famous by the radio-active thermal station of Badgastein, and rejoins the No. 3 secondary itinerary at Lend: Innsbruck-Salzburg, via Zell am See.

Gastronomy: Eastern Tyrol cooking is the same as that of the Tyrol, except, owing to its geographical situation, it comes under Italian influence.

PRINCIPAL SIGHTS

CHURCH: Parish church of Heiligenblut. CASTLES: Liebburg at Heiligenblut; Matrei. MUSEUMS: Heiligenblut, Rauris. VIEWS: Waterfalls at Lend, and Badgastein.

★ BRUCK

N. 107 14 km

From Bruck, head south down the Fusch Valley to Dorf Fusch (805m), from which a road runs towards Bad Fusch (1,239m), thermal station with radio-active springs. A floral gateway indicates the Fusch toll-house. The road runs via the Bärenschlucht (Gorge of the Bear) to:

★ FERLEITEN

(1,145m), small holiday resort. The road climbs steeply, with four bends, to the **Piffkar** car-park (1,620m). View over the Wiesbachhorn (3,570m). From there to the Hochmais car park (1,850m), then, by the "Witches Kitchen" and the "Wall of the Edelweiss" to the car park of the Oberes Nassfeld (2,374m). 150 m further on a road (maximum gradient 1 : 8) forks towards the Edelweiss-Spitze (2,557m), from which there is a panorama of 37 mountains exceeding 3,000m and 19 glaciers.

The road runs round the Torköpfl and leads to the Fuscher Törl (2,465m). Car park. Monument to the builder of the road, the engineer Wallack, and to the 11 workers who were killed in accidents during its construction. Continuous view of the Brennkogel Glacier and the Grossglockner. Slight descent from the car-park towards the tiny Fuscher Lacke (2,262m), through the Mittertörl Tunnel, 117m long, and climb to the Hochtortunnel.

A Recommended Hotel

Ferleiten: ∗ Hotel Lukashansl.

HOCHTORTUNNEL ★

(2,506m), highest point of the road, frontier between Salzburg and Carinthia. Car park at exit of tunnel. The road drops down again by the Fallbichl to the Tauerneck. First sight of the Grossglockner and the Schober. Then by four bends to the Ankehr car park (192m) and to Guttal (1,859m). *A road to the west, 8.2 km, leads*

to the **Franz-Josefshöhe** *(2,418m), up-to-date hotel with every convenience. Three car parks. Terrace overhanging the giant Pasterze Glacier at the foot of the Grossglockner. This glacier of 32 square kilometres is 10 km long and at the top reaches a width of some 5 km. 500m from the hotel is a fourth car park with a view over the upper section of the glacier. Each year in June, when the road opens to traffic, the Grossglockner Race is held, a famous ski test on the Pasterze Glacier, marking the end of the Austrian winter season.* At the Guttal fork, the road makes a sharp left-hand bend, crosses the Guttal stream and climbs again to the Kasereck car park (1,913m). Beautiful view of the Grossglockner.

HEILIGENBLUT ★

(1,301m). Holiday resort, climbing, summer ski-ing and winter sports. To compensate for the absence of a ski-lift, a motorcoach service is continuously in operation to take skiers up the Grossglockner road above the resort. Mountaineering school at Heiligenblut.

In the 15th-century **Gothic church** there is a beautiful carved altar and a treasury which contains, according to legend, a flask with drops of the blood of Christ which St Briccius was carrying when he perished in a storm not far from the

Pasterze Glacier. Fearing robbers, St Briccius slashed a hole in his leg in which to hide the flask. The day after his death, peasants found at the foot of the Grossglockner three blades of wheat which had pierced the snow and indicated where the saint's body lay. A chapel was built there, around which grew up Heiligenblut, a name which means "sacred blood". Via Putschall, Döllach, Mörtschach, and Winklern to the Iselsberg Pass.

Some Recommended Hotels

Heiligenblut: ★★ Kaiser-Franz-Josef-Haus.   ★ Hotel Glocknerwirt.

★ BAD ISELSBERG

(1,204m). Summer resort and thermal station, sulphur springs. Swimming pool, tennis courts, winter sports. The Iselsberg Pass divides Carinthia and the Eastern Tyrol.

(margin: ↗ Z · km 107 ↺)

★ LIENZ

(pop. 10,000 - 676m). Capital of the Eastern Tyrol. All the usual distractions of a small town. Twice weekly, in the evening, open-air concerts are given by the municipal band in national costume. In summer, regional band contest. Every day there are Tyrolean evenings at the Hotel Post. Best restaurants: Hotel Traube, Post, Dolomiten, and Grossgasthof Rose. Typical crafts: wrought-iron shops for the sale of souvenirs; earthenware stoves and Tyrolean hats. Principal business streets: Hauptplatz, Johannesplatz, Rosengasse, Schweizergasse. **Liebburg Castle** (16th century) in the Kaiser-Josefsplatz with two fine round towers.

Lienz is the birthplace of one of the greatest Austrian painters, Egger-Lienz, whose tomb is found in the Ex-Servicemen's Chapel, decorated with his own frescoes, at the side of the **Pfarrkirche** (15th century), which contains the monument of the last Count of Görz. To visit the chapel, ask for the key at the Forcher joiner's shop, Pfarrplatz.

The Municipal Museum housed in Bruck Castle, on the Schlossberg, former residence of the Counts of Görz, contains more than 60 pictures by Egger-Lienz, art and natural history exhibits, and finds from excavations at the Roman town of Aguntum of which the remains were brought to light 4 km east of Lienz, between Nussdorf and Dölsach *(open daily, 9-12 and 2-6, except Monday)*.

Beautiful surroundings with numerous mountain lakes and the opportunity for climbing excursions in the Grossglockner, Venediger, and Dolomite ranges. Starting point for tours of the Iseltal and neighbouring valleys: Defereggen, Kalser, and Virgental. *Lienz lies only 32 km from the Italian frontier (Venice direction). Customs at Arnbach. Near the frontier is* **Sillian** *(1,097m), health resort and winter-sports centre.*

A Recommended Hotel

Lienz: ★ Hotel Post.

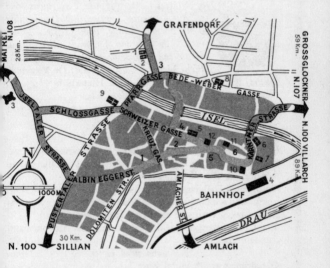

1 Ex-Servicemen's Chapel. 2 St Andrew's Church. 3 Bruck Castle. 4 Station. 5 St Mary's Church. 6 Hospital Church. 7 St Anthony's Church. 8 St Michael's Church. 9 Klösterle-Kirche. 10 Post Office. 11 Hotel Traube. 12 Hotel Post.

1 Messinggasse. 2 Rosengasse. 3 Patriasdorfer-Str. 4 Jahnplatz. 5 Johannesplatz. 6 Stadtplatz.

The Iseltal: Lienz-Matrei i. Osttirol (30 km):

The road runs north-west to **St Johann.** *1 km further on, on left of road, the Kienburg ruins, and immediately afterwards, on right, a superb view of the Grossglockner.* **Huben** *(832m): fork to the east: the Kalsertal, 13 km as far as* **Kals** *(1,322m), health resort and starting point for the easiest and quickest climb of the Gross-glockner. Peasant theatre.*

From Huben, a road running west leads to the **Defereggental** *(28 km). Gradient 1 : 10. Via Hopfgarten to St Veith, St Jakob, and Erlsbach, also bases for mountaineers.*

Continue along the Iseltal to the health resort of **Matrei i. O.** *(975m). Ferruginous and sulphur water cures. Cinema, theatre, swimming pool, shooting, fishing. Folklore fêtes. To be visited: the collection of minerals, Weissenstein Castle and the monument to Emperor Joseph. From Matrei towards the west: the* **Virgental** *(16 km) with* **Prägraten** *(1,312m) and* **Hinterbichl** *(1,331m), summer residence of the Vienna Boys Choir.*

From Lienz, via Dölsach and Nikolsdorf, a road takes you into Carinthia.

★ OBERDRAUBURG

(620m), in Carinthia. From here, a road runs south via Kötschach and the **Plöcken Pass** (1,360m) to the Italian frontier, in the direction of Tolmezzo.

Go through **Dellach**. At Greifenburg, a road (11.5 km) with many steep sections leads to the **Weissensee**, Austria's warmest Alpine lake, with the resort of **Techendorf** (946m).

Steinfeld, Obergottesfeld, small thermal station, and Sachsenburg.

A Recommended Hotel

Oberdrauburg: ★ Hotel Post.

★ MÖLLBRÜCKE

(558m). Road No. 100 here takes the southerly direction, through Spittal and ending at Villach, centre of the warm lake region of Carinthia. *(See Itinerary No. 10.)*

We re-enter Salzburg by the north-west. Bad going from Mühldorf, until after Penk, before Obervellach.

N. 100 21 km

N. 100 40 km

N. 106a 27 km N. 106 and

MALLNITZ ★

(1,185m), Summer holiday and health resort. Tennis, shooting, fishing. The road ends here, and cars are taken by railway through the Tauern Tunnel (12 km). Several services a day. Fare: S 75 per car, plus S 3.40 per passenger.

A Recommended Hotel

Mallnitz: ★ Alpenhotel Alber.

BÖCKSTEIN ★

at the end of the tunnel, small picturesque village frequented by artists (camping site). Starting point for many excursions. Cure treatment in the galleries of the old Böckstein gold-mine. Owing to the powerful radio-activity of the atmosphere in the gallery, entrance is allowed only with medical permission. (Administered by the Management of the Badgastein cure.)

BADGASTEIN ★

(1,086m), the greatest thermal station in Austria with a world-wide reputation, and also a major winter-sports resort. Luxury hotels, casino (roulette and baccarat), international clientele, leading artistes, orchestras, and theatre companies. Very beautiful walks in the neighbourhood, and the Gasteiner Ache waterfalls. Cure treatment throughout the year. The strongest radio-active springs in the world gush up at 116° F. in the heart of the resort. *Visits to thermal springs from May to October, Tuesday and*

1 Casino. 2 Waterfalls. 3 Station. 4 Post Office. 5 Cable railway for Stubnerkogel. 6 Bellevue ski-lift. 7 Ski-lift for the Höllbrunn and the Grankogel. 8 Hauptstr. 9 Kötschacher-Str. 10 Kaiser-Franz-Joseph-Str. 11 Kaiserin-Elisabeth-Walk. 12 Catholic church. 13 Protestant church.

N. 167   8 km

Friday, at 10 and 11. Departure, Hotel Moser. Length of tour: 1 hour. The radio-active waters are piped to the hotels and boarding houses of Badgastein; the cure (normal duration: 21 baths in 24 days) is thus followed actually at the hotel. Badgastein has been nicknamed the "Fountain of Youth". Treatments: rheumatism, lumbago, sciatica, nervous disorders, circulatory troubles, endocrine glands, and metabolism, blood pressure, old-age troubles, and general weaknesses. Tennis, fishing, shooting. Four ski-lifts, two cable railways with several coaches on the Stubnerkogel (2,245m). Winter-Sports Weeks, national and international ski contests, and ski-joring on the road to Böckstein. The healing waters of Badgastein are also taken, without loss of radio-activity or temperature, by insulated pipelines to the neighbouring resort of Bad Hofgastein.

Some Recommended Hotels

Badgastein: *** Hotel Astoria. ** Grand Hotel Gasteinerhof. * Hotel Grüner Baum.

Böckstein: * Kurhaus Rader.

★ BAD HOFGASTEIN

N. 167   25 km

(869m), less fashionable, same directions for cure. Shooting, fishing. Camping site. Ski-lift and winter sports. Then through Dorfgastein.

Some Recommended Hotels

Bad Hofgastein: *** Grand-Hotel Gross. ** Hotel Moser Zum Goldenen Adler. * Kurhaus Luisenhof.

★ LEND

N.159   7 km

(636m). Here we join the secondary Itinerary No. 3. Beautiful waterfalls.

★ TAXENBACH

N. 159   12 km

(716m). Starting point for the Rauris Valley (28 km), formerly noted for its gold and precious stones, and the Kitzlochklamm Gorge. **Rauris,** *holiday resort and winter-sports centre. Old houses (16th century) and regional museum.*

Via **Gries** we reach the starting point of the Grossglockner mountain road.

★ BRUCK

SALZBURG
AND THE SALZKAMMERGUT

All the region east of Salzburg was in the long-ago a vast stretch of water. When the waters retreated, they left 15 lakes in the hollow they formerly filled, in a countryside of rare beauty. This area, which is shared by three of the Federal "Countries": Salzburg, Styria, and Upper Austria, was christened *Salzkammergut*, because of its richness in salt. However, it was not the salt mines which made it famous, but the beauty of its scenery which won it international renown as a holiday centre. The operetta *White Horse Inn* did much to bring fame to the villages of the Salzkammergut, especially St Wolfgang.

It is a chain of lovely watering-places on the lake-sides, where sailing boats glide and on which festivals and floral carnivals are held.

Gastronomy: While in Salzburg you must taste the *Salzburger Nockerln* and the balls of chocolate "*Mozart*". In the Salzkammergut are found the specialities of the three provinces wich share it, and, in addition, salmon trout and lake grayling. Nor must you miss tasting pastries in one of the finest Austrian pastry-shops: the *Zauner Pâtisserie* at Bad Ischl. The great speciality of the Salzkammergut is the Traunkirchen cake.

PRINCIPAL SIGHTS

Salzburg: CHURCHES: Cathedral, Franciscan church, St Peter's, University Church, St John at Mülln. CASTLES: Hohensalzburg, Leopoldskron, Hellbrunn. MUSEUM of Natural History. ABBEYS: Nonnberg, Capucine. PALACES: Residence and Mirabell. MONUMENTS: Carillon, Birthplace of Mozart, Catacombs, St Peter's Cemetery, Festspielhaus with Rock Riding-school, Horses Trough, Mozarteum.

Salzkammergut: CHURCHES: Mondsee, Gmunden, Traunkirchen, Hallstatt, St Wolfgang. CASTLES: Mondsee, Gmunden. MUSEUMS: Gmunden, Bad Ischl, Hallstatt, Bad Aussee. VIEWS: The Kaiservilla at Bad Ischl; the glacier caves of the Dachstein; salt mines of Altausee; Alpine Garden of Bad Aussee.

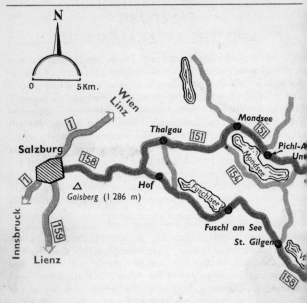

★ SALZBURG

(pop. 100,000 - 412m). Capital of the Federal "country" of
Salzburg. City of Mozart. City of the Festival. Founded in 690,
on the ruins of the Roman Juvavum, by St Rupert, patron saint
of Salzburg, who built the St Peter's Monastery there. The
bishops and later, after 803, the prince-archbishops, of this city
stamped it, through the Gothic, Renaissance, and even the
baroque, periods with the seal of their powerful personalities.
The city owes its present architectural beauty to the Prince-
Archbishop Wolf Dietrich. Brought up in Rome, son of the
Renaissance, elected Archbishop of Salzburg at the age of 28
in 1583, he dreamed of making Salzburg the Rome of the North.
He decided to change the tortuous streets of this city on the left
bank of the Salzach into great squares and avenues. To do this,
he calmly demolished entire districts, and it is said that the
burning of the old 8th-century basilica was not entirely accidental,
because Wolf Dietrich had planned to build a cathedral there
surpassing St Peter's at Rome in size and beauty. The pleasure

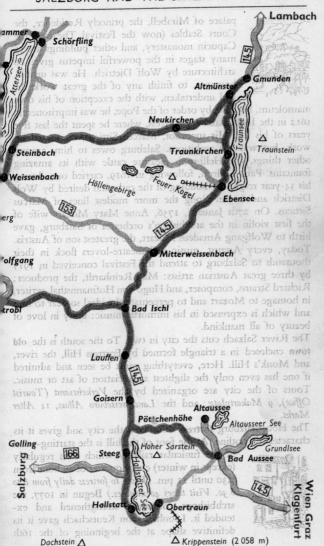

palace of Mirabell, the princely Residence, the Court Stables (now the Festival Theatre), the Capucin monastery, and other buildings are so many stages in the powerful impetus given to architecture by Wolf Dietrich. He was unable, however, to finish any of the great works he had undertaken, with the exception of his own mausoleum, because, by order of the Pope, he was imprisoned in 1612 in the Hohensalzburg fortress, where he spent the last five years of his life. His successor, Marcus Sitticus, continued his work, but was less ambitious. Salzburg owes to him, among other things, the Hellbrunn pleasure castle with its amazing fountains. Paris Lodron, following in 1619, carried out, during his 34-year reign, the building of the cathedral desired by Wolf Dietrich and begun along the more modest lines of Marcus Sitticus. On 27th January, 1756, Anne Mary Mozart wife of the first violin in the archbishop's orchestra of Salzburg, gave birth to Wolfgang Amadeus Mozart, the greatest son of Austria. Today, every August, music and theatre-lovers flock in their thousands to Salzburg to attend the Festival conceived in 1917 by three great Austrian artists: Max Reinhardt, the producer; Richard Strauss, composer, and Hugo von Hofmannsthal, writer, in homage to Mozart and to perpetuate the ideal so dear to him and which is expressed in his immortal music: unity in love of beauty of all mankind.

The River Salzach cuts the city in two. To the south is the **old town** enclosed in a triangle formed by Fortress Hill, the river, and Monk's Hill. Here, everything must be seen and admired if one has even only the slightest appreciation of art or music. Tours of the city are organized by the *Verkehrsamt (Tourist Office), 9 Makartplatz*; and the *Landesreisebüro Albus, 11 Alter Markt*.

The Hohensalzburg **fortress** dominates the city and gives it its characteristic outline. At the foot of the hill is the starting-point

of the funicular railway which runs regularly (except in winter) every quarter of an hour from 7.30 until 11 pm. *(Visits to fortress daily from 8 to 6.30. Visit takes 40 minutes.)* Begun in 1077, the archbishops constantly strengthened and extended it. Leonhard von Keutschach gave it its definitive shape at the beginning of the 16th

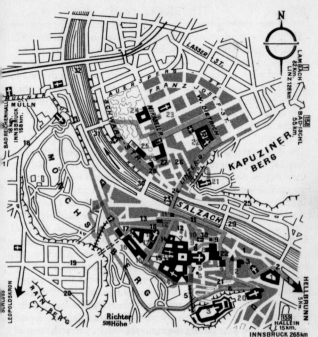

1 Law Courts. 2 Chiemseehof. 3 Hohensalzburg Fortress. 4 Post Office. 5 Cathedral. 6 Pferdeschwemme. 7 Residence. 8 Carillon. 9 Mozart Statue. 10 St Michael's Church. 11 Rathaus (Town Hall). 12 Mozart's Birthplace. 13 Franciscan Church. 14 Abbey and Church of St Peter. 15 Festival Hall. 16 Natural History Museum. 17 Old University. 18 University Church. 19 University Chapel. 20 Nonnberg Monastery. 21 Capucine Convent. 22 St Sebastian Cemetery. 23 St Andrew's Church. 24 Mirabell Palace and Gardens. 25 Mozarteum. 26 Landestheater.

1 Hellbrunner-Str. 2 Rudolfs-Pl. 3 Pfeifer-Gas. 4 Chiemsee-Gas. 5 Drahtseilbahn. 6 Festungs-Gas. 7 Kapitel-Pl. 8 Residenz Pl. 9 Mozart Pl. 10 Waag Pl. 11 Rudolfs Kai. 12 Alter Markt. 13 Getreide-Gas. 14 Sigmund-Haffnergas. 15 Reinhardt-Pl. 16 Universitäts Pl. 17 Sigmunds-Pl. 18 Augustiner-Gas. 19 Neutorstr. 20 Rainberg-Str. 21 Herren-Gas. 22 Kai-Gas. 23 Staats-Brücke. 24 Platzl. 25 Stein-Gasse. 26 Priesterhaus-Gasse. 27 Makart-Pl. 28 Bismarck-Str. 29 Mozart-Steg. 30 Museums-Steg. 31 Müllner-Steg. 32 Eisenbahn-Brücke.

century and installed in it the *Bull of Salzburg*, a massive mechanical instrument like an organ with 300 brass pipes. It can play 12 different tunes. It can best be heard at the eastern end of the cathedral. The instrument makes a bellowing noise at the beginning and end of each tune—hence its nickname. The fortress is linked with the town by underground passages, and it was a refuge for the prince-archbishops in time of peril. The restaurant of the fortress has ancient rooms, with a terraced garden giving a fine view over the city. On the way down, do not forget to take a glass of beer at the *Stieglkeller*, a tavern standing on the slope of the hill.

The Festungsgasse leads straight to the Kapitelplatz (Chapter Square) with a marble drinking trough for horses (1732). Opposite is the cathedral (Dom). Entry is free except between 12 and 2. Entrance is by the Cathedral Square (Domplatz). In the centre of the square is a statue of Our Lady by Hagenauer, a sculptor many of whose works are found in Salzburg.

The **cathedral**, built according to the plans of Santino Solari in the first half of the 17th century, on the site of the Roman basilica built in 767 A.D. by St Virgil, is 101m long and its transept measures 69m. It can hold some 10,000 people. The magnificent façade is in marble, of baroque style. It provides the setting for the mystery play of *Jedermann*, by Hugo von Hofmannsthal, performed several times a year during the Festival (26th July to 30th August), on the parvis. Between the two towers are the blazons of Marcus Sitticus and Paris Lodron, between Moses and Elias dominated by a statue of Our Lord. Below are the four Evangelists. At the entrance, St Rupert and St Virgil, and finally St Peter and St Paul, added in 1697. The interior of the cathedral is very simple. Marble altars. Above the high altar is the famous *Resurrection* by Arsenio Mascagni. On either side of the high altar are the tombs of Marcus Sitticus and Paris Lodron. The baptismal fonts are the only relics of the old basilica (the lions date from the 12th century). Interesting Treasury containing, among other objects, a Monstrance studded with 1,792 precious stones. The inaugural Mass written by Horace Cenevoli, with its 16 vocal sections shared by 8 different choirs installed on the 12 balconies, and with 34 instrumental sections backed by the cathedral's three organs, was worthy of the musical and artistic tradition of Salzburg. Even in 1618, the opera *Andromeda* had been performed at the Peter of Hellbrunn Theatre, the oldest German-language open-air stage, and from 1591 the archbishop's court had its own orchestra.

In summer there are daily organ recitals at 11 o'clock. Every Sunday and on feast-days, high Mass at 10 am with church musical recital. North of the cathedral is the Residence Square created by Wolf Dietrich, who had 100 houses demolished to clear the front of the **Residence**, built by his orders at the beginning of the 17th century. Visit the impressive rooms on the second floor. *(Open: May–September: daily from 9–12 and 2–6; January–April, opening days: 10–12 and 2–4. Saturdays, Sundays and holidays: 10 to 12. Tour takes 30 minutes.)*

Opposite the Residence is the **Carillon** with 35 bells and small bells (1695) which ring daily, except Friday, at 7, 11, and 6. It can be visited: entrance in Mozart Platz in which stands a statue of the great composer (1842). Charming courtyard at No. 4 in this square. On the west side, St Michael's Church with a very beautiful rococo grill. Take the little Waagplatz, adjoining Mozart Platz, and follow the **Judengasse** (Lane of the Jews) which runs through one of the oldest sections of the town, to the **Alter Markt** (former market) with the St Florian fountain (1734). (Roman soldier martyred in 300 in Upper Austria, who has become the patron saint against fire and flood.) Throughout Austria the image of this saint extinguishing flames is found, painted on houses and especially on firemen's barracks. Have a look at the laboratory of the Prince-Archbishop's apothecary, founded in 1591 and still standing unchanged. Opposite, is the oldest café in Salzburg. A little further on is the **Rathaus** (Town Hall), then the Getreidegasse (Wheat Alley).

No. 9 is the **birthplace of Mozart.** The third floor houses the Mozart Museum, in his own rooms: his first violin, his spinet, his musical scores, letters, etc. On the second floor are models of scenery and settings for his operas. *(Open daily, 9–12 and 2–6. Sunday, from 1st October to 30th June, mornings only. Tour takes 1 to 2 hours.)* Return to beginning of Getreidegasse, take the **Sigmund-Haffner-Gasse** which, with the Judengasse and the Getreidegasse, are the principal business streets with a wealth of wrought-iron signs. At the end of the Sigmund-Haffner-Gasse is the **Franciscan Church**

(Franziskanerkirche), most interesting because it combines the three main styles of European architecture: Roman, Gothic, and baroque. The statue of Our Lady on the baroque altar is all that remains of the high altar by Michael Pacher, Austria's greatest sculptor (end-15th century). Beautiful altar rail. Opposite the southern doorway is the Franciscan monastery which now houses the studios of the transmitting station Red-White-Red. Around the north-east corner an archway leads into a square. In the centre, a fountain with statue of St Peter (1673). Note the baroque roof and railing of the fountain in front of the Benedictine abbey of St Peter's, the oldest monastery in Austria. St Peter's Church, where the Renaissance, baroque, and rococo styles succeed each other. Below the porch is a beautiful grill. At back, the great organ on which Mozart often played. The picture above the high altar is the work of Kremser Schmid, one of the great Austrian painters of whose work there are several examples in this church. Statue of Our Lady with the Child on altar in north transept (15th century); tomb-stone of St Vitalis with a lily growing from the heart, in the south transept (15th century). Tombs of St Rupert and of the father of Wolf Dietrich. Go through the arch on right of the entrance to St Peter's to visit the **catacombs.** They probably date from the beginning of the 3rd century and were the hiding-places of the first Austrian Christians. At the entrance, there are several tombs, including that of Mozart's sister, Nannerl. In front of the catacombs is the Kreuzkapelle (13th century) and **St Peter's Cemetery,** with ancient tombs and vaults of which the rails are real masterpieces. In the centre is St Margaret's Chapel (1490). Entry to St Peter's Church and the cemetery is free *(visit to the catacombs with guide, daily from 8 to 12 and 1 to 7).* On right of entrance to catacombs is St Peter's Cellar (Stiftskeller), a very old tavern set in the actual rock, famous for its cellar.

The path along the Mönchsberg leads to the **Festspielhaus** (Festival Theatre), situated in the Max-Reinhardt Platz. The

building was formerly a stable for the archbishop's horses. Behind the Festspielhaus is the **Riding School of the Rocks** which, during the Festival, is used as the setting for operas and concerts *(visit with guide daily, except Sunday, from 9-12, and 3-6; Saturday: 9-12. Tour: about 15 minutes).* Beside the Festival Theatre is the

Natural History Museum, very comprehensive and up to date. *(Open daily, 9–12 and 2–5. Closed on Thursdays, from October 1 to April 30.)* Opposite is the Old **University**, of which only the faculty of theology and the library remain, the latter containing over 100,000 volumes. On the first floor is the Aula, in which congresses are held and where church music recitals are given during the Festival. In the University Square is the **University Church** (Kollegienkirche), the work of Fischer von Erlach, the greatest Austrian architect of his day. This church for him was a kind of preliminary test before he built the church of St Charles in Vienna. The University chapel is found in the west wing of the University building, in Sigmund Platz. High altar by W. Hagenauer. Admission free. In the square, beside the Neu-Tor, 123m long tunnel built under Wolf Dietrich, the monumental **Horse-trough** (Pferdeschwemme). The path beside the Mönchsberg leads to the Church of St Blaise. A little further on, on right, the oldest bakery in Salzburg (1429) and, on left, the new entrance to the Lift, with two mosaics representing views of Salzburg in 1553 and 1818. This lift leads to the **Mönchsberg** and to one of the best known cafés in Salzburg: the *Café Winkler*, from which there is a beautiful view over the city. Not far away are remains of the 15th-century fortifications. Climb up to the Richterhöhe to admire the view over the fortress and the mountains to the south. Descend by the Hoher Weg to **Nonnberg**, where there is a monastery founded in 700, destroyed by fire and rebuilt in the 15th century. Very fine high altar of the beginning of the 16th century. Follow the **Kaigasse**, picturesque lane lined with old houses, to the river, take the Rudolfskai on left up to the Staatsbrücke bridge and cross over to visit the **New Town** on the right bank of the Salzach.

After the Platzl (little square) comes the **Linzergasse,** one of the two oldest streets on the right bank. The other, the **Steingasse,** goes at right angles along the river. In olden days it was one of the main arteries of the city. Note the strange shape of the roofs, especially noticeable at Nos 43 and 45 in this street. The Linzergasse runs along the Kapuzinerberg. Climb the stairway which leads up from 14 Linzergasse. Stations of the Path of the Cross along the staircase. Beautiful view from the Felix Pforte. The road on the right leads to the Capucine church and **monastery**

(Kapuziner Kloster), built at the end of the 16th century. Descend again and follow the Linzergasse as far as **St Sebastian's Church**, with a beautiful grill and the tomb of Paracelse, alchemist and scientist, who died in 1541. There are several interesting tombs in St Sebastian Cemetery: that of the father and the wife of Mozart, that of the mother of the composer Weber, etc. The St Gabriel Chapel, mausoleum of Wolf Dietrich which he built during his lifetime. Still continuing along the Linzergasse, turn right at the end of the road: here is St Andrew's Church and, opposite, the **Palace** and **Gardens of Mirabell** (open to the public). Wolf Dietrich had this palace built for his mistress, Simone Alt. Completely rebuilt at the end of the 18th century. Staircase by Raphael Donner, marble hall and chapel of St John Nepomucene with a beautiful grill in the south-east corner. The gardens adjoining the palace were probably laid out by Fischer von Erlach. The Pegasus in front of the palace dates from 1661. Multitude of statues in gardens. On the west, a small maze and the **Mozarteum**, to which access is gained by the Schwarzstrasse, famous Conservatory with two concert halls and a Mozart library. *(Visit with guide on weekdays at 11.30. An organ recital is included in the tour. Duration : 1 hr.)* During the Festival, a visit is made at the same time to the small **house of the Magic Flute**, in which Mozart composed his famous opera. This house was brought from Vienna to the Mirabell gardens and contains a collection of Mozart souvenirs. Also in the Schwarzstrasse is the **Landestheater** and, behind it, Makart Platz and the Mario-nettes Theatre which is considered the best in the world. Per-formances daily during the Festival season, especially Mozart operas. On the north side of the platz is the Church of the Most Holy Trinity, built in 1699, to the plans of Fischer von Erlach, surrounded by old palaces.

This brings us to the end of a very complete tour of historic Salzburg. We can now take a glass of the finest beer in Salzburg, a city which possesses several breweries of great renown, at the *Augustiner Bräustübl*, 4 Augustinergasse. We take a seat at one of the rustic tables after being served with a big tankard of beer, sausages, cheese, and bread. Other typical restaurants are: the Sternbräu-Grossgasthof in the Griesgasse; the Eulenspiegel, in-stalled in an old building at 2 Hagenauerplatz, where one can eat and drink in little rooms with a medieval setting, and the Goldener Hirsch at 37 Getreidegasse, where the waiters are dressed in Salzburg huntsman costume in a setting dedicated to Nimrod. Do not miss tasting the *Salzburger Nockerln*, a delicious light omelette. The best cafés, apart from the Café Winkler on the Mönchsberg, are the Bazar, the Tomaselli, and the Pitter. There are numerous bars and dance halls throughout the city. In summer, Salzburg is not only Festival Town, but also the headquarters of Catholic University Weeks, of the Summer Academy of the Mozarteum, and university holiday courses in the German tongue and of German culture. The medical and surgery rooms of the provincial hospital, rebuilt in 1952 according to the latest principles, are worth a visit, as is the Central Professional School in the Ignaz-Harrerstrasse 2, built in 1952. On leaving Salzburg, remember to take away some "Mozart Balls", the chocolate and marzipan sweet speciality of Salzburg. Other souvenirs of Salzburg: ornamental jewellery with the Salzburg hunting motif (Scheibl, Griesgasse, and Dallinger, Rathaus Platz), popular art objects (Heimatwerk, Residence Platz), art works in Salzburg marble (Moser, Eichstrasse 51, Krieger, Churfürststrasse 1, and Hattinger, Schwarzstrasse 12), little figures in Salzburg dress (Hattinger, Schwarzstrasse 12, and Schatz, Getreidegasse 2) and fine articles in leather (Makart-Platz 8).

Some Recommended Hotels

Salzburg: ★★★★ Hotel Mönchstein, 26 Mönchsberg. ★★★ Hotel Fondachhof, 46 Gaisbergstrasse. ★★ Hotel Maria-Theresien-Schlössl, Morzg. ★ Hotel Eder, 20 Gaisbergstrasse.

Environs of Salzburg:

Mülln, on the other side of the Mönchsberg. Follow the Franz-Josef-Kai to the end of the Mönchsberg, turn left. Pass in front of the Lepers House (13th century), now a home for the aged. Mülln church, consecrated to Our Lady (1453), rebuilt in baroque style, one of the most elegant churches in Salzburg. The arch which crosses the road leads to the Augustine monastery built by Wolf Dietrich. The Benedictines are the owners today. Bräustübl, a very popular drinking-saloon. Further on, a masterpiece of Fischer von Erlach: St John's Church. The **Leopoldskron Castle,** 1 km south of the city. Reached by the road running round the Nonnberg. Fine, well-preserved castle which was the home of the producer Max Reinhardt, one of the founders of the Festival. **Hellbrunn,** country palace of the arch-bishops (17th century). Follow the Alpenstrasse (continuation of the Rudolfskai to the south), turn right at the first crossing (5 km; *tour with guide from 1st May to 30th September, daily from 8.30 to 6. Fee: S 3*). First see the fountains in the gardens, created by Marcus Sitticus in 1615. Also attributed to him is the palace, carried out by Santino Solari, the architect of the cathedral. Visit the Theatre of Stones, an open-air theatre in a natural cave, and the deer park in which chamois and other mountain game live in their natural surroundings of rock and woods. In the gardens, note the statue of the Empress Elisabeth of Austria, wife of Francis-Joseph, assassinated at Geneva in 1898, and the statue of dwarfs of the court of Marcus Sitticus.

THE SALZKAMMERGUT

LENGTH OF ITINERARY: 252 KM.

On leaving Salzburg by the Schallmooser Hauptstrasse (continuation of the Linzergasse), the route runs along the Kapuzinerberg and passes beside the Gaisberg (1,286m) up which runs a narrow, but good, road (1 : 9). 7 km further on, turn left, going through Thalgau. This is the gateway to Upper Austria.

★ MONDSEE

(481m), watering-place on Lake Mondsee, the warmest in the Salzkammergut (80° F.). Ancient Lacustrian city. Beautiful 15th-century church, much rebuilt: façade and altars (baroque), high altar (Renaissance). Visit the castle. Follow the north shore of the lake, passing the fine hotel Pichl Auhof, very modern, on the lake-side.

Some Recommended Hotels

Mondsee: ★★ Hotel Post.   ★ Hotel Krone.

★ UNTERACH

(468m), on the Attersee, the biggest of the Salzkammergut lakes, 15 km long, 3 km wide, and 171m deep. Go round the southern bay via Burgau, Weissenbach, and Steinbach. Leave the lake after this village and take the Traunsee road.

(margin left, top to bottom) N. 158   27 km   N. 157   13 km   N. 145

This road runs through Neukirchen, then **Altmünster,** where Wagner composed *Tristan and Yseult.*

Some Recommended Hotels

Altmünster: ⋆⋆ Katharinenhof. ⋆ Gasthof Reiberstorfer.

39 km ★

GMUNDEN

(425m), important watering-place on the Traunsee with big modern beach, open-air theatre, dance-halls, sports contests. It is particularly renowned for the fishing. Floral fêtes on lake. From the **Lake Walk** there is an admirable view over the water and the Traunstein (1,691m). Local museum. Notable high altar (1678) in the parish church. Visit **Orth Castle,** almost opposite the beach, a meeting place for Gmunden's guests. This castle, built in 1062 on an artificial island, was the property of Archduke Salvator who, in 1891, took the name of Johann Orth. **Gmunden Pottery** is world-famous, and a piece bought on the spot is a souvenir of value. In summer, international university holiday schools are held here. Tourist information office and travel agency. In the neighbourhood are the Traun Falls with hydroelectric plant. Take the road again towards Altmünster, following the lakeside towards the south.

N. 145   13 km

Some Recommended Hotels

Gmunden: ⋆⋆⋆ Hotel Austria. ⋆⋆ Hotel Elisabeth. ⋆ Bahnhof.

TRAUNKIRCHEN

★

N. 145   4 km

(430m). Romantic old village on a steep peninsula, opposite the Traunstein. In its church is the famous **altar** by an unknown artist representing the Miraculous Draught of Fishes. Fine procession of flower-decked boats on Corpus Christi Day. An arcaded road has been hewn in the rock. Make a point of tasting a *Traunkirchen tart.* Very fine road leading to Ebensee.

Some Recommended Hotels

Traunkirchen: ⋆⋆ Hotel Post. ⋆ Hotel am Stein.

EBENSEE

★

(426m), at the end of the Traunsee. Big saltworks in which

the salt waters piped from Hallstatt and Bad Ischl are treated.
Cable railway up the **Feuerkogel,** in the Höllengebirge
(1,625m). The road runs through Mitterweissenbach.

Some Recommended Hotels

Ebensee: ★★★ Sporthotel Steinkogel. ★ Berghotel Feuerkogel.

BAD ISCHL

(pop. 10,000 - 468m). International spa.
Salt springs. Ultra-modern cure establishment with salt water swimming pool.
Treatments: respiratory, circulatory, and
gynaecological troubles, rheumatism, rickets. Methods: baths, mud and oxygen
baths, inhalation, taking the waters. **Kaiservilla** (Villa of the Emperor), summer residence of Emperor
Francis Joseph who took the cure at Ischl every year. The
gardens can be visited. **Lehar Museum** in the villa which
the composer made his home at Bad Ischl. Town for
medical and other congresses, international university
holiday courses. Theatre, open-air concerts, shooting. Do
not miss taking coffee and cakes at *Zauner's,* one of the
most famous pastry-shops in Austria which had the patron-
age of Emperor Francis-Joseph. The road runs through
Lauffen.

Some Recommended Hotels

Bad Ischl: ★★★ Hotel Post. ★★ Hotel Austria. ★ Hotel
Goldenes Schiff.

★ GOISERN

(500m). Spa with iodized sulphur spring. Treatment: nerve
troubles, anaemia, rheumatism, arteriosclerosis, diabetes,
digestive tract troubles. The famous mountain boots are
produced here.

Leave the main road for a secondary road on right, via Steeg.

A Recommended Hotel

Goisern: ★ Hotel Post.

★ HALLSTATT

(511m), on the **Hallstätter See,** in a unique setting opposite
the **Dachstein** (2,996m), small town built on the side of

the Salzberg (Salt Mountain). The houses are linked by stairways and arcades. A covered stairway leads to the parish church, from which there is a lovely view over the lake. The interior contains a beautiful work in carved wood, the altar triptych in the nave. Visit the cemetery, with its amazing ossuary. School of wood carving. **Hallstatt Museum** containing objects found in the numerous prehistoric tombs in the district. The salt-mines of Hallstatt were being worked 2,000 years before the Christian era. As at Traunkirchen, the Corpus Christi Day procession is held on the lake. The officiating priest, surrounded by numerous flower-decked boats, reads passages from the four Gospels while, from the banks and the mountain, guns are fired. The Hallstatt Lake, 8 km long and 2 km wide, is surrounded by mountains rising up to 2,000m. The townsfolk do not see the sun from mid-November to February. The road runs round the lake, leading to Obertraun.

A Recommended Hotel

Hallstatt: * Hotel Grüner Baum

(500m). Terminal of cable railway up the Dachstein. The first section climbs to the Schönbergalpe (1,342m), at the entrance to the Dachstein ice caves, and was opened in 1952. The second section, up the Krippenstein (2,058m) is still under construction. Departure station 3 km behind Obertraun. The Dachstein ice caves date from the Tertiary period. Visits *(daily from 8 to 4)* are not in the least dangerous. The caves, galleries, chapels, and enormous domes with fantastic ice shapes, are lit by electricity. Wear warm clothing *(the tour lasts about 1½ hours)*. A little lower down, 20 minutes walk, is the Mammouthöhle, a non-glacial cave. It is the biggest limestone cave in Europe, with 30 km of galleries of which only one section is accessible *(tour lasts about 1½ hours)*. A direct, but bad, road (15 km 1 : 5) leads to Bad Aussee. (It is better to return via Hallstatt and Steeg, turning right by the Pötschenhöhe, frontier between Upper Austria and Styria.)

OBERTRAUN

★ BAD AUSSEE

(657m) hydro-mineral resort with some of Europe's richest brine springs; international tourist centre. Treatments: respiratory troubles: bronchitis, asthma, rheumatism, gout, neuritis, gynaecological troubles, etc. Visit the **Alpine Garden** with its 5,000 specimens of mountain plants from every continent. The local museum houses a fine collection of costumes of Archduke Johann's days. Open-air concerts, theatre, swimming pool, tennis courts, shooting. The Aussee Carnival, held at the beginning of February, is very interesting, with a masked procession in which only men dressed as women take part. Visit the salt building. Aussee Weeks for music students during July. Tourist information bureau at the Kurhaus; travel agency.

The dress of the women of Aussee, the Ausseer Dirndl, is considered the most beautiful of the Austrian Dirndls.

Ski-lift up the Tressensattel (1,079m). Excursion to the Grundlsee, renowned for its fishing (good road, 12 km).

A fine road (4 km, 1 : 9) leads to **Altaussee** *(720m) on Lake Altausseer See. Watering-place in a very beautiful setting. An hour's walk away is the* **Ausseer Salzberg** *(Aussee Salt Mountain, 948m), apply to the Steinberghaus for tickets to visit the salt mine. Visitors don miners' clothing, all white with big black buttons, and go from gallery to gallery on toboggans. Exit from the mine is made on little trucks down a steep slope which suddenly emerges into the open-air.*

Rejoin the road leading to Bad Ischl, leaving this resort in a westerly direction. We are now in the Salzburg country. 12 km from Bad Ischl, via **Strobl** (543m), a little holiday resort on the Wolfgangsee with bar, dance-hall, and beach, a road (6 km) leads *to* **St Wolfgang** *(Upper Austria, 550m), also by the lake. The operetta* White Horse Inn *brought fame to St Wolfgang. The inn actually exists there. Visit the church and see a world-famous masterpiece: the* **altar** *by* **Pacher.** *Take the little rack-railway up the Schafberg (1,783m). Splendid view over the Salzkammergut lakes. Follow south bank of the lake.*

Some Recommended Hotels

ltaussee: ★ Hotel am See.

ad Aussee: ★ Hotel Kaiser von Österreich.

Wolfgang: ★★ Grandhotel. ★ Hotel Peter.

trobl: ★★★ Grandhotel am See.

SANKT GILGEN

50m). Watering-place at the north-east tip of the Wolfangsee. Note the twin-bulb Roman belfry. Birthplace of Mozart's mother. A minor road (5 km, 1 : 9) leads to the Valdhotel Kreuzstein, a very up-to-date hotel in a delightful situation beside the Mondsee.

Some Recommended Hotels

ankt Gilgen: ★★ Hotel Billroth. ★ Hotel Lueg.

FUSCHL AM SEE

69m), on the Fuschlsee. On the opposite bank is the chlosshotel Fuschl am See, former hunting lodge of the rince-Archbishops of Salzburg, transformed into an hotel 1948.

Some Recommended Hotels

uschl am See: ★★★ Schlosshotel Fuschl. ★ Strandhotel Seerose.

he road runs beside the lake for 4 km, goes through Hof, nd ends at:

SALZBURG

N. 158 7 km ★

N. 158 25 km ★

SALZBURG-GRAZ-KLAGENFURT

For motorists who do not wish to include Vienna in their trip, e give below the direct itinerary Salzburg-Graz-Klagenfurt. part from the visit to the Gesäuse, this itinerary has little traction apart from the fact of being the most direct.

After running through the Salzburg country and Bad Ischl, we ter "Green Styria", so named because of the immense forests hich cover half its area, and its numerous meadows and mounin pastures. This country, inhabited since the remotest days, nevertheless the third ranking in Austria for density of popution, with 1,105,000 inhabitants. Despite its vast forests, the mber industry is not the most important, but metals, thanks to

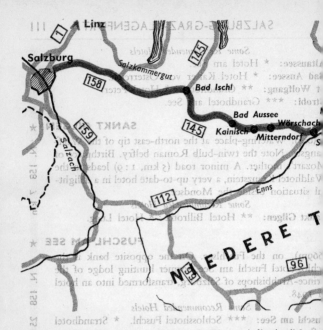

its underground wealth, are: iron ore (at Eisenerz), lignite (Murta
and Köflach basins) and vast deposits of magnesite at Veitsch, the
biggest in the world. And finally, a rather unexpected but
flourishing business, there is the export of snails to France. Styria'
mountain forests have rich stocks of game which make thi
federal country the favourite hunting ground of Austria. The
road runs down the Enns valley for 14 km; then, from Liezen
(from which a trip to the *Gesäuse* can be made by one of the mos
impressive roads in Austria), it follows the valley between the
Eisenerz Alps, on the east, and the Niedere Tauern on the west
and rejoins at Sankt-Michael national highway No. 17, and ou
No. 9 Itinerary, which leads to Graz and Klagenfurt.

PRINCIPAL SIGHTS

CHURCHES: Parish and Spitalkirche of Rottenmann; parish church of Kalwang. MONASTERY of
Admont. VIEW: Valley of the Gesäuse.

★ SALZBURG

N. 158
92 km

Leave Salzburg by the Schallmooser Hauptstrasse leading to the Salzkammergut. Follow in the reverse direction the route Bad Aussee-Salzburg described in Itinerary No. 5. From Bad Aussee, via Kainisch, to:

★ MITTERNDORF

N. 145
14 km

(pop. 2,500 - 797m), holiday resort and winter-sports centre at the junction of the Enns Valley road. On the Kulm is a giant ski-jumping platform from which leaps of up to 130m can be made. Very fine swimming pool, and baths formerly used by the Romans.

A Recommended Hotel

Mitterndorf: ★ Hotel Alpenheim.

★ STAINACH

N. 112
6 km

(pop. 1,600 - 660m), big rail junction. Stainach, Friedstein, and Trautenfels Castles in the neighbourhood.

★ WÖRSCHACH

N. 112
8 km

(650m). Spa at the foot of the Warscheneck; sulphur spring. Thermal establishment of Bad Wolkenstein nearby. Wild gorge and ruins of Wolkenstein.

★ LIEZEN

N. 113
24 km

(659m). Summer resort and business centre of the Enns Valley, at the foot of the Pyhrn Pass, frontier between Upper Austria and Styria. Manufacture of artistic ceramics. Swimming pool, tennis courts, shooting, fishing.

Excursion to Admont and Hieflau, via the Gesäuse: 42 km. *By road No. 12, rather poor after Liezen, then turn right after 17.5 km.*

Admont (641m), *health resort with the famous* **Benedictine monastery of Admont,** *founded in 1074. Destroyed by fire in* 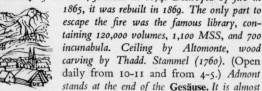 *1865, it was rebuilt in 1869. The only part to escape the fire was the famous library, containing 120,000 volumes, 1,100 MSS, and 700 incunabula. Ceiling by Altomonte, wood carving by Thadd. Stammel (1760). (Open daily from 10-11 and from 4-5.) Admont stands at the end of the* **Gesäuse.** *It is almost*

*a gorge, at the bottom of which the River Enns cuts its noisy path.
The road, very good, runs by the rocks overhanging the river and
makes a striking impression on the traveller. At the exit of the
Gesäuse stands* **Hieflau.** *From there a road leads straight to
Leoben, but it is in poor condition. It is therefore better to return
to Liezen by the Gesäuse, which it is a pleasure to traverse a
second time.*

At the exit from Liezen, leave the National Highway No. 12
which becomes a secondary road, turning right. Via **Selzthal,**
another big rail junction on the Vienna-Bischofshofen line,
the road runs in front of the very ancient fortress-castle
of Strechau, then, to **Rottenmann** (674m), a charming old
fortified town surrounded by wooded mountains. Industrial
town and winter-sports resort. On the main square (Hauptplatz) is the 15th-century parish church, beside the ancient
monastery of the Augustine Canons. West of the town is
the Gothic Hospital church, built in 1446.

TRIEBEN ★

(pop. 1,800 - 708m). Holiday resort and winter-sports
centre. Near this village, at Sunk, are big graphite and
magnesite plants. From here, Road No. 114 towards the
south leads directly to Klagenfurt, 130 km. *(See secondary
Itinerary No. 9.)* Climb of 1 : 5 after Trieben, drop of 1 : 15
just before Sankt-Georgen where we rejoin the National 17.
Via **Wald** (847m), on the Schober Pass, a quiet holiday
resort surrounded by beautiful forests, and winter-sports
centre, to **Kalwang** (767m). Magnificent **sculptures** by
Thadd. Stammel (1750) in parish church.

ST MICHAEL ★

(pop. 3,500 - 570m), at the head of the Liesing Valley, which
forms a continuation of the Paltenbach and Enns valleys. Here
we link up with the *secondary Itinerary No. 9.* By the National 17,
south, 138 km: **Klagenfurt** (via Knittelfeld and Judenburg); to
the north-east, 175 km: **Vienna** (via Leoben, Bruck, and Wiener
Neustadt). From Bruck (25 km from Sankt-Michael), the
National 67 to the south leads to **Graz,** 53 km. *(See Page 174.)*

SALZBURG-VIENNA

The Salzburg-Vienna itinerary can be divided into two
sections: Salzburg-Linz and Linz-Vienna.

For this journey, the motorist has the choice between a direct itinerary and a secondary itinerary. The direct road Salzburg-Linz, apart from the town of Wels, has little attraction except that it is the quickest. The secondary itinerary, from Lambach onwards, allows for visits to two of the loveliest abbeys in Austria: Kremsmünster and St Florian. It also includes Steyr, an important industrial town of Upper Austria. The population is dense (1,138,000 inhabitants for an area of 11,978 square kilo-

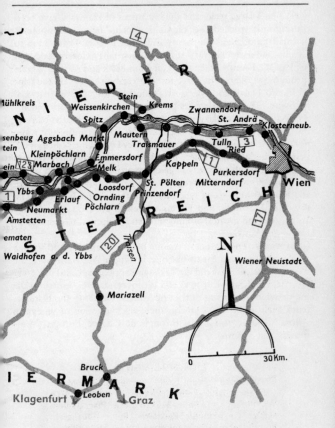

metres) and there is a busy industry, even though half the population earn their living in agriculture. The scythes and knives of Upper Austria (Steyr, Krems, and Alm Valleys) are known the world over and have been exported for centuries. Heavy industry has its centres at Linz, Wels, and Steyr, and Austria's biggest aluminium plant is found at Ranshofen. Finally, this province produces textiles, paper, cement, chemical products (nitrogen), and glass. Lignite is mined on the Hausruck (north of Vöcklabruck) on a large scale, and the salt mines of Hallstatt have been continuously worked since the Celtic epoch. The country abounds in small game; and the rivers and lakes in fish. From Linz to Vienna, the main itinerary at first follows fairly closely the south bank of the Danube, then turns off from Melk and runs to Vienna through St Pölten. The three most interesting towns on the trip: Ybbs, Pöchlarn, and Melk, are found slightly off the national highway. The little detours to these towns are warmly recommended. The secondary itinerary at first hugs the north bank of the Danube, then the south bank. This road is infinitely more picturesque. It runs through the legendary land of the Nibelungengau and the Wachau, where proud castles dominate the river and everything seems to have the gaiety appropriate for a land where the grape flourishes. This region is the orchard of Lower Austria, and is a ravishing scene when the fruit trees are in blossom. The towns of Dürnstein and Krems as well as the Göttweig Abbey are among the greatest architectural and sculptural treasures to be found in Austria.

Gastronomy: The regions stretching between Salzburg and Vienna is principally noted for its pastries: in Upper Austria there is the *Linzer Torte*, almond and nut cake with apricot jam, and in Lower Austria, the *Krapfen*, fritters and turnovers. Lower Austria is the major wine-producing district of Austria. All along the Danube, from Melk to Klosterneuberg, there is a succession of vineyards whose produce is famous throughout Central Europe (Wine museum at Krems).

PRINCIPAL SIGHTS

CHURCHES: Paura; Old Cathedral, St Mary's Cathedral and Seminarkirche of Linz; Lorch; Waidhofen a. d. Ybbs; Sankt-Pölten; Pfarrkirchen; Steyr; Christkindl; Pöchlarn; Spitz; Dürnstein; Spitalkirche, Piaristenkirche and Pfarrkirche of Krems. ABBEYS: Melk; Kremsmünster; Göttweig; Klosterneuberg. MONASTERY of Sankt-Florian. MUSEUMS: Ried im Innkreis; Linz; Krems. CASTLES: Enns; Waidhofen a. d. Ybbs; Grein; Schönbühel; Aggstein; Dürnstein. HISTORIC MONUMENTS: Hans Sachs' House at Wels; Bemaltes Haus at Schärding am Inn; English Girls' Institute at Sankt-Pölten; Mathematics Tower of Kremsmünster. VIEWS: The Nibelungengau; the Wachau.

SALZBURG ★

Leave Salzburg by the Schallmooser Hauptstrasse and take
Road No. 1. Go through **Strass** and Henndorf (on left,
the Wallersee, another Salzkammergut lake), Neumarkt
and **Strasswalchen**. Soon after, the road runs from the
Salzburg country into Upper Austria. The road goes through
Frankenmarkt and runs round **Vöcklabruck**, along the River
Ager, through **Schwanenstadt**.

*Just before Lambach, a left fork of the road leads north-west to
Braunau on the German frontier, running through the district
known as the Innviertel. The road is good up to Haag, then
becomes bad on the journey from Geiersberg to Ried im Innkreis
(pop. 12,000 - 454m): pretty little transit and business town.
Many baroque houses on the Stadtplatz. In the parish church,
also baroque, there is a beautiful altar by Schwanthaler and a
fresco dating from 1520. The Museum of History and Popular
Art (Volkskundemuseum) contains numerous works by the
Schwanthaler family of sculptors, born at Ried. Via Kirchheim,
Pollin, Altheim, and St Peter, to Braunau am Inn (pop. 12,000 -
352m), frontier town where Adolf Hitler was born. At 18
Johann-Fischer-Gasse is a beautiful old house, the Glocken-
giesserhaus. Gothic-style parish church built in 1486. Tower
of the Gate of Salzburg. Spitalkirche, built between 1417 and
1430, with high altar by Hagenauer (1697). The town is linked
by a modern bridge to Simbach in Bavaria, where the German
Customs Office is found.
To the east and west of Braunau are the great lakes of the Inn
dam which supplies the hydroelectric plants of the district. On the
road to Ranshofen, west of Braunau, is a big aluminium plant.*

Some Recommended Hotels

Braunau am Inn: ★★★ Hotel Zur Post. ★ Hotel Fink.
Ried im Innkreis: ★★★ Hotel Gärner. ★ Hotel Barth.
Schwanenstadt: ★ Hotel Ammering.

LAMBACH ★

(366m), little old town with houses with beautiful 18th-
century façades. Great Benedictine abbey, founded in 1032.
A quarter of an hour away from Lambach, on the right
bank of the Traun, is the pilgrim church of **Paura**, built

N. — 80 km

N. I 15 km

in 1724 by Prunner of Linz, one of the rare triangular churches. Dedicated to the Holy Trinity, it has three towers, three altars, three organs, etc. High altar by Altomonte. The road henceforth follows the left bank of the Traun as far as the suburbs of Linz (a second road leads to Vienna via Steyr and Enns, along the Danube): *(see secondary itinerary below)*.

★ WELS

N. I 30 km

(pop. 37,000 - 317m). Industrial and agricultural centre of Upper Austria on the Traun. The picturesque old town lies on the left bank of the river. Notable **Stadtplatz** with Lederertor (gate) and massive tower of the Pfarrkirche, which contains tombs of the Polheims. Statue of Emperor Joseph II on the Kaiser-Josefsplatz. Go by the Burggasse to Burg Wels, where Emperor Maximilian I died in 1519. Visit the **house of Hans Sachs,** where the poet worked as a cobbler in 1513 and where he wrote his first poems. The municipal museum houses relics of the Roman and Germanic epochs. Wels is famous for its great popular festival, the *Welser Volksfest,* which is held in the Volksgarten every other year (even-figure years, first week in September).

The Vienna Spanish Riding School moved to Wels in 1946. The road runs through **Marchtrenk** and enters the suburbs of Linz by the Wiener Reichsstrasse, lined with big metal plants.

A Recommended Hotel

Wels: ★ Hotel Post.

★ LINZ

(pop. 182,000 - 264m). Capital of Upper Austria. Third largest city in Austria, Danubian port and industrial city. A bridge 208m long links the two sections of the city. Follow the Landstrasse, a continuation of the Wiener Reichstrasse. On left, the Volksgarten (public garden)s, then the Schillerplatz and, on right, the Ursulinenkirche. At the corner of the Domstrasse is the

Alter Dom (old cathedral). On left of entrance, monument to the great composer Anton Bruckner who was organist at Linz Cathedral from 1858 to 1868. The Landstrasse runs into the Hauptplatz, with the Town Hall, beautiful private houses, and the New Gallery of the city of Linz, an art gallery devoted to 19th- and 20th-century works. In the centre of the square is the Holy Trinity column. Behind the square, to right, is the parish church which contains, beneath a slab of red marble, the heart of Emperor Frederick III who died in 1493. Go past the main Post Office building, take the Graben and the Museumstrasse to the **Provincial Museum** of Upper Austria, with a natural history collection, applied arts, and prehistoric relics from Hallstatt. Continue along the Museumstrasse, then, on right, the Hümerstrasse, and finally the Harrachstrasse to the remarkable little **Seminarkirche** (seminary church) built in 1725, with high altar by Altomonte and side altars by Kremser Schmidt. Take the Humboldtstrasse on left; then the Göthestrasse on right as far as the Landstrasse which is crossed to continue along the Volksgartenstrasse and the Herrenstrasse as far as the **Marien-Dom** (St Mary's Cathedral), begun in 1862 and completed in 1924, in French Gothic style. Continue and pass in front of the Bischofshof and the monument to the writer Adalbert Stifter who died at Linz on 28th January, 1868. The road ends at the Promenade, with the Landhaus dating from 1564 with a beautiful arched courtyard. Visit the Stein Hall there (1582). The **Minorite Church** beside the Landhaus contains beautiful paintings by Kremser Schmidt. Opposite the Landhaus is the Provincial Theatre; open-air concerts are given on the promenade in summer. Then via the Klosterstrasse, back to the Hauptplatz.

There are vineyards north-east of Linz in the Mühlviertel, but the area produces mainly an excellent cider (apple and pear) which the people of Linz drink at table, and between meals. There are several fine taverns where it can be tasted, such as the Kremsmünster Weinstube and the Dürnsteiner Weinstube, Graben 27. Do not forget to order a *Linzer Torte* (the pastry speciality of this city) in one of the many cafés of Linz. The busiest shopping street is the Landstrasse. The Tourist Information Bureau and the travel agency are found at 9 Hauptplatz; the ÖAMTC at 15 Volksgartenstrasse.

Some Recommended Hotels

Linz: ★★★ Parkhotel, Christian-Coulin-Strasse-Figuly-strasse. ★★ Hotel Achleitner, 18 Hauptstrasse. ★ Hotel Oberndorfer, 1 Schubertstrasse.

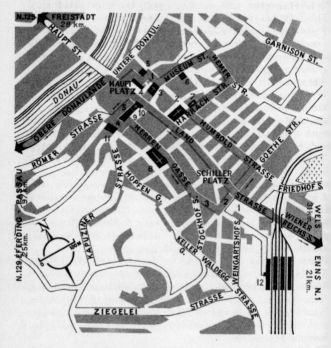

1 Graben. 2 Stelzhamer-Str. 3 Volksgarten-Str. 4 Promenade. 5 Klosterstrasse.

1 Volksgarten. 2 Ursulinenkirche. 3 Alter Dom. 4 Rathaus (Town Hall). 5 Stadt Pfarre. 6 Museum. 7 Seminarkirche. 8 Marien-Dom. 9 Landhaus. 10 Minoritenkirche. 11 Theatre. 12 Station.

*We would recommend the motorist who arrives by the direct itinerary to make the lovely excursion to **St Florian**, 10 km south of Linz. Leave by the Wiener Reichsstrasse, cross road No. 1, turn left after 8.5 km. For a description of St Florian, see Page 130.*

From Linz, a fine road to the west leads to Passau, on the German frontier towards Regensburg.

The road runs along the right bank of the Danube. Via Wilhering, with a Cistercian convent founded in 1146, at the foot of the Kimberg, to **Eferding** *(pop. 3,700 - 271m). Town which is mentioned in the Song of the Nibelungen. In 1626, it was the centre of the War of the Peasants in Upper Austria. In the parish church (late-Gothic) there are some interesting tombstones, portraits of 1467, and a very beautiful double corkscrew staircase. Opposite Eferding is the castle of the princes of Starhemberg with a sumptuous interior (open to public).*

The road leaves the Danube, which at this point cuts its way through the granite and gneiss mountains of the Böhmerwald, to the north, and the Sauwald to the south. Waizenkirchen, 368m, contains the last work of Kremser Schmidt, the altar reredos: Birth and Resurrection of Christ (1800). Peuerbach, Taufkirchen, and **Schärding am Inn** *(pop. 6,300 - 313m): small town of medieval streets in a beautiful setting. Biggest Austrian centre of the milk industry. Cure establishment, Kneipp method. In the picturesque Stadtplatz, opposite the Town Hall, is the famous house with the painted façade* **(Bemalte Haus).** *The road runs along the Inn as far as* **Passau,** *in Bavaria, at the junction of the Inn and the Danube. Straight road to Regensburg (Germany): 122 km.*

From Linz, several roads branch off towards Czechoslovakia. The best is the most easterly road. *Leave Linz by the Freistädter Strasse. Via Gallneukirchen and Neumarkt to* **Freistadt im Mühlkreis** *(pop. 5,600 - 558m): medieval town with many Gothic houses. Notable parish church in 15th-century Gothic style, and Liebfrauenkirche dating from 1470. The castle, also dating from the Middle Ages, houses a Museum of Popular Art.*

The road crosses the Kerschbauersattel just before **Unterheid,** *Czech frontier and Customs, 41 km from Budapest and 197 km from Prague.*

LINZ ★

Leave Linz by the Wiener Reichstrasse, turning left after clearing the suburbs.

N 21 km

ENNS ★

(pop. 7,600 - 280m). The oldest town in Upper Austria, on the left bank of the Enns, built on the site of a camp of the Roman legions, *Lauriacum*, and dominated by **Ennsegg Castle** (beautiful park). In the centre of the Stadtplatz is the Town Tower, erected in 1564. On the east side of the square is the old Town Hall with Municipal Museum containing principally Roman relics. On the south, the 15th-century parish church with the Walser Chapel added later. Just north of the station can be seen the very old village of Lorch which, up to the 5th century, was the site used by the civilian section of the legionaries camp. **Lorch Church** was the first to be built in Austria. It was probably originally a Roman temple which the early Christians converted into a church. It was here that St Florian was martyred. Near the church are the foundations of the Roman Forum.

The frontier between Upper and Lower Austria follows the Enns up to Steyr. The bridge across the river at the exit from Enns is actually one of three compulsory routes for entrance and exit to the Soviet Occupied Zone.

We advise motorists following the road which forms the principal itinerary to make the necessary detours for visits to the loveliest places in the Danube Valley *(see secondary itinerary below, pages 131 to 134).* They can also take the roads which hug the left bank of the Danube, from Grein to Krems, and the right bank, from Krems to Vienna. Cross the Enns Bridge. The road runs parallel to the Danube. Via **Strengberg** and **Oed** to Amstetten.

A Recommended Hotel

Enns: ★ Hotel Goldener Ochs.

★ AMSTETTEN

Napoleon won a victory over the Russians here on 5th November, 1805.

Road No. 121 forks to the south, leading (26 km) via Kematen

to **Waidhofen a. d. Ybbs** *(358m). Picturesque little town of 5,600 inhabitants, with many old houses and arcaded courtyards. In the Middle Ages, Waidhofen was an industrial centre with many forges using the iron ore from the mountains of the Ybbs Valley. It is still surrounded by old walls. The Town*

N. 1 36 km

N. 1 40 km

Tower, built in the 16th century to commemorate the victory over the Turks in 1532, indicates the hour of the triumph. Opposite the parish church (15th century), late Gothic, is the **Burg,** *dating from the 16th century, now the headquarters of the forestry administration. Interesting regional museum containing fine examples of wrought ironwork. North-east of the town is the* **Sonntagberg,** *a 704m peak, which is reached by a road forking east just before reaching Waidhofen. On this mountain stands one of the masterpieces of Jakob Prandtauer, the* **Pilgrim Church,** *completed in 1732: magnificent ceilings decorated with frescoes by D. Gran, and interesting Treasury.*

14 km from Amstetten, just before reaching Neumarkt, a road to the left leads to **Ybbs** *(see page 131)*. The road runs through Erlauf. 1.3 km after this town, left fork towards **Pöchlarn** *(see page 132)*. Go through **Ordning;** the road closely follows the Danube and runs round:

MELK ★

(pop. 3,100 - 228m). Melk Abbey is one of the finest baroque buildings in the world, in a truly magnificent situation 57m above the Danube. Below it is the little town, former Roman castle, which was the residence of the Babenbergers, the reigning princes, from 976 to 1100. The centre of the town is the Hauptplatz. On left, the Rathausplatz with the 16th-century Town Hall and the Koloman Fountain (1687). The Post Office is a fine building dating from 1790. Fine middle-class houses, particularly along the Hauptstrasse. Picturesque lanes running down to the Danube. The Stiftsweg climbs to the **Abbey** *(visits with guide daily from 9-12 and 2-5)*. In 976, margrave Leopold II of Babenberg built a fortress on this rock, which in 1111, Leopold III handed over to the Benedictine monks of St Lambrecht. The abbey was fortified during the 14th

1 Koloman Fountain. 2 Town Hall. 3 Post Office. 4 Abbey. 5 Station.

century, but suffered badly during the wars of the 15th and 16th century. Badly neglected in later years (the noblemen of the district being Protestants) it regained importance during the Counter-Reformation. Following a fire, it was completely rebuilt in its present form by the Tyrolean architects Jakob Prandtauer and his pupil Franz Munggenast, between 1702 and 1736. The southern façade is 362m long. Access to the abbey is through an entrance flanked on right and left by statues of St Leopold and St Koloman, patron saints of the abbey; through a first courtyard and porchway, to the courtyard of the Prelates, with ornamental fountain. Opposite is the House of the Prelates which contains numerous valuable paintings, the records, and treasury of the church, of which the best known item is the **Cross of Melk** (1363). This 60cm cross

 in chaste gold is covered with precious stones. The main staircase leads to the first floor of the south wing and to the Passage of the Emperors, some 200m long, with pictures of the Austrian regents. In the marble hall a fresco decorates the ceiling (P. Troger, 1732). Along the great terrace, from which there is a magnificent view of the church façade, entry is gained to the Library, containing more than 700,000 volumes and 1,800 9th-century MSS; note the ceiling paintings by P. Troger. A spiral staircase leads down to the abbey church, baroque construction by Prandtauer (1702-1726). Magnificent interior. The cupola above the nave is 64m high. The carved crucifix dates from 1478: below the church porch is the tomb of the first Babenberg. In the south tower hangs the **Petri-Pauli Bell** (St Peter and St Paul, to whom the church is consecrated); it weighs nine tons.

The road continues east, while the Danube curves to the north. Go through Loosdorf and Prinzersdorf.

★ ST PÖLTEN

(pop. 40,700 - 267m). Fine old town and bishopric since 1784. Its main industries are paper, cloth, and the manufacture of machines. The Tourist Information Bureau is housed in the Town Hall. At the Riemerplatz, where the main roads meet, take the Rathausgasse as far as the Marschallplatz with its Column of the Holy Trinity (1782), the Town Hall (16th century; restored in baroque), the Carmelite Church, built in 1712 by Prandtauer, and, on right, the Franciscan church, a great rococo building completed in 1768.

Then by the Prandtauergasse to the Linzer Strasse, in which stands the **Institute of the English Girls** (Institut der Englischen Fräulein), begun in 1715, one of the finest specimens of baroque style, and the Municipal Museum *(open: Saturday and Sunday, 3-5)*. Next, along the Wiener-Strasse with its beautiful baroque houses, to the Herrenplatz, with the Virgin's Column (1718) and memorial to the dead. In the Domplatz is the cathedral, with three naves, originally Roman, remodelled in 1750 in baroque style to plans by Prandtauer. Inside is the noteworthy **Rosary Chapel** (13th century). In the same square is the bishop's palace, a former Augustine convent. *Towards the south a road follows the Traisen and leads to the famous place of pilgrimage of* **Mariazell** *(see Itinerary No. 9), 77 km away.*

The road crosses the Traisen on leaving St Pölten. Via Pottenbraun, Kapelln, and Mitterdorf to Sieghartskirchen and **Ried.** After several turnings up the Riederberghöhe (480m), fine view over the foothills of the Alps and the Vienna Woods, into which the road now runs. On left is the Riederberg (417m); on right, the Weideck (419m). Along the Gablitzbach to Purkersdorf, where the road crosses the River Wien and follows its right bank; then through Weidlingau and into Vienna.

A Recommended Hotel

St Pölten: ★ Hotel Pittner.

VIENNA ★

N. 1 63 km

SECONDARY ITINERARY:
VIA KREMSMÜNSTER AND ALONG THE DANUBE: 395 KM.

SALZBURG ★

Leave Salzburg by the Schallmooser Hauptstrasse, turn right outside the city and follow, in the reverse direction, Itinerary No. 5, Gmunden — Bad Ischl — Salzburg (pages

158 and 145

96-7). From Gmunden, via Steyrermühl and Roitham, to Lambach *(see main itinerary)*. After Lambach, turn right.

★ KREMSMÜNSTER

(345m). **Benedictine Abbey** founded in 777 by Bavarian Duke Tassilo III. In the Prelates Court is the twin-tower abbey church which houses the famous **Chalice of Tassilo,** known throughout the world. Dating from 780, it is the oldest piece of jewellery of the Austro-Bavarian lands. Near the Oak Door (Eichentor) is an interesting fish-pond composed of five basins surrounded by arcades, dating from 1692. In the great garden is the Observatory, with the **Mathematical Tower** (1748) of a strange design, containing remarkable natural history exhibits. In the abbey itself are historical and art collections and a library. On first floor is the Emperor's Hall (paintings by Altomonte). *(Tour of the abbey and the Mathematical Tower can be made daily: duration, 1 hour.)*

★ BAD HALL

(380m). Thermal station with iodo-bromide springs, the strongest in Central Europe. Treatments: scrofula, rickets, arteriosclerosis, blood diseases, gynaeco-logical troubles, neuralgia, rheumatism, ophthalmic and skin diseases. Provincial hospital. Open-air concerts, swimming pool, tennis courts, theatre, parks. Beautiful woods in the neighbourhood. Nearby, at **Pfarrkirchen,** is an exquisite little rococo church with ravishing internal decorations. Go through **Sierning.**

Some Recommended Hotels

Bad Hall: ★★ Kurhotel Landessanatorium. ★ Hotel Tassilo.

★ STEYR

(pop. 39,000 - 303m). Centre of the iron industry since 1800, at the junction of the Steyr and the Enns. Tourist Information Bureau at the Town Hall. On the eastern boundary are the famous motor-car and motor-cycle work

of Steyr – Daimler – Puch.
The iron which is the basis
of Steyr's industry comes
from the nearby Innerberg,
whose mineral resources
have been worked since
the Middle Ages. Industrial
museum, permanent exhi-
bition. The centre of the
town, which is dominated
by the fortress-castle of
Steyr, is the Stadtplatz,
with the Town Hall in
rococo style (1765), the
Bummerlhaus, a fine Gothic
building, and numerous
houses with picturesque
courtyards (Nos. 9, 12, and
14, in particular), as well as

1 Stadtplatz. 2 Innerberger
Kornspeicher. 3 Parish Church.
4 Station. 5 Castle. 6 Ennser-
Strasse. 7 F. D. Roosevelt-Str
8 Kircheng. 9 Zwischenbrücken.
10 Grünmarkt. 11 Enns-Kai.
12 Redtenbachergasse. 13 Christ-
kindlweg.

the *Madlsederhaus* at No. 39. Also in this square is the
Dominican Church: baroque interior with rich stucco
decoration. In the centre of the square is the Leopoldi
Fountain (around 1680). From the square, go straight to
the Innerberger Kornspeicher (Innerberg Silo, 1612), with
the municipal museum, then up through a lane to the
parish church, one of the biggest Gothic churches in the
country. It was built in 1443 by Hans Puchsbaum, the
architect of St Stephen's Cathedral in Vienna. At the south
end of the church is St Margaret's Chapel and the Pfarrhof,
where Bruckner completed his *Sixth Symphony.* On the
north is the Messnerhaus with Bruckner's room. From
there the Pfarrgasse runs back to the Hauptplatz, off which
runs the very picturesque **Engengasse.** To the west of Steyr
lies the hamlet and pilgrim church of **Christkindl.** The
church dates from 1706. It is one of the
masterpieces of Carlone. *Christkindl* means
"Little Jesus". Austrian children therefore
address their Christmas present request
letters not to Father Christmas, but to
Christkindl. All letters bearing this address
are forwarded by the Austrian Post Office

to this Styrian hamlet, where a special Post Office is installed around Christmas time. The staff send replies to all
children who have enclosed a stamped, addressed envelope
for a reply, affixing the seal of Christkindl, a reproduction
of the Virgin and Child which appears on the wall of
the church.

Road No. 115, towards the south, leads to Leoben (128 km)
(see Itinerary No. 9). Take the same road in a northern
direction and turn left at **Dietachdorf.** Go through **Hofkirchen.**

A Recommended Hotel

Steyr: ★ Hotel Münichholz.

★ **ST FLORIAN**

(248m). In the Market Square (Markt-
platz), take road on left up the Speiserberg,
on which stands the **Canons Monastery** of
St Florian, founded in 555 in honour of
this saint, a Roman legionary martyred at
Enns in 304 and who is the "guardian"
against fire and flood. His likeness is found
on many Austrian houses. (The following prayer is addressed
to him by peasant folk: "St Florian, spare my house: rather
burn that of my neighbour.") His statue, carved in wood,
is found in the monastery, which was built over his tomb.
The present building is a baroque masterpiece begun in
1686 by Carlo Carlone and completed in 1751 to the design
of Prandtauer *(open daily 9-11 and 3-6)*. Take particular
note of the staircase, courtyard, and southern wing of the
monastery. Visit the **Marble Hall** with its magnificent
ceilings by Altomonte, and a fine collection of paintings
including a cycle by Altdorfer (about 1520), master of the
Danubian School; library of 110,000 volumes and 885
9th-century MSS; the Emperor's Chamber and the church
of the Monastery with Anton Bruckner's organ, one of
the greatest Austrian composers. Left an orphan very young,
he was brought up in St Florian's monastery, and was a
choir-boy at the Music School. He became the headmaster,
was appointed to St Florian and became organist at the
monastery church from 1845 to 1858. He was buried in
the crypt, below the church organ. A public concert is
given there daily at 4.30. From St Florian, a road running

N. 1 and N. 123   13 km

east (2 km) links up with national highway No. 1 at **Asten**.
Bearing left, the suburbs of Linz (8 km) are reached, and,
to the right, (5 km) **Enns** *(see main itinerary).*

Leave Enns, heading north, and follow the left bank of
the Enns. Cross the Danube.

MAUTHAUSEN ★

(pop. 3,600 - 244m). Old town which owes its lugubrious
renown to the great concentration camp built by the
Germans near the Mauthausen quarries. Visits can be made
to this camp, which is preserved as a memorial to the
thousands who died there. Mauthausen possesses an impressive parish church and a regional museum housed in
the old Pragsteiner Castle (1491), on the banks of the Danube.
On leaving Mauthausen, turn right and follow the Danube,
through **Mitterkirchen.**

GREIN ★

(pop. 2,600 - 218m). Picturesque holiday resort on the
Danube, dominated by the **Greinburg** (castle) of the end-
15th century, with a splendid Renaissance courtyard.
Grein is proud of having the oldest Austrian theatre, while
in the church there is a high altar by Altomonte.

SARMINGSTEIN ★

Frontier between Upper and Lower Austria.

PERSENBEUG ★

See its castle dominating the Danube, one of the oldest in
the region, built in the 10th century and reconstructed in
1621. Persenbeug is the start of the famous **Wachau** Gorge,
a beautiful countryside, rich in castles, churches, vineyards,
orchards, and forests.

YBBS ★

(pop. 4,500 - 216m). On the opposite bank of the Danube
(car-ferry), ancient little town which was the *Pons Isidis*
of the Romans. On its quays is the old wine-toll building.
In the main square stands the great Gothic parish church
(1490), the Roland Fountain (1600), a statue of the Virgin
and a funereal memorial of 1350. Ybbs is the first town of

N. 123 34 km

N. 3 7 km

N. 3 12km

N. 1 9 km

the **Nibelungengau** which stretches up to
Melk and which forms part of the **Wachau**.
The *Lied der Nibelungen* is for German
speaking people what the Song of Roland
is to the French. The manuscript of this
epic legend, discovered in the Vorarlberg,
in the 18th century, inspired Richard
Wagner's great cycle of operas. It was through the region
we now approach that King Gunther, One-Eyed Hagen
and his knights rode to the court of Etzel (Attila) where
they had been summoned by Kriemhild, sister of Gunther
and wife of Etzel, with the sole purpose of avenging the
death of her first husband, Siegfried, killed by Hagen.
Neither Gunther nor his men ever saw the Rhine again.
They fell to the last man after an heroic battle.

*From Ybbs, a road to the south-east links up with the main
itinerary, which is followed as far as Melk (see main itinerary).*
After **Erlauf**, a road to the left leads to:

★ PÖCHLARN

(pop. 3,000 - 212 m). Opposite **Kleinpöchlarn**, birthplace of
the famous painter Kokoschka, and **Marbach** with the
pilgrim place of **Maria Taferl**. This is the old *Bechelaren*
of the *Nibelungenlied*, headquarters of the Margrave
Rüdiger. Here One-Eyed Hagen threw into the Danube the
chaplain who, according to an oracle, would be the only
one who would return home again. The chaplain succeeded
in swimming to the opposite shore, so Hagen, after the
landing of the knights, burned his boats. The two towers
Welserturm and *Urfahrturm*, are the last traces of the might
fortifications of the Middle Ages. In the **church** are reredos
by Kremser Schmidt and a bas-relief of the Mount of
Olives dating from 1500.

A road to the south-east links up with national highway
No. 1 at **Ordning**.

*After Melk, along road No. 33, the impressive
Schönbühel Castle, built between 1819 and
1821 on the old foundations and ruined walls
of a fortress of the Middle Ages. Nearby, to left
is the little Servite monastery. Still continuing
along the right bank of the Danube, **Aggsbach***

N. 3 17 km

Dorf, *with a very beautiful church of the end-14th century.
2 km further on are the ruins of the* **Aggstein Castle-fortress**
*on a rock rising 320m above the river, one of the best-known
and most strongly fortified positions on the Danube.*

Return to Melk, taking the car ferry which takes you to
Emmersdorf on the opposite side of the Danube.

AGGSBACH MARKT ★

Holiday resort, with camping site and beach on the Danube,
in one of the prettiest sites of the Wachau.

SPITZ ★

(197m). Holiday resort surrounded by
vineyards ranking among the finest in
Austria, on the slopes of the Tausendeimer-
berg, which means the Hill of the Thousand
Buckets of Wine. The **parish church,** a
basilica with three naves, has a rather
unusual appearance: the axis of the choir

forms a sharp angle with the bay. Inside are several reredos
by Kremser Schmidt (1799) and the 12 Apostles on the
rood-screen of the organ (1240). Beautiful old houses,
especially the Aggsteiner Hof in the market square (Markt-
platz). Fine Town Hall.

Shortly after Spitz, the fortified church of **St Michael,**
founded in 987. The present building was erected in 1500.
Through Wösendorf and Joching.

WEISSENKIRCHEN IN DER WACHAU ★

(190m). Charming holiday resort with beach, one of the
most picturesque places in the Danube Valley, dominated
by the fortified parish church which is approached by a
covered stairway built in 1531. The church fortifications
run round the 16th-century Teisenhofer Hof with its
arched courtyard and the Town Hall. The road now
follows the curve made by the Danube.

DÜRNSTEIN ★

(207m). Pleasant little medieval town surrounded by walls
and defence towers on the slope between the Danube and
the **Castle-fortress of Dürnstein.** The **parish church** (Pfarr-

N. 3
8 km

5 km

6 km

6 km

kirche) is one of the finest examples of baroque church architecture, a masterpiece by Munggenast (1725). Beautiful interior decoration. Path of the Cross and Crib by Johann Schmidt (1722). In the main street (Hauptstrasse) are the Town Hall and beautiful private residences. On the banks is the Starhemberg Castle (1633), and not far away, beside the enclosure, the ruins of the Kunigundenkirche, erected in the 13th century, with an ossuary of two storeys. From here, a stairway-path leads (25 minutes) to the **ruins of Dürnstein,** impressive remains of the fortress in which Richard Coeur de Lion was imprisoned from 1192-1193. Throughout the town, signs and the names of the inns recall the memory of this illustrious prisoner: "At the Sign of the Minstrel Blondel", "Richard Lion Heart", etc. Here, too, on 11th November, 1805, 5,000 French under General (later Marshal) Mortier, held back 30,000 Russians. A memorial to this feat of arms is found on the road leading to Krems, via Stein.

A Recommended Hotel

Dürnstein: ⋆ Gasthof Zum Richard Löwenherz.

⋆ STEIN

Small town whose surrounding vineyards are famous. Make a point of sampling, in one of the bars, the best produce of the region.

⋆ KREMS

(198m). Small market town on the western boundary of the Wachau, one of the oldest in Austria, which has retained its medieval character which is mentioned in manuscripts dating from 995. Krems is noted for roses and apricots. In the Obere Landstrasse, on right, is the Town

Hall (15th century), the **Spitalkirche** and beautiful **old houses** (particularly Nos. 10, 21, and 32). At the end of the road is the Steiner Gate (Steiner Tor) dating from 1480. Before the gate, on right, through an alley, is the Körnermarkt (Corn Market) with St Mary's Pillar (1683) and, at No. 4,

2 km

18 km

a beautiful rococo-style
house. In the Theater-Platz
is the former Dominican
church, now the **Municipal
Museum** which houses
paintings by Johann Martin
Schmidt, known as Krem-
ser Schmidt, one of the
greatest Austrian painters,
whose pictures and reredos
adorn many Austrian
churches. In the building
adjoining the monastery is
the Wine Museum. A
little further on, the **parish
square with the church,** containing paintings by Kremser Schmidt (ceiling). At
No. 5 in this square is the
Pfarrhof, parish courtyard,
with arcaded court. To the
north, by a partly covered
stairway, is the Frauenberg

1 Town Hall. 2 Spitalkirche.
3 Steiner Tor. 4 St Mary's
Column. 5 Körnermarkt. 6 Old
Dominican Church (Museum).
7 Wine Museum. 8 Parish Church.
9 Pfarrhof. 10 Piaristenkirche.
11 Sgrafittohaus. 12 Donau-
lände. 13 Ring-Str. 14 Herzog-
str. 15 Dreifaltigkeitsplatz. 16
Ob. Landstrasse. 18 Theater-
Platz. 19 Hoher Markt. 20 Gar-
tengas. 21 Spitalgas. 22 Juden-
gas. 23 Unt. Landstr.

with the **Piaristenkirche,** a beautiful Gothic church several
times remodelled in the 15th and 16th centuries. Beautiful
southern doorway and reredos by Kremser Schmidt. To the
east, via the picturesque upper market *(Hoher Markt),*
with its beautiful old houses, is the old Hofburg (13th
century) and the Hercules Fountain (1682). At 5 Margareten-
strasse is the *Sgrafittohaus* (1560). Return to parish square.
Go back to Stein and take the bridge over the Danube
leading to **Mautern.** *Follow road to the south to visit the*
Benedictine abbey of Göttweig, *which can be seen from the road.*
(Visits: Opening days 8-11.30; holidays 10.30 to 11.30 and
from 2.30 to 6.30.) *The most beautiful part of this abbey is the
Emperor's Staircase (Kaiserstiege), a masterpiece of baroque with
decoration by Kremser Schmidt and painted ceilings by Paul
Troger. In the upper storey, the Altmannssaal with a ceiling
painted by Joh. Rud. Buss (1731). Following this room are the
four ducal chambers, including Napoleon's Room, with magnificent
Gobelins tapestries.*

Back to the road leading to Mautern, and, just before,
cross bridge over the Traisen.

★ TRAISMAUER

Former Roman citadel of *Trigisanum*, with rectangular
enclosure; then the road runs through **Gemeinlebarn**. Take
first road on left, and, via **Zwennendorf** to:

★ TULLN

(pop. 5.500 - 181m). Old Danubian town where, according
to the *Song of the Nibelungen*, Attila met his fiancée Kriemhild, the widow of Siegfried. Alongside the parish church,
whose western doorway dates from 1220, is an early 13th-
century ossuary. Via **St Andrä**, to:

★ KLOSTERNEUBURG

(pop. 16,000 - 168m). From 1938, this has
been the 26th district of Vienna, at the foot
of the Kahlenberg and the Leopoldberg,
surrounded by vineyards. Its **beach** is one
of the biggest and most up to date in the
Vienna region, with more than 1,000
cabins and where beach huts and chalets
can be rented. Tennis courts, concerts, open-air cinema,
dance-halls, and restaurants. In 1106 the Margrave, Leopold-
the-Holy, founded the **Abbey of the Augustine Canons**
there, of which the massive building can be seen far out on
the Danube *(visits: weekdays by arrangement; Sunday: 2 tours
with guide in the afternoon)*. Emperor Charles VI (1711-1740)
wanted to make it an imperial residence and, at the same
time, a monastery, on the lines of the Escurial in Spain,
but his ambitious plans were carried out only in part. The
abbey was built between the 12th and 14th centuries and
remodelled in the 15th, and then extended during the
Renaissance. Alongside the abbey church (1114-1136) is
the **New Building,** the work of Donato Allio, which was
used as an imperial residence. In St Leopold's Chapel (the
old Chapter House) is the famous **Verdun Altar,** one of
the finest examples of enamel work in the world, by
Nikolaus of Verdun (1181), with 51 scenes from the Old
and New Testaments. Make a point of taking a meal at

N. 33   26 km
N. 33   24 km

the Stiftskeller (brasserie-cellar of the Abbey) and tasting
the *Strohwein*, a very sweet local wine. Every year on
15th November there is a big public festival, the Leopoldi-
Feier, at Klosterneuburg.
Follow the Danube and, via the Heiligenstädter Strasse,
down into Vienna.

VIENNA ★

VIENNA

(pop. 1,760,000 - 170m). Capital and cultural centre of Austria,
seat of Government and the Federal authorities as well as the
provincial governments of Vienna and of Lower Austria.

Vienna stands on the site of an old Celtic colony, *Vindobona*,
transformed into a stronghold by the Romans in 90 A.D., and
where the Roman Emperor Marcus Aurelius died in 180. The
stronghold does not appear to have survived the subsequent
invasions. In 881, however, a document mentions *Wenia* on
this same site. The name "Wien", (Vienna) first appeared in 1030.
Since the days of Leopold of Babenberg, who chose Vienna
as his home in 1140, the city has been the residence of counts,
princes, kings, and emperors, with brilliant courts and a flourishing
trade. It was under the Habsburgs, who made their capital the
centre of an empire "on which the sun never sets" from the 15th
century and particularly under Charles VI (1711-40) and Maria
Theresia (1740-80), that Vienna knew its greatest splendour. The
city then attracted artists, scientists, architects, musicians, noblemen, and wealthy traders all anxious to live near the brilliance
of the imperial court. Palaces rose in the lanes and the small
squares of the centre of the city, in the "Viennese Baroque" style
which even today sets its seal on the heart of Vienna.

During the Congress of Vienna in 1814 and 1815 it was the
meeting-place for all Europe and the city enjoyed unparalleled
prosperity which had its influence not only on architecture, but
also on the minds and way of life of its inhabitants. After the
revolutions of 1848, Emperor Ferdinand abdicated in favour of
his nephew, Francis Joseph, then 18, who reigned over the vast
Austrian Empire (60 million souls) for 68 years. The walls still

surrounding the city were demolished in 1865, and the suburbs were linked to the city by the Ring, lined with theatres, museums, and impressive administrative buildings, which gave definite shape to the city. At the end of the First World War, Vienna was the capital of a country totalling only six and a half million inhabitants, impoverished and out of work. The municipal authorities then launched important social reforms and solved the housing problem by building, in the suburbs, giant blocks of flats at low rentals which remain a model of their type. Occupied by the Germans in 1938, Vienna for the next seven years ranked only as a provincial city. During the last days of the war it was bombed 53 times. 20 % of the houses were destroyed, and the Opera House and museums badly damaged. But since 1945, the Viennese, with funds donated from all over Austria, have begun to rebuild their city at such a rate that it has practically resumed its pre-war appearance.

Under the Habsburgs, Vienna was an artistic centre. Among the nobility and wealthy tradesmen, many patrons of the arts encouraged painters to settle in Vienna. As for music, it received its first impetus in 1498 with the foundation of the *Hofmusik-kapelle*, the orchestra of the imperial court. It was Vienna that saw the reformation of opera by Gluck, the flowering of the genius of Mozart, and so many other musicians. Here, too, the waltz was born, eternally linked to the name of the Strauss family. Vienna has often been called "The Paris on the Danube", because its atmosphere is so propitious for the flowering of the arts and because its people have that lightness of spirit associated with the French. It is not surprising, therefore, that it has become an important fashion centre, and that its Haute Couture School and its creations have influenced fashion throughout Central Europe.

Gastronomy: The Viennese are fond of eating, and like copious helpings. They used to have a mid-morning snack at 11 o'clock, consisting of a big portion of *goulash* or of Vienna sausages served with a *goulash* sauce, but this custom has died out and is almost unknown today. But the Viennese is a real gourmand when it comes to hot desserts and pastries, which are unrivalled in the world. First place goes, without doubt, to the *Sacher Torte*, a chocolate cake created by the master-cook Sacher for Chancellor Metternich. Then come the *Krapfen*, the famous *Zwetschgenknödel*, and the various *Strudel*, with fruit or cream. This does not mean that Viennese cooking lacks specialities other than pastries. Everybody knows the Vienna sausage and the *Wiener Schnitzel*. Don't forget to order, especially in the Spring, a Vienna-style chicken, that is to say fried. The soups are excellent in Vienna. The *goulash* soup, very spicy, is taken principally after an evening out. Another Viennese speciality is stuffed carp. Finally, we must mention Vienna coffee which connoisseurs maintain is the finest in Europe, served for preference with whipped cream *(Schlag-obers)* and always with a big glass of iced water.

PRINCIPAL SIGHTS

CHURCHES: Kapuzinerkirche; Stefanskirche; Augustinerkirche; Minoritenkirche; Maria-am-Gestade; Ruprechtskirche; Votivkirche; Karlskirche; Mariahilferkirche. PALACES: Winter Palace of Prince Eugene; Archbishop's Palace; Lobkowitz; Neue Hofburg; Hofburg; Liechtenstein; Kinsky; Hungarian Guard Palace; Schwarzenberg; Belvedere; Schönbrunn. MONASTERY of the Scots. MUSEUMS: Art History; Clock-making; State Archives; Natural History; Arts and Crafts: Sezession; Wagenburg at Schönbrunn; Technical of Industry and Commerce. HISTORIC BUILDINGS: Opera House; Winter Riding School; National Library; Chancellery; Town Hall; University; Theater an der Wien; Gloriette. FOUNTAINS: Donner; Andromeda; Joseph. SQUARES: Michaelerplatz; Josefplatz; Ballhausplatz. PARKS: Volksgarten; Stadtpark; Belvedere; Schönbrunn; the Prater; Tiergarten. VIEWS: Grinzing; Cobenzl; Kahlenberg; Porcelain Works of Augarten; Marx-Hof Workers' City.

The city of Vienna is divided into 23 districts. The most interesting is the 1st, the old city, encircled by the Ring, 6 km long, and the Franz-Josefs-Kai to the north, on the bank of the Danube canal. For the visitor who has only a little time to spare, we recommend the following walk: From the Opera House by the Burggarten to the Burg, then by the Kohlmarkt and the Graben to St Stephen's

Square. Visit the cathedral and return via the Kärntnerstrasse to the Opera House. If he has a whole day at his disposal, the same itinerary can be followed in the opposite direction and then follow the Ring by the Parliament building and the Town Hall. In the afternoon: visit to Schönbrunn and finish the evening in a small tavern of Grinzing.

In the 1st District, each little street is of interest. Apart from the itineraries given below, the visitor with time to spare will find a thousand things to see in aimless stroll through the alleys between the Franz-Josefs-Kai, to the north, the Tuchlauben on the west, the Ring on the east, and the Himmelpfortgasse to the south.

(1st) OPERA HOUSE, CATHEDRAL, MICHAELER-PLATZ, JOSEFSPLATZ

The Vienna Opera House was the first great building erected on the Ring after the demolition of the walls in 1865, by August Siccardsburg and Edward van der Null. It was inaugurated on 25th May, 1869, by a performance of Mozart's *Don Juan*. The interior, façade, and the roof were completely destroyed by bombing on 12th March, 1945. The façade and roof have been completely rebuilt, and also much of the interior. As yet, only exhibitions are held there, but rebuilding will be completed by the autumn of 1955. Opera performances are staged at the *Theater an der Wien*, Lehargasse 5 (6th), and at the *Volksoper*, Währingerstrasse 78 (9th district).

The **Kärntnerstrasse** (Carinthia Road) is the most important and elegant street in Vienna with fine fashion and lingerie stores. The **Neuer Markt** (New Market), of modern appearance thanks to the new buildings surrounding it, was badly hit by bombing. Of the old palaces and big houses, only the *Maysederhaus* (No. 15) remains. In the centre of the square is the **Donner Fountain** (rebuilt in 1949), the loveliest fountain in Vienna, masterpiece of Raphael Donner (1739). On the west side is the **Kapuzinerkirche**, a baroque building of 1632. In the open chapel to left of entrance, monument by H. Mauer to Marco d'Aviano, "the soul of the liberation of Vienna", during the struggle against the Turks in 1683. Below the church is the Kaisergruft or **Kapuzinergruft** (crypt of the emperors or Capucines), family vault of the Habs-

burgs with 144 coffins in which lie, among others, 12 emperors
and 15 empresses. Only the bodies of members of the imperial
family are buried there; their hearts are found in the Augustine
church and their intestines in the cathedral catacombs. Note the
double sarcophagus of Empress Maria Theresa and her husband
Francis I of Lorraine, and the luxurious sarcophagus of Emperor
Charles VI († 1740) decorated with four crowned death's heads.
(Open daily, 10-12.)

Return to the Kärntner-Strasse opposite the Himmelpfortgasse
in which stands, at no. 9, the **Winter Palace of Prince Eugene**,
a baroque masterpiece by Fischer von Erlach the Elder, completed
in 1724 by Lukas von Hildebrandt.

St Stephen's Square (Stephansplatz) forms the
centre of the city. Here stands the **Stephanskirche**
(St Steven's Cathedral), one of the biggest
Gothic monuments in Central Europe, insignia
of the capital. Of all Vienna's monuments, the
cathedral was hardest hit by the war. In April
1945, the cross-fire of the Germans in retreat
showered over the capital for several days and set fire to all the
houses around the cathedral. On 12th April, fire broke out,
destroying the organ and the roofing which was supported by
3,000 wooden beams. The "Great Pummerin", a bell cast from
the bronze of 200 Turkish cannon, toppled from its tower. The
roof of the nave stood up to the pressure of ashes, but the central
roof collapsed and this part of the church burned for several
days. Only a few days after the disaster, the Viennese began to
clear the wreckage and to rebuild their cathedral with the
generous help of all Austria. The work which, up to the end of
1949, had cost 15 million schillings, was entirely financed by
subscriptions and coin collections. Since 1950, green and white
tiles similar to the original ones again covered the roof, resting
on a metal framework. Each province contributed, one the new
stained glass windows, another the stalls, etc., and 26th April,
1952, saw the triumphal "progress" of the new Pummerin,
recast at St Florian, through the country to Vienna where, amid
general rejoicing, it was once again placed in the tower of this
church dedicated to the patron saint of Vienna. On the same day
the choir, completely reconstituted, was returned to the faith.
The Riesentor (Doorway of the Giant) in the western façade,
which probably dates from 1230, had been walled up before the

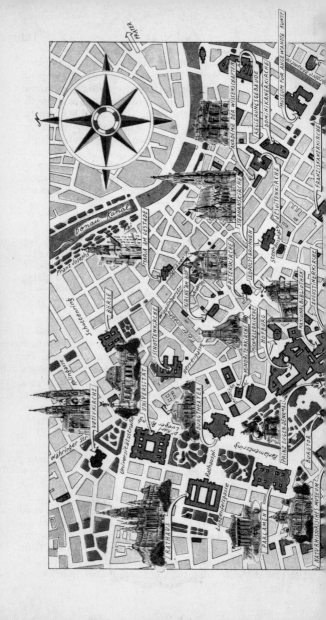

bombing and was thus spared. This door derived its name from an enormous bone which hung for centuries over the door and which was reputed to be the leg-bone of a giant drowned in the Flood. In actual fact, it was the tibia of a mammoth. In making a tour of the outside of the cathedral, to the right, a Turkish cannon ball can be seen buried in the second pillar of the structure, to left of the tower. This is not attached to the nave, but to the transept. 136m high, it was erected between 1350 and 1433. The Viennese affectionately call it the "Steffel". It can be climbed as far as the firemen's post (72m). *(Open daily from 9-12 and 2-5, except on Friday.)* After the tower comes the Singertor. On the north side is the pulpit where Johann Capistran preached in 1451 for the crusade against the Turks, and the little portico used for the funerals of the poor, one of whom was Mozart. Then comes the Bischofstor. The choir of the cathedral was built from 1304 to 1340 and the nave from 1359 to 1450. Inside, a magnificent **Gothic pulpit** by Anton Pilgram (1510), at the second pillar on left. In the St Barbara Chapel is the **Madonna of the Maidservants,** one of the loveliest statues of the Virgin. In the choir, rebuilding has been going forward speedily. The Gothic stalls by Rollinger were wiped out by the fire, but the altar of Wiener Neustadt (1447) was saved. The marble tomb of Emperor Frederick III (1493), work of Nik. von Leyden, was only slightly damaged. *(Visit with guide: daily from 9-12 and 2-4, Sunday: 2-4.)* On the north side of the square stands the **Archiepiscopal Palace,** the first dwelling in baroque style built in Vienna, erected from 1638 to 1669. On first floor, the Archiepiscopal Museum of the cathedral and diocese, museum of religious art, which contains, among other works of Christian inspiration, the altar of St Veith of Schäuffelein. *(Visits: Daily 9-12, except Wednesday.)* The **Graben,** another street with fashionable shops and the *Pestsäule*, column of the Holy Trinity, in baroque style (1682), by Rauchmiller. The reliefs on the pedestal are by Fischer von Erlach the Elder. This column was erected as the result of a vow by Emperor Leopold I to commemorate the end of the plague in 1679. In front and behind the column are two fountains (1804), bearing the statues of the patron saints of Austria: St Leopold and St Joseph-the-Fosterfather. Then right, via the Jungferngasse to the **Peterskirche** (St Peter's Church), said to have been founded by Charlemagne in the 9th century, and completely rebuilt in 1702 by Lukas von Hildebrandt. It is the most sumptuous baroque church in Vienna, with three altar pictures by Altomonte. The **Kohlmarkt** (Cabbage Market) also has elegant shops, particularly antiquaries and book-shops. In the courtyard of No. 7 is a library of historic works in French.

The **Michaelerplatz** (St Michael's Square), with the northern façade of the Imperial Palace. On left, the Michaelerkirche (St Michael's Church), one of the oldest in Vienna, dating in part from the first half of the 13th century, former parish church of the Imperial Court. Outside is a wood-carving, the *Mount of Olives* (1494), the most popular medieval work in Vienna. At the corner of the square and the Herrengasse, the first modern house built at the beginning of the century, in the old city, by the architect Loos, a building which aroused much criticism at the time.

Along the façade of the **Winter Riding School** used by the Spanish Riding School, built by Fischer von Erlach the Younger in 1730. The Vienna School of Spanish Riding is the most famous *haute école* which carries out training in the style of 300 years ago. The riders mount, without stirrups, their Lipizzans, horses which are as white as snow, although born

almost black. It has its actual headquarters at Wels, in Upper Austria. The Riding School is linked by an archway to the Stallburg (Castle of the Stables) (1560). The **Josefsplatz** is a har-monious square surrounded by baroque build-ings: the Redoutensaal, the National Library, the Augustine Abbey, the Palffy Palace, and the Pallavicini Palace. In the centre is an equestrian statue of Emperor Joseph II. In the Redoutensaal (Hall of the Masked Balls), the Opera Company give performances from time to time.

National Library *(Nationalbibliothek)*, built from 1723 to 1726 by Fischer von Erlach the son, following plans by his father. Its façade, and the hall behind it, take up the whole length of the Josefsplatz. *(Open daily, except Sunday, at 11 precisely.)* Entry to reading room on all opening days *(9-4; Saturday 9-1)*. The Library contains over 35,000 manuscripts, 85,000 autographs, over 8,000 incunabula, 1,370,000 volumes, 135,000 geographical maps, etc.

Opposite the National Library is the Palffy Palace, damaged

during the bombing. After the National Library comes the Abbey of the Augustines and, in the Augustiner-Strasse, the **Augustiner Kirche** (1330), where Royal marriages were celebrated including that, by proxy, of Napoleon and Maria Louisa. As the size of Napoleon's finger was not known, a dozen wedding rings· of different sizes were blessed and sent to Paris. In the Loretto Chapel stands 54 urns containing the hearts of members of the imperial family. Opposite the entrance is the· **tomb of Archduchess Maria Christina,** daughter of Maria Theresia, Canova's masterpiece. In the crypt, below the high altar, is buried the famous preacher P. Abraham a Santa Clara, who died in 1709. Opposite the church is the **Lobkowitz Palace,** built in 1687 by Pietro Tencala and modernized in Viennese baroque style by Fischer von Erlach the Elder.

Alongside this palace are the municipal pawnshop and auction-rooms. At the end of the road, on right, is the **Albertina**, with collections of drawings of all masters and all schools from the 15th century up to modern times (some 26,000 sheets), and more than 600,000 engravings on wood and copper. Collection of Albrecht Dürer drawings in the Study Hall. The same building houses the musical collection of the National Library. *(Visits Study Hall: Monday, Tuesday, Thursday, 10-2; Wednesday, Friday, 3-6, Saturday 10-1. Escorted tours daily at 11. Exhibition: Wednesday, Friday, 10-6; other opening days, 10-1.)*

In front of the Albertina is the Danube Fountain *(Donaubrunnen),* 1869, badly damaged during the war. It represents the Danube and its tributaries. On the other side of the square is the *Hotel Sacher*, one of the most famous hotels in Vienna, for long the meeting-place of the aristocracy. In its private rooms, decisions were often taken which affected the history of all Europe. Its most famous guests autographed a tablecloth there. The proprietress of the hotel, Anna Sacher, who smoked fat cigars, embroidered the signatures, now totalling 140, on the cloth, making an original kind of Golden Book which is considered the most precious possession of the hotel. Its cooking is among the best in Vienna. Opposite the Hotel Sacher is the Opera House.

(2nd) BURG, SCHOTTENSTIFT, AM HOF AND OLD TOWN

Through the Burggarten, with the equestrian statue of Emperor Francis I by Balthasar Moll (1781) to the Burgtor (Palace Gate)

by Peter Nobile, built in 1824 to commemorate the battle of the
nations at Leipzig. Inside is the 1914-1918 war memorial, the
work of Rudolf Wondracek (1934). On ground floor, Tomb
of the Unknown Warrior; above, the Hall of Honour. Through
this gate to the Heldenplatz (Square of the Heroes), with two
beautiful equestrian statues by the sculptor Fernkorn. On right,
that of Prince Eugene of Savoy, born in Paris, son of the Count
of Soissons and Olympia Mancini, who died in Vienna in 1736.
On left, that of Archduke Charles, a statue of
astounding balance in which the whole mass
rests on the hind hooves of the horse. On right
the Heldenplatz is the **Neue Hofburg** (1894) of
which the pendant, on left of the square, was
never built. It contains the collections of the
Museum of the History of the People *(open:
daily, 10-1, except Monday)*, and several sections of the Natural
History Museum collection *(open: Sunday 9-1; Wednesday 10-1)*
of which the most interesting is the collection of ancient weapons.
In addition, there are collections of old musical instruments,
antiquities (belonging to the History of Art Museum), and models
of a proposed museum of Austrian culture.
Finally, a collection of portraits from the National
Library *(open: daily, 9-12)*. In the left corner of
the Hofburg is the entrance, marked with a big
red flag, of the Casino for Soviet Officers. The
Hofburg (imperial palace) was the home of the
imperial family. It is made up of several buildings
of different styles grouped around the Burg, built in the 13th
century by Rudolf of Habsburg, and since constantly altered and
extended. In the interior courtyard: monument to Emperor
Francis II (1792-1835) by Marchesi. On right, the **Schweizerhof**
(Court of the Swiss), the oldest part of the palace, rebuilt between
1536 and 1552 by Ferdinand I, younger brother of Charles V.
The only decoration of this quiet square is the Schweizertor
(Doorway of the Swiss): Renaissance porch with arms and titles
of Ferdinand. From the Schweizerhof, a stairway leads to the
Chapel of the palace, made famous by the Vienna Boys Choir.
open only on Sundays at 10 am for Mass. On left of the Schweizertor is the Leopold wing, built between 1547 and 1552, and
extended between 1660 and 1668, when it was completely
destroyed by fire. In less than two years, it was entirely rebuilt.

Empress Maria Theresia lived in this wing, where she had the apartments decorated in rococo style. They are now used as offices and reception rooms for the President of the Republic. Opposite the Schweizerhof is the Amelia wing, begun in 1575 under Maximilian II and completed in 1605 under Rudolf II. The Empire Chancellery wing forms an extension, and ends in St Michael's wing. The Chancellery wing was begun in 1723 by Lukas von Hildebrandt and completed in 1730 by Fischer von Erlach the Younger. The entrance to the apartments is found beneath the gilded cupola, 54m high, of the Michaelertrakt. Beautiful wrought-iron grill at entrance. The apartments of Francis Joseph I and those of Empress Elisabeth have been used, since 1948, for an exhibition of Austrian art from the Middle Ages to 1900, displaying works from the former Austrian Gallery. Exit on St Michael's square. Via the Schauflergasse to the **Ballhausplatz** (Rackets Square), built, with the Chancellery, in 1719 by Lukas de Hildebrandt. From here, Metternich directed the fate of Austria for 34 years and, in 1814 and 1815, presided over the Congress of Vienna. Chancellor Dollfuss was assassinated in this building in 1934. The Chancellery today is the seat of Government and the Foreign Ministry. The State records are housed in the wing added later alongside the Minoritenplatz. *(Open daily, 9-4; Sunday 9-1.)* Opposite the Chancellery is the Austrian Home Office.

In the Minoritenplatz is the **Minoritenkirche** with the stump of its hexagonal tower, the top of which was blown off by a Turkish cannon ball. Beautiful main doorway, the work of the monk Jacques de Paris (1340). Inside, in the left side nave, is a famous copy in mosaic of the *Last Supper* by Leonardo da Vinci, executed between 1806 and 1814 by Giacomo Rafaeli on the order of Napoleon. North of the church is the Ministry of National Education, the former Starhemberg Palace built in 1661, of, west of the church, the **Palace of the Reigning Prince of Liechtenstein,** with a magnificent doorway of 1705. This palace, begun in 1694 to plans by Domenico Martinelli, and completed in 1705 by Gabrieli, is the most sumptuous baroque palace in Vienna. Its main façade overlooks the Bankgasse, through which the Herrengasse is reached. At No. 13 is the Langhaus (Prefecture) and at No. 8 the Hochhaus (skyscraper) erected in 1932, with a terrace restaurant on the 16th storey from which there is a beautiful view over Vienna. At No. 9 is the Clary Palace which now houses the Provincial Museum of Lower Austria (closed at the moment). At No. 7 is the entrance to the Home Office installed in the former palace of the Duchess of Modena. The **Freyung** (Freedom) in the Middle Ages was a sanctuary where fugitives could not be seized. The house forming the west corner of this square (No. 4) is the **Palace of Prince Kinsky,** a masterpiece by Lukas von Hildebrandt (1713). The arms of the Kinskys—three boars' tusks—are reproduced on the pediment of the palace. At No. 3 is the Palace of the Counts of Harrach, begun in 1702 by Domenico Martinelli, disfigured by remodelling in 1845. On the roof are the arms of the Harrachs: three ostrich feathers. North side of the square, the Schottenkirche and behind it the **Schottenstift,** Scots Monastery, Benedictine abbey. In the monastery is the *Schottenstiftskeller,* a very old tavern. In centre of square, the Austria Fountain of 1846.

The **Am Hof** square was the first residence of the Dukes of Austria. In the Middle Ages, public festivals, knightly tournaments, etc., were held in this square where, just before Christmas, the famous *Christkindlmarkt* (Little Jesus market) was held. Christmas trees and decorations, toys and cakes were sold; it was a child's paradise, a fairyland, particularly at night when the traders lit their lamps. In the middle of the square is the column of the Virgin overthrowing the Dragon (1664), the work of Carlone, decorated with angels symbolizing victory over war, pestilence, famine, and heresy, by Balthasar Herold. To the north-west is the former arsenal; on the east, the *Jesuitenkirche zu den Neun Chören der Engel* (Jesuit Church of the Nine Choirs of Angels), of which the façade is overlaid on the original façade by Carlone in 1667. Via the narrow Pariser-Gasse to the **Judenhof.** At No. 2 is the **Clockmakers Museum** in which the thousands of watches on exhibition illustrate the development of the craft from its earliest days. *(Open: Tuesday, Wednesday, and Saturday at 10; Saturday and Sunday at 3.)* On the façade of the museum is a relief of 1421 depicting the expulsion of the Jews from Vienna. In the Wipplinger Strasse is the Böhmische Hofkanzlei, built between 1708 and 1714 by Fischer von Erlach the Elder, now the High Court of Justice. Opposite is the old Town Hall. In the courtyard of this building is one of the finest works of Raphael Donner (1741): the **Fountain of Andromeda.**

The **Maria am Gestade** (Mary-on-the-Bank Church) is a Gothic masterpiece built between 1394 and 1414 by Michael, the master. Beautiful heptagonal tower 57m high. Via the Salvator-Gasse with the Sankt-Salvator Chapel to the **Hoher Markt,** heart of the old town where, in Roman times, stood the Forum of *Vindobona* with the Praetorium. In the Middle Ages, a pillory was erected here with a giant basket in which bakers guilty of selling bad bread were placed; the cage and the baker were then ducked in the neighbouring Danube Canal. In the centre of this square is the Joseph Fountain, better known as the **Vermählungssäule** (wedding column), by Fischer von Erlach the Younger (1732). In the eastern corner of the square is a modern mechanical clock (no longer working) with ten figures (one of them Charlemagne). Via the Judengasse, very picturesque, to the oldest church in Vienna, the **Ruprechtskirche,** said to have been founded in the 8th century and which is mentioned in records of 1161. Only the tower is Roman. Back to the Opera House by the lanes of the **old town:** Kohlmesser-Gasse, Griechen-Gasse (with the Griechenbeisel, one of the oldest and best restaurants in Vienna), the Fleischmarkt (meat market), the Postgasse, and the Jesuitengasse to the Dr Ignaz-Seipel-Platz, with the twin-towered University church, and the old Aula University, built in 1755 by John Nicolas Jadot of Ville-Issey, and since 1857 the headquarters of the Austrian Academy of Science. Via the Wollzeile, one of the oldest streets in Vienna, and the Seilerstätte to the Akademie-Strasse and via the Mahlergasse to the Opera House.

(3rd) THE RING

Head west from the Opera House. The Opernring. On right, the Goethe memorial, and on left, that of Schiller. Behind the latter is the Academy of Fine Arts. Picture Gallery open every afternoon. Behind the Academy of Fine Arts is one of the buildings of the School for Higher Technical Studies. The Babenberger-Strasse, a little further on, on left, is the continuation of the Maria-Hilfer-Strasse, the main shopping road of Vienna. The Burgring. On right, the Burggarten and the Burg (see 2nd excursion). On left, the **Kunsthistorische Museum** (Museum of History of Art), built between 1870 and 1891 from plans by Karl Hasenauer and Gottfried Lemper. In 1945, its cupola was destroyed and several rooms badly damaged. It is only since May 1953 that this magnificent museum, almost completely rebuilt, has once again housed its famous collections which make it one of the greatest museums in Europe.

The mezzanine floor contains Egyptian and Greek antiquities, and a suite of 17 rooms displays collections of sculpture, ornamental art, and pictures of the Flemish, Dutch, Italian, and English schools.

The **Egyptian antiquities** are arranged in five rooms. Among the finest specimens are: the chamber of worship of Prince Kaninisut (2500 B.C.) and the statue of the Orator of Thebes (1900 B.C.). The **Greco-Latin antiquities** rooms are almost completed (the cameo show-cases are not yet available). The provisional arrangement of the other rooms comprises the following groups: I — Sculpture and painting of the Italian Renaissance, ivories. II — Ivories, rock crystal, jewellery, sculpture, and tapestry of the 18th century. III — Tapestries, jewellery of the French Renaissance and Limoges; painted enamels. IV — **German sculpture and painting of the Renaissance**, the *Most Holy Trinity* by Dürer, B. van Orley, J. van Cleeve. V — Italian mannerist painting of the 16th century and Italian bronzes. VI — 16th-century Dutch school. VII — Sculpture and applied art of the Middle Ages. VIII — Ornamental art of the 16th century (rock crystal containers and precious stones, jewels, etc.). IX — Dutch primitives (15th century) and so-called Burgundy enamels. X — **Rubens**. XI — **Rembrandt**. XII — 18th-century paintings (Italian and English), and lead sculptures of the same period. The first floor is reached by a great stairway on which stands the Canova group: *Theseus Overthrows the Minotaur* which symbolizes Napoleon taming the Revolution. As half of the first floor is being reconstructed, only part of the collections can be seen. The collection which was exhibited abroad and which occupied the new rooms on the first floor was replaced in November 1953 by a rich selection of Italian, Spanish, Flemish, and Dutch pictures of the 17th century. Fifteen **Breughels** are already in their final position, including *The Marriage* and *The Peasant Fair*. The coin collection is on the third floor. Almost all schools of painting are represented in the museum by outstanding examples. There are 40 by Rubens, including the *Triptych of St Ildefonse* and a **Portrait of the Artist by Himself.** With the sole exception of the Prado, no other museum possesses such a rich selection of works by Velasquez. Among the finest are the *Portrait of the Infante Philip Prosper* and that of the *Infanta Margareta Theresia.* Also noteworthy are the works by G. Bellini, Giorgione, a beautiful **Raphael Madonna,** numerous canvases by Titian, including two *Madonnas,* beautiful works by **Tintoretto** (Diana and Callisto, **Susannah in the Bath** and several portraits). Among Flemish works is the **Portrait of Cardinal Albergati** by John van Eyck. The reredos of the *Crucifixion* by Roger van der Weyden, the works of Hans Memling, Jerome Bosch, and among German and Austrian painters: Martin Schongauer, Michael Pacher, the *Crucifixion* by Lucas Cranach the Elder, portraits of *Queen Jane Seymour* and a *London Merchant* by Hans

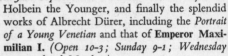

Holbein the Younger, and finally the splendid works of Albrecht Dürer, including the *Portrait of a Young Venetian* and that of **Emperor Maximilian I.** *(Open 10-3; Sunday 9-1; Wednesday 10-12; closed Monday.)*

The **Maria-Theresien-Platz,** with the monument of Maria Theresia by Zumbusch (1888), 20m high, representing the Empress Maria-Theresia surrounded by diplomats. At her feet is the Chancellor Prince Kaunitz, promoter of the alliance with France. At bottom of pedestal are equestrian statues of her great generals. On right, above Von Swieten, Empress's doctor, Gluck, Haydn, and the young Mozart. Behind the monument is the square and Palace of the Fair, formerly the imperial stables, built in 1725 by Fischer von Erlach the Elder. In front of the south-west corner of the Palace, two groups by the sculptor Friedl: *The Horse-Tamers* (1892). The Natural History Museum is an exact replica of the History of Art Museum, built at the same time. Mineralogical, palaeontological, and zoological collections. *(Open daily, except Tuesday, 9-1.)* Film shows daily at 9.30, 10.30 and 11.30. The **Parlamentsring:** on left, the Schmerlingplatz with, at back, the Law Courts built in 1881 before which stands the Monument of the Republic representing Victor Adler and two other Socialist statesmen who played a leading part in the proclamation of the Republic on 11th November, 1918. Erected in 1928, then taken away in 1934, the monument of Hanak was re-inaugurated on 11th November,

1948. On right of the Law Courts is the monument to the poet
Anzengruber († 1889) by Scherpe. Behind the Law Courts is
the Volkstheater (Popular Theatre) inaugurated in 1889, the
Palace of the Hungarian Guard by Fischer von Erlach the Elder
(1712), one of the finest in Vienna, and the Auersperg Palace.
The **Parliament** building, erected in 1883 after plans by Theophilus Hansen. Grand approach with four horse-tamers in bronze
by Lax, and 8 statues of Greek and Roman historians; in the
pediment, Emperor Francis Joseph I. In front of
the building is the great Minerva Fountain
(Pallas-Athene-Brunnen) by Kundmann (1902).
Opposite, to right of the Ring, is the **Volksgarten**
with the Tilgner Fountain, memorial to the
greatest Austrian dramatist Grillparzer (1792-
1872), that of Empress Elisabeth assassinated at

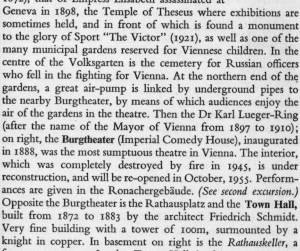

Geneva in 1898, the Temple of Theseus where exhibitions are
sometimes held, and in front of which is found a monument
to the glory of Sport "The Victor" (1921), as well as one of the
many municipal gardens reserved for Viennese children. In the
centre of the Volksgarten is the cemetery for Russian officers
who fell in the fighting for Vienna. At the northern end of the
gardens, a great air-pump is linked by underground pipes to
the nearby Burgtheater, by means of which audiences enjoy the
air of the gardens in the theatre. Then the Dr Karl Lueger-Ring
(after the name of the Mayor of Vienna from 1897 to 1910);
on right, the **Burgtheater** (Imperial Comedy House), inaugurated
in 1888, was the most sumptuous theatre in Vienna. The interior,
which was completely destroyed by fire in 1945, is under
reconstruction, and will be re-opened in October, 1955. Performances are given in the Ronachergebäude. *(See second excursion.)*
Opposite the Burgtheater is the Rathausplatz and the **Town Hall,**
built from 1872 to 1883 by the architect Friedrich Schmidt.
Very fine building with a tower of 100m, surmounted by a
knight in copper. In basement on right is the *Rathauskeller,* a
famous restaurant. In the Town Hall is the
Historical Museum of Vienna, now under reconstruction. At the moment, only small exhibitions are held there, but the banqueting hall
can be visited (free) every day from 9-4, apply
by telephone (B 40.500, extension 127). Between
the gardens and the Ring are 8 statues; left-hand

side: Duke Henry who chose Vienna as his residence in 1158;
Duke Rudolf who founded the University in 1365; Count
Starhemberg, commander during the siege by the Turks in
1683; Fischer von Erlach the Elder, the great architect. On
right: Duke Leopold VI who gave Vienna her communal
freedom; Count Salm, who defended Vienna against the Turks
in 1529; Count Bishop Kollonitsch, famed for his charity during
the siege of 1683; the jurisconsult Sonnenfels, who in the 18th
century succeeded in abolishing torture. In the gardens, on the
far left, memorial to Johann Strauss the father (1804-49) and to
Lanner (1801-43); bas-reliefs of waltzing couples. On extreme
right, memorial to the painter Waldmüller († 1865).

The University was founded by Duke Rudolf IV in 1365 and
reorganized by V. Swieten in 1752. The present building dates
from 1884. It was hit by 18 bombs, but one can still visit the

Court of Honour with its numerous statues of
famous professors, as well as the staircases, and
it is possible to attend (without formalities)
lectures on the arts, with films, in Room 21.
The Vienna University is the oldest in the
German-speaking countries, and its library of
1,200,000 volumes is the biggest university
library among these countries. It is housed in the section of the
University overlooking the Reichsrats-Strasse. The University
is open from 9 to 8 (in August and September 9-1). Opposite
is the monument to Mayor Liebenberg, killed during the Turkish
siege of 1683. A plate on the house at No. 8 Mölkerbastei recalls
that Beethoven lived there, at intervals, from 1804 to 1815. His
rooms on the fourth floor can be visited. Apply to door porter.
Through the Votivpark to the **Votivkirche**, built from 1856 to
1879 by H. v. Ferstel to fulfil the wish of Archduke Maximilian
the later unlucky Emperor of Mexico, in thanksgiving for the
failure of an assassination attempt against his brother Francis
Joseph in 1853. Inside is the tomb of Count Niklas Salm (about
1540). Behind this church is found the district of clinics, where
many doctors live. The **Schottenring:** on left, ruins of the Sühn-
haus, destroyed in 1945, revenue building raised on the site of
an opera house destroyed by fire in 1881. At first, rents paid
by tenants of this building were used for the education of the
orphans of the 400 people who died in the fire. On right, at
No. 16, the Stock Exchange, built from plans by Theophilus

Hansen. Behind is the Börseplatz and the central telegraph office, open night and day. Further along the Schottenring, on left, the monument and barracks of the Deutschmeister Regiment. The **Franz-Josefs-Kai** borders the canal which, despite its name, is a branch of the Danube and has its source at Nussdorf. The Franz-Josefs-Kai was the hardest-hit street in Vienna. Practically all its houses were wiped out by bombing or destroyed by fire. In addition, the Germans in retreat blew up all the bridges linking the quay with the 2nd district. Only the Schweden-brücke (Swedes Bridge) opposite the Schwedenplatz, has so far been rebuilt. The other bridges are temporary. The Franz-Josefs-Kai ends at the Aspernplatz in which stands the Urania, public university institute. View over the great wheel of the Prater which is reached over the Aspern Bridge leading to the Praterstrasse.

The **Stubenring**: on left, former War Ministry, entirely rebuilt, now the seat of various Government services. In front of the building is a fine equestrian statue of Radetzky by Zumbusch (1892). On right of the Ring, the G.-Coch-Platz, with Savings Bank, National Lottery office, Chamber of Commerce. Further on, on left, the School and **Museum of Arts and Crafts,** built in 1871 by Ferstel, containing one of the finest collections of carpets in the world. In addition, remarkable collections of porcelain from the potteries of Vienna, Meissen, and Sèvres. Enamels, ceramics, cloth, embroidery, etc. *(Open daily 9-4, except Monday. Sunday: 9-1.)* Behind the museum, the other side of the Wienfluss, is the Bürgertheater. On right in the Ring, the Dr Karl Lueger-Platz with memorial to Mayor Lueger (1844-1910). On left, the **Stadtpark** (City Gardens), with the Volksgarten, the most popular open-space in Vienna. Several monuments, including those to Schubert and Bruckner and the famous *monument of Johann Strauss* playing the violin. Charming fountain of the Danube Sirens (Donauweibchen-Brunnen). At southern end, the Kursalon, café-restaurant with terrace, very pleasant especially on summer evenings. Opposite the Kursalon is the Skating Rink next to the Konzerthaus *(see later)*. Via the Schubertring (on left the Ö.A.M.T.C., Automobile and Touring Club of Austria) to the Schwarzenbergplatz with memorial to Marshal Schwarzenberg, Austrian Ambassador to Paris and Commander-in-Chief of the Austro-Russian-Prussian armies from 1813 to 1814. At the corner of the Ring and the Schwarzen-

bergplatz is the former Palace of Industry and Electricity, now
headquarters of the Interallied Commission. At back, Raphael
Donner monument, the Stalinplatz and the Schwarzenberg
Palace *(see later)*. Via the Kärntnerring (on left, Hotel Imperial,
Soviet headquarters; on right, Grand Hotel taken over for
Russian families, and the Hotel Bristol, inhabited by the Ameri-
cans), to the Opera House.

(4th) KARLSKIRCHE, SCHWARZENBERG PALACE, BELVEDERE. KONZERTHAUS

From the Opera House via the Operngasse to the Girardi
monument by Hofner (1929) and the **Sezession,** art gallery, with
open-work dome formed of 300 laurel leaves and 700 acorns,
built in 1898 by Olbrich, who gave his name to a school of
Viennese painting at the beginning of the 20th century. In front
of the Sezession is a bronze group, *Mark Anthony,* by Strasser
(1899), member of the Sezession. Via the Papageno-Gasse with
the Portico representing Schikaneder, the librettist of the *Magic
Flute,* in the role of Papageno which he created
in 1791. The **Theater an der Wien** dates from
1797. It saw the first performance of *Fidelio* in
1805, Beethoven's only opera (commemorative
plate) and, later, the *premières* of *The Bat* by
Strauss and *The Merry Widow* by Lehar.

Across the Naschmarkt, fruit and flower market
which forms the boundary between the Russian
and French sectors, to the Friedrichstrasse. On left, the Österreichische Verkehrsbureau (Austrian Rail Travel Agency). In
the Karlsplatz stands the loveliest baroque church in Vienna,
the **Karlskirche,** the church of St Charles of Borromea, masterpiece of Fischer von Erlach the Elder, completed in 1739 by
Fischer von Erlach the Younger. On each side of the porch, two
columns decorated with spiral reliefs, constructed by Christoph
Mader and Martinelli. Inside, altar pictures by Altomonte and
Daniel Gran. To the east of the church is a house in which
Schubert lived and, to the west, the school of Higher Technical
Studies. In square, memorials to Brahms, Madersperger, and
Ressel, who invented the marine propeller. On north of the
square, the Künstlerhaus (Artists House), art gallery, and the
Musikvereinsgebaeude (1869) where concerts are given by the
Vienna Philharmonic Orchestra.

The **Stalinplatz:** This name has been given to the section of the Schwarzenberg Platz between the Lothringer-Strasse and the Schwarzenberg Palace. In the centre of this square is the Hochstrahlbrunnen, a great fountain illuminated at night, which is in front of the Red Army Memorial inaugurated in 1945, completed in 1946, representing a Soviet warrior at the top of a column in front of which stands a Russian tank. At back of the square, the **Schwarzenberg Palace,** on slightly higher ground, begun in 1697 by Fischer von Erlach the Elder and completed in 1715 by his son. Badly damaged in the 1945 bombing, it is now being rebuilt. It cannot be visited. One part of the palace now houses the club of the "International House". The main façade overlooks a garden decorated with several groups by the sculptor Martinelli. *(Open daily from 1st May to 30th September from 7 to 6. Entry free.)* Follow on left the Rennweg, with the little Church of the Holy Cross (Kirche zum Heiligen Kreuz), former church of the Guards, now the church of Vienna's Polish colony. It was built in 1763 and is the only Vienna church with a rococo interior. At No. 6, entrance to the **Belvedere.** This imperial residence with its two castles, the Minor Belvedere and the Major Belvedere separated by the Park, is one of the loveliest creations of secular baroque architecture. Lukas von Hildebrandt built it between 1700 and 1723 for Prince Eugene of Savoy, conqueror of the Turks. The Minor Belvedere, which includes the Orangery, the Modern Gallery (beside the Schwarzenberg Palace), served as the residence of Mme Royale, daughter of Louis XVI, when she left the Temple prison. Before the war, the Museum was housed in the Minor Belvedere. As the two castles are under reconstruction, the interior cannot be visited (the finest room was the marble hall with magnificent stuccoes and painted ceilings by Martin Altomonte). Some of the pictures are on show at the Hofburg. The Park is open all day. There are sculptures everywhere. The beautiful wrought iron gates are the work of the Tyroleans Arnhold and Konrad Küffner (1728). From the Minor Belvedere there is a fine view of the Major Belvedere. Prince Eugene's niece sold the Belvedere to the Emperor, who had an art gallery installed in the major castle. It was later inhabited by Archduke Francis-Ferdinand, heir to the throne, assassinated in 1914 at Sarajevo. It has since held the Gallery of

19th-Century Art. The composer Bruckner died there in 1896 (commemorative plaque in annexe on right of main building). It will soon be possible to visit the Sala Terrena with the Four Giants, the beautiful staircase, and the Golden Cabinet which escaped the bombs. (The Golden Cabinet was badly damaged by fire in March 1950.) The two castles, after restoration, have again become art galleries. They also house the Museum of Austrian Art which illustrates the development of Austrian art from the Middle Ages up to modern times. Return to Minor Belvedere, follow on right the Marokkaner-Gasse which leads to the Heumarkt. The **Skating Rink** of the Wiener Eislaufverein (Vienna Ice-skating Club) is the biggest open-air artificial rink in Europe. Important skating competitions are held there in winter, international ice-hockey matches, and performances of the *Ice Revue of Vienna*. Next to the rink is the **Konzerthaus**, with its great Concert Hall, the Mozart Hall, and Schubert Hall, in which the Vienna Symphony Orchestra gives concerts. Opposite the skating rink is the Beethoven Platz with memorial to the great composer by Zumbusch (1880). Via the Fichtegasse to the Schubertring and back to the Opera House.

SCHÖNBRUNN

At the Opera House, take the Operngasse and the Naschmarkt, then follow the Linke Wienzeile through the 6th district, home of the fur merchants and button-makers, to the Schönbrunn. (By car, instead of the Linke Wienzeile, take the Rechte Wienzeile to the Heumühlgasse, then the Schönbrunner Strasse. Enter Schönbrunn by the Meidlinger Tor.) Schönbrunn is an old imperial pleasure palace which was begun under Emperor Leopold I in 1694, after plans by Fischer von Erlach the Elder, but was not completed until 1749 under Maria-Theresa, by Paccassi, who made big changes from the original plans. He it was who created the interior of this grandiose palace with its 1,400 rooms and halls. Napoleon made it his headquarters in 1805 and 1809. Francis Joseph was born there in 1830 and died there in 1916. In 1945, over 300 American bombs fell in the grounds of Schönbrunn. The great courtyard of the castle is lined by two wings and flanked by two obelisks with Napoleonic eagles. It is the classic Court of Honour. In the west wing is the Schönbrunner Schloss-theater (Schönbrunn Castle Theatre). Through the arch on right, the **Wagenburg** is reached, the finest carriage museum in the world. Among the historic coaches see that used by Napoleon at Milan, and the coaches, sedan-chairs, and sleighs of Empress Maria-Theresia; then the travelling Berlin in which Maria-Theresia visited France in 1810 and, among the perambulators, that of the King of Rome which he used at the Tuileries. *(Open daily, 10-4.)* In the central building, a staircase leads to the 44 rooms open to the public. *(Visits: daily, 9-5. Escorted tours each half-hour.)* The most interesting rooms are in the apartments of Emperor Francis Joseph and those of the Empress Elisabeth; the Hall of Mirrors where Mozart, aged 5, played the harpsichord before Maria-Theresia; the Chinese Room; the Blue Room, where Emperor Charles handed over his resignation to the Republican Government on 11th November, 1918; the Lacquer Room, Napoleon's study, and Napoleon's Room, in which the Duke of Reichstadt died. Finally, the **Hall of the Million** with its walls decorated with Persian and Indian miniatures; the Hall of Tapestries (Brussels); the Grand Gallery. Loveliest part of the Schönbrunn is its **Park,** entered by a five-arched gateway in the central building. It is laid out in French style, by John Trehet. The left avenue leads to the Obelisk, the central alley to Neptune's Fountain (beside the "Roman Ruin", artificial ruins erected in 1778). Nearby is the *Schöne Brunnen*, the "Beautiful Fountain", which gave its name to the castle. Beautiful view of the castle from the fountain. Zigzag paths lead from there to the **Gloriette,** a pillared building, built in 1775 from plans by F. v. Hohenberg. From its roof there is a beautiful panorama of all Schönbrunn and the mountains of the Vienna Woods. Towards the left, facing the castle, is the **Tiergarten** (Zoo), which can also be reached direct from Neptune's Fountain. It is the oldest zoological gardens in Europe, founded in 1752 by Francis of Lorraine. Most of the animals were killed in the 1945 bombings, but it has been partly re-stocked. In the centre is a charming pavilion, the work of Jadot. Forming a continuation of the zoo is the botanical gardens, the famous palm-house of which, though wrecked by bombing, has already been rebuilt. The Park,

Gloriette, and Zoo are open daily from 9 to dusk. Return by the Mariahilfer-Strasse, Vienna's main shopping street, 5 km long. At No. 212 is the **Technical Museum of Industry and Commerce,** with the Post Office Museum and the Railway Museum, which are very interesting. *(Guided tours daily from 10 to 2; Sunday at 2. Open to the public Sunday morning from 9 to 1.)* From October to May, Saturdays at 3.30 and Sundays at 10, film shows. This museum illustrates by models, blue-prints, tools and experimental machines the development of all branches of industry.

At the junction of the Mariahilfer-Strasse and the Gürtel is the West Station. Memorial to the composer Haydn, who died in 1809 aged 77, at 19 Haydngasse (Haydn Museum, now closed). Behind the memorial is the **Mariahilferkirche** built by Prince Esterhazy at his own cost after the Turkish siege of 1683.

LIFE IN VIENNA

The gaiety of bygone days has gone forever, but there is a "night life" in Vienna. One still finds a passionate love of music there, but it is mainly grand opera, of which performances are given, pending reconstruction of the National Opera House, at the Theater an der Wien (Lehargasse, entrance by the Wienzeile) and at the Volksoper (Währinger-Strasse). Vienna's orchestras, the celebrated *Wiener Philharmoniker* and the *Wiener Symphoniker,* give magnificent concerts in the halls of the *Gesellschaft der Musikfreunde* (Dumbastrasse) and at the *Grosse Konzerthaussaal* (Lothringer-Strasse). These concerts have a faithful audience and it is advisable to book seats in advance. Operetta is by no means neglected in the city of Lehar and Strauss. Three theatres give regular performances: the Volksoper, the Stadttheater (Skodagasse), and the Raimundtheater (Wallgasse). In Vienna, the word "bar" means "night-club". The best known are the *Casanova Bar* and *Gipsy,* both in the Dorotheergasse, the *Renaissance Bar* in the Singerstrasse, and the *Splendid Bar* in the Jaromirgottstrasse. There is also the *Moulin Rouge* (Walfischgasse), a cabaret like the Bal Tabarin in Paris, on a smaller scale. The best restaurants, and most typically Viennese, are found principally in the 1st district. Here are a few of the names: *Restaurant am Franziskanerplatz* (Franziskanerplatz), *Stadtkrug* and *Zu den 3 Husaren* (Weihburggasse), *Hochhaus-Restaurant* (Herrengasse 6-8, evening dances), *Wiener Rathauskeller* (Neues Rathaus),

Deutsches Haus (behind cathedral), *Hotel Sacher* (opposite Opera House), and *Griechenbeisel* (Griechengasse).

The Viennese, as soon as it is fine, prefer to dine at one of the open-air garden restaurants. Among the best are: *Kursalon* (Stadtpark), *Linde and Lindenkeller* (Rotenturmstrasse 12, founded in 1435, Viennese music), and the open-air restaurants of the Prater. Much has been said and written of the *Vienna cafés*, where the true citizen spent much of the day reading the newspapers, playing cards or chess, where the quantity of milk in the coffee was designated by picturesque names: the *Capuchin* (more coffee than milk), the *Einspänner* (black coffee with whipped cream served in a glass), etc. These cafés still exist, but are gradually losing ground to the "espressos" opened since the war. The best-known cafés are the *Opernkaffee*, the *Grabenkaffee*, the *Kaffee Carlton* and the *Kaffee Schwarzenberg*, all in the 1st district. The two best-known pastry-shops are the *Konditorei Demel* (Kohlmarkt) and the *Konditorei Lehmann* (in the Graben). Good beer and fine wines are found in the "Kellers" (cellars). Ancient and picturesque, and frequently with orchestras or quartets. The Viennese love to spend their leisure time in the setting of a beautiful landscape. For this reason, among the bars, the *Kobenzl-Bar* is popular in fine weather. In summer, the small suburban taverns *(Heurigen)* draw the crowds, for here new wine and last year's vintages can be obtained. They are also the best places for an evening's fun, and you will soon be drawn into the *gemütliche Stimmung*, the incomparable atmosphere of Vienna.

Some Recommended Hotels

1st—**** Hotel Ambassador (Krantz), Neuer Markt 5. **** Hotel Sacher, Philharmonikerstrasse 4. *** Hotel Astoria, Kärntner Strasse 32. ** Hotel Altenburgerhof, Walfischgasse 5. * Hotel Adlerhof, Hafnersteig 7.

2nd—** Hotel Continental, Praterstrasse 7.

3rd—** Hotel Goldene Spinne, Linke Bahngasse 10. * Hotel Roter Hahn, Landstrasse Hauptstrasse 40.

4th—*** Hotel Erzherzog Rainer, Wiedner Hauptstrasse 27-29. ** Hotel Carlton, Wiedner Hauptstrasse 23-25.

5th—** Hotel Jägerhorn, Wiedner Hauptstrasse 108.

6th—*** Hotel Kummer, Mariahilfer Strasse 71a. ** Hotel Mariahilf, Mariahilfer Strasse 121b.

7th—** Hotel Wimberger, Neubaugürtel 34-38. * Hotel
Fürstenhof, Neubaugürtel 4.

8th—*** Hotel Weisser Hahn, Josefstädter Strasse 22. ** Hotel
Goldener Hirsch, Alser Strasse 33. * Hotel Josefstadt,
Lerchengasse 3-5.

9th—*** Hotel Bellevue, Althanstrasse 5. ** Hotel West-
minster, Harmoniegasse 5. * Hotel Auge Gottes, Nussdorfer
Strasse 75.

12th—** Hotel Wienzelle, Dunklergasse 3.

ENVIRONS OF VIENNA

The Prater, the Old Danube, Heiligenstadt, and Grinzing.

Via the Aspernbrücke *(see excursion No. 3)* to the Praterstrasse,
one of the widest and busiest streets of Vienna. At No. 54 is
the house in which Johann Strauss the younger composed, in
1867, the *Blue Danube Waltz* which made him famous overnight.
The Praterstrasse ends at the Praterstern, a circus from which
radiate 7 roads. Tegetthoff monument by Kundmann and
Hasenauer (1886). The Heine-Strasse, on left, leads to **Augarten**
where the famous Porcelain Works of Vienna are situated *(visit
only on special application)* and the Augarten Palace, winter home
of the Vienna Boys Choir. Nearby, the Rotunda, the building
for exhibitions at the Vienna Fair, and the Venedigerau, an
up-to-date children's garden.

Via the Ausstellungsstrasse to the **Prater**, a
magnificent natural park which is the Viennese
equivalent of Hyde Park in London, or New
York's Central Park. In the 16th century the
Prater housed a zoological gardens and was the
scene of splendid fêtes given by the Imperial
Court. It was thrown open to the public in
1766 by Emperor Joseph II. Between the Ausstellungsstrasse and the Hauptallee is the **Wurstelprater,** (a name
which comes from the German word *Hanswurst* [buffoon] and
not the word *Wurst* [sausage] as so many foreigners think).
Its famous **Big Wheel** is 64m high. Numerous restaurants and
taverns in the open-air. Start of the miniature railway running
to the Vienna **Stadium** which can hold 60,000 spectators and
the arena where big national and international football matches

are played—the favourite sport of the Viennese. The *Wonderteam*, Austria's national XI, is one of the finest in Europe. The Hauptallee, 5 km long, leads to the *Lusthaus*, former Imperial hunting lodge, which is now a café. Opposite the Wurstelprater, on right, is the circus and school of sculpture of Vienna. On left, the Fair grounds with five exhibition halls. The great Vienna Fair which is held twice yearly, in the spring and autumn, is held partly in these halls and partly in the Palace of the Fair behind the Ring *(see excursion No. 2)*. Also on the left is the racecourse (trotting) and the great stadium, then the swimming stadium and the golf-course of Freudenau (18 holes; length of course 2,500m). Behind the Lusthaus is the great Freudenau Racecourse. Return to the Praterstern and, via the Lassalle-Strasse, to the **Bridge of the Red Army**. On left, a red obelisk erected in honour of the Russian Army; on right, a modern church built in 1898 on the model of a Roman basilica on the occasion of Francis Joseph I's 50 years on the throne. Continue as far as the **Old Danube,** the real Blue Danube of the song. Several beaches. Continue along the Old Danube towards the mountains of the north, **recross** the Danube by the Malinowsky Bridge (formerly the **Floridsdorf** Bridge) and cross the canal.

Heiligenstadt: In the long Heiligenstätter-Strasse is the **Karl Marx-Hof**, the biggest workers' city built by the Socialist council after the first world war, containing 1,200 flats. Scene of the battles of February 1934. Heiligenstadt was made famous by Beethoven, whose favourite holiday resort it was, and where he composed some of his works. He lived at 2 Pfarrplatz, where he composed the *Pastoral Symphony*. He composed the *Testament of Heiligenblut* at 6 Probusgasse. He also lived at 26 Kahlenberger-Strasse and, finally, at 92 Döblinger Hauptstrasse, in the suburb of Döbling, where he composed the *Eroica Symphony*.

The Grinzinger-Strasse leads to **Grinzing,** famous village of the wine-growers, where an evening should be spent in one of the little taverns *(Heurigenschenken)* indicated by a branch of pine suspended from a long pole, where the *Heurigen* (new wine) is drunk to the strains of Schrammel's music usually played by a quartet comprising two violins, a guitar, and an accordion, and popular Viennese songs.

The Höhenstrasse: From Grinzing, follow the Höhenstrasse built between 1934 and 1936, a very fine road which, with several turnings, runs up to the wooded heights north of Vienna. The **Cobenzl** (350m), former property of Baron von Sothen, bears the name of Count Cobenzl who signed the Peace of Campo Formio. The restaurant, with bar, has a splendid view over Vienna. The castle (end-18th century) has been transformed into a luxury hotel. At the moment it is a displaced persons camp. Continue along the heights. On right, a fork road leads down to the popular restaurant of *Krapfenwaldl*, with swimming pool. The **Kahlenberg** (483m). Charles of Lorraine and John Sobiesky left here with the Imperial army in 1683 to repel the Turks, thus freeing besieged Vienna. In St Joseph's Church, built in 1734, is the Black Virgin of Tschenstochau, patron saint of Poland. A few steps away is the *Kahlenbergrestaurant* with its several terraces and, five minutes walk away, the Kahlenberg Observatory, 22m high, from which there is a magnificent view of Vienna and the Vienna Woods as far as the Schneeberg.

The **Leopoldsberg** (423m), 226 m above the Danube, is the most easterly buttress of the Vienna Forest and the range of Alps which begin in the Bay of Genoa end here. On its summit is the little Leopold Church, rebuilt by Leopold I after the victory over the Turks, on the site of the fortress of the Babenbergs which stood here from 1115 to 1529. Also on the ruins of the fortress is a castle dating from 1705, now converted into a restaurant. Make a tour of the building to obtain a magnificent view over the Danube.

VIENNA-GRAZ-KLAGENFURT

The direct road from Vienna to the Semmering runs through Wiener Neudorf and Wiener Neustadt. A little to the west of this road, another of less importance provides much more interest for the tourist. It is the road which goes through Mödling, Baden, and Bad Vöslau, names also dear to the wine-lover, for this part of Lower Austria is famous for its good vintages. This road also affords an opportunity to visit Heiligenkreuz and Mayerling. Lower Austria has a population of 1,270,000 of whom more than half are engaged in farming. Industry is concentrated mainly in the Vienna basin. There, machinery and railway rolling stock is built. Glass, metals, leather, and rubber are other industries. This federal country, in addition, has big oil-wells; actually, they do not contribute to the Austrian economy, as they are exploited by the Soviet authorities as war reparations.

From Wiener Neustadt to Bruck an der Mur there is only one road, which runs through the Semmering, on the frontier between Lower Austria and Styria. After Neunkirchen, we come again to the familiar scene of mountain peaks rising on each side of the road; to the south, the mountains of the Wechsel; to the north, those of the Schneeberg, the Rax, and the Schneealpe. Then the road follows the River Mürz between the Hochschwab and the Fischbach Alps. At Veitsch, north of Mitterdorf, are the biggest magnesite deposits in the world. From Kapfenberg, a road leads to Mariazell, the famous place of pilgrimage.

At Bruck, two roads again present a choice for the motorist. One follows the Mur towards the west, via Leoben, Knittelfeld, and Judenberg, through the industrial heart of Styria with its iron ore and lignite deposits near Leoben, and the blast furnaces of Donawitz and Knittelfeld, and reaches Klagenfurt via Neumarkt, Friesach, and Sankt-Veit. The other road also follows the River Mur, but in a southerly direction. It is a very beautiful road, running beside numerous waterfalls, old forges, and the famous Peggau Caves, before entering Graz, the capital of Styria. From Graz to Klagenfurt the road beats a path between the numerous mountain ranges of Western Styria and Eastern Carinthia, going via Voitsberg and Köflach, alongside a vast lignite field, part of which is worked by the open-cast system. Then through the Packsattel, frontier between Styria and Carinthia, the road takes the Lavanttal to avoid the Saualpe which rises to the west, by-passes it at Völkermarkt, and ends at Klagenfurt, capital of Carinthia.

Gastronomy: The southern part of Lower Austria at the beginning of this itinerary produces excellent wines. They are more fruity and stronger scented than those of the northern sector. The best-known are: the *Gumpoldskirchner*, the *Goldeck von Schlumberger*, the *Sosser Muskateller*, the *Rotgipfler*, the *Zierfandler*, and the *Neuberger*. The wines of Styria, particularly those of southern Styria, are also very good. The most popular in Austria and for the foreigner are: the *Schilcher* (sour but refreshing), the *Portugiese*, the *Sylvaner*, the *Riesling*, the *Weisser Burgunder*, the *Traminer*, and the *Weisser Klevner*. In addition, Styria is renowned for its sheep and fat pullets.

PRINCIPAL SIGHTS

CHURCHES of: Wiener Neustadt; Kapfenberg: Mariazell; Frohnleiten; Maria Strassengel; Graz; Maria Trost; Voitsberg; Friesach. ABBEYS of: Heiligenkreuz. Rein; CASTLES of: Gloggnitz; Rabenstein; Eggenberg; Forchtenstein; Friesach. MUSEUMS of: Mürzzugschlag; Graz. MONUMENTS: Town Hall of Mödling; Roman spring of Baden; Military Academy of Wiener Neustadt; Kornmesserhaus at Bruck; Burgtor, Paulustor, Clock Tower, Gemaltes Haus, Landhaus, and Mariensäule at Graz; Jew's Head at Judenberg. VIEWS: Lurgrotte at Peggau; Schlossberg and Municipal Park at Graz; Semriach Caves; the Geiersberg; Piber Stud.

PRINCIPAL ITINERARY, VIA GRAZ: 375 KM.

VIENNA ★

The direct road (No. 17) from Vienna to Semmering runs through Wiener Neudorf, Traiskirchen and Wiener Neustadt (48 km). We advise the secondary road via Mödling, Baden, and Bad Vöslau, it is more interesting.

At the approach to Wiener Neudorf, turn right and enter

MÖDLING ★

(pop. 15,000 - 240m). Very picturesque old town. Notable 16th-century **Town Hall**, the Herzoghof of the 15th century, and the Gothic-style **Church of St Othmar** (1454), on a height, with a 13th-century Roman ossuary. Beethoven lived at Mödling during the summers of 1818, '19 and '20, at 79 Hauptstrasse, and 6 Achsenauergasse, where he composed the *Missa Solemnis*. Near Mödling, on the western boundary of the town, is the Kalenderberg rock with the Black Tower and the Liechtenstein fortress, facing which stands Liechtenstein Castle. From Mödling, a direct road (13 km) leads to Baden, via **Gumpolds-kirchen**, where one of the finest wines in Austria is grown, the *Gumpoldskirchner*.

But there is a very beautiful detour to make: leave Mödling in a westerly direction by the Neuer Weg. On left, reuins of the castle stronghold of Mödling, built in the 11th century by the Babenbergs, destroyed in 1683 by the Turks. Go through Vorderbrühl. Via the Königswiese to **Hinterbrühl**, a charming holiday place with several old inns, of which the most famous is the *Radetzky Restaurant*, in a beautiful setting on a height. Leave Hinterbrühl by the road leading south-west which crosses the Mödlingbach near Höldrichsmühle (where Schubert lived and composed several of his works) and which then by-passes the Schweizerberg (471m). Via Gaaden to

★ HEILIGENKREUZ

(305m). Fine **Cistercian abbey** founded in 1135 by Duke Leopold-the-Holy. Escorted tours daily at all times of the day. The church formed part of the original Roman-style building and its nave is in strange contrast to the Gothic-style choir, dating from 1295. Note the Path of the Cross executed from 1220 to 1250. In the Chapter House is the tomb, mutilated by the Turks, of Duke Frederick-the-Bellicose, the last of the Babenbergers, who died in 1246. Very beautiful **carved stalls** by Giovanni Giuliani (1707), in the organ gallery. Fine courtyard surrounded by arched buildings of the 18th century. Continue west, taking the first fork towards the south:

★ MAYERLING

Hunting lodge of Archduke Rudolf of Austria, heir to the throne, who committed suicide there with Baroness Vecsera on 30th January, 1889. The Emperor Francis Joseph transformed the castle into a Carmelite convent. The chapel of the convent was built to commemorate the tragedy which occurred at Mayerling. Going east, take the road which follows the right bank of the River Schwechat by the Helenental, to:

BADEN ★

(pop. 23,000 - 233m). Famous spa with
15 sulphur springs ranging from 73° to
79° F, the largest and richest in sulphur in
Europe. Treatments: rheumatic pains
(joints, muscles, nerves), gout, neuralgia
and neuritis. Modern thermal beach which
will hold 15,000 people, built in 1926.
400 trucks of seaside sand were brought to make this
artificial beach, 140m by 40. The two great swimming
pools are filled with water from the Marienquelle (95° F).
Notable **Roman spring** with supply pipes dating from the
year 1, A.D. Fine Kurpark. Restaurant, café, etc. on beach.
In the main square (Hauptplatz) is the Town Hall (1815)
with the column of the Holy Trinity erected to recall the
plague epidemic of 1714. The parish church of St Stephen's,
Gothic, bears a strange resemblance to St Stephen's Cathedral in Vienna. At No. 10 Rathausgasse, Beethoven composed most of his Ninth Symphony. Mozart wrote his
famous *Ave Verum* at 4 Renngasse. Schubert, Johann
Strauss, Suppé, Millöcker, Grillparzer, and a great number
of Austrian composers and poets also lived at Baden,
and the town is studded with memorials erected in their
honour by the municipality. The Tourist Information
Bureau is at No. 2 Hauptplatz. Apart from its springs,
Baden is a vine-growing centre producing excellent wines.

Some Recommended Hotels

Baden: ★ Hotel-Restaurant Brusatti. ★ Hotel-Pension
Ebruster.

BAD VÖSLAU ★

(275m). Thermal station on the eastern slopes of the Harz-
berg, sheltered from the wind and enjoying a very mild
climate. Its three thermal baths of 75° F are beneficial for
general weakness, rheumatic troubles, neuralgia, and gout.
As at Baden, a big beach has been built to cater for 15,000
people. The Vöslau vineyards produce one of the best red
wines in Austria: the *Goldeck* of *Schlumberg*. Via Leobers-
dorf to:

★ WIENER NEUSTADT

BADEN 23 Km.   WIEN 48 Km.

NEUNKIRCHEN 16 Km.

1 Burg. 2 Neuklosterkirche. 3 Town Hall (Rathaus). 4 Cathedral. 5 Station. 6 Badenerstr. 7 Wienerstr. 8 Neunkirchner-Strasse. 9 Neuklostergasse. 10 Niederlandergasse. 11 Hauptplatz. 12 Ungar-Gasse. 13 Domplatz. 14 Pogner-Gasse. 15 Eyersperg Ring.

N. 17 29 km

(pop. 31,800 – 270m). Founded in 1194 and rebuilt after a fire in 1834. Imperial residence under Frederick III. Before the last war, Wiener Neustadt was the industrial centre of Lower Austria. The Germans erected big aeroplane factories there. Bombing wiped out this industry and wrecked a great part of the town. Wiener Neustadt was famous for its **Maria-Theresia Military Academy**, housed in the castle-fortress of the Babenbergs (begun in 1192) from 1752 to 1919. At this castle, visit the St George's Chapel, in the west wing, where Maximilian I is buried. (He was born in 1459 at the Wiener Neustadt castle.) From the chapel, go along the Neuklostergasse to the **Neuklosterkirche** (Church of the New Convent): magnificent tombstone on the funeral monument of Empress Eleanor of Portugal. Follow the Ungargasse to left as far as the Hauptplatz (main square), to the Town Hall and beautiful Gothic houses with arcades. To north is the Liebfrauenkirche (former cathedral), 13th century. Inside is the very beautiful tomb of Cardinal Khlesel, carved by G. L. Bernini (around 1630) and 12 statues of the apostles by Lorenz Luchsperger (1485). Via Neunkirchen to:

★ GLOGGNITZ

(437m). Holiday resort dominated by the **Gloggnitz Castle**, former Benedictine abbey built in 1084. This is the start of the Semmering railway, the first mountain railway built in Europe, by the engineer Karl von Ghega between 1848 and 1854, and the Semmering road which climbs (1 : 16) via Schottwien to the Semmering Pass (980m), frontier

N. 17 16 km

between Lower Austria and Styria, the most eastern of the
Alpine passes. This pass has been used since the Middle
Ages, and the first carriage road was built in 1728. The
present road dates from 1841.

SEMMERING ★

1,000m). Famous health resort and winter-
sports centre, on right of the road, with
all-round protection by forests. Big luxury
hotels, of which the best known are the
Panhans, with swimming pool in the hotel,
and the Hotel du Sud, with open-air
swimming pool, tennis courts. Big international ski competitions are held here. (The World
University Games ski contests are often held at Semmering.)

A Recommended Hotel

Semmering: ★ Südbahnhotel.

The road drops sharply via Spital am Semmering to:

MÜRZZUSCHLAG ★

pop. 13,000 - 672m), at the foot of the Semmering. Ski-
lift on the Ganzstein (900m). Beautiful old patrician houses
and **Ski Museum.** Mürzzuschlag was, in fact, the cradle
of ski-ing in Central Europe. Max Kleinoschegg and Toni
Schruf, proprietors of the Hotel Post, introduced the sport
in 1889 and organized the first international competition
in 1893. On left of the road are the ruins of the castle-
fortress of Hohenwang, and, on right, Neu-Hohenwang
Castle.

A Recommended Hotel

Mürzzuschlag: ★ Hotel Post.

KRIEGLACH ★

Birthplace of the great Styrian poet Peter Rosegger (1843-
1918). His house, tomb, and the Rosegger Museum can
be visited.

MITTERDORF ★

small town which gained importance thanks to the great
magnesite plants of **Veitsch,** reached by a road on the right
5 km). These deposits are the biggest in the world. Note

Pichl Castle on the road from Mitterdorf to Veitsch (17th century).

Cross the River Mürz, through Wartberg and past the oldest church in Styria, Sankt-Georgi Church, on a hill to the right.

★ KINDBERG

(565m). Summer resort dominated by Oberkindberg Castle, baroque; inns in typical Styrian style.

Go through Mürzhofen, Allerheiligen, and Sankt-Marein.

A Recommended Hotel

Kindberg ★ Hotel Gruber.

★ KAPFENBERG

(pop. 21,000 – 508m). Industrial town with the great Böhler iron-works. Iron has been worked at Kapfenberg since the 15th century. Just at the approach to the town, on left, is the pilgrim church of Maria Rehkogel, on the slopes of the Rennfeld. At the entrance to the town is a great stadium with an indoor swimming pool, very up to date. Parish church dating from 1490 and, in the cemetery, a notable church of the end-Gothic epoch: **Church of Sankt-Martin.**

From Kapfenberg, road No. 20 (poor condition with gradient up to 1 : 5) runs north to **Mariazell** *(862m), the greatest place*

of pilgrimage in all central Europe. It is visited by some 100,000 pilgrims every year. It is also a big health resort and winter-sports centre, at the foot of the Bürgeralpe (1,267m), up which runs a cable railway. Mariazell was founded in 1157 by a Benedictine monk who arrived from over the mountains to preach the faith. He always had with him a statue of the Virgin, 45cm high, carved in lime tree wood. According to legend, the mountain opened to give him passage when he was at the end of his strength, allowing him to reach the sheltered valley where he built a church. The miraculous statue of the Virgin is to be seen on a silver altar in the **basilica,** *which is Gothic and the biggest church in Styria and has a façade ornamented with three towers. The high altar is the work of Fischer von Erlach. It is in red and black marble with an ebony crucifix.*

The road follows the Mürz as far as its junction with the Mur.

A Recommended Hotel

Mariazell: ** Hotel Laufenstein.

BRUCK AN DER MUR ★

(pop. 14,000 - 487m). In the Town Hall square is a very well-known Gothic building, the **Kornmesser-haus,** with arches and loggias and a notable Renaissance fountain made of wrought-iron. *Motorists in a hurry, coming from Vienna or Salzburg, can make straight for Klagenfurt by National Highway No. 17 (see second-ary itinerary) which runs through Knittelfeld and Ju-denberg.* Leave Bruck to the south and follow the Mur. After leaving Kirchdorf, **Pernegg** can be seen on the opposite bank of the Mur,

1 Town Hall. 2 Kornmesserhaus. 3 Fountain. 4 Travel Agency. 5 Station. 6 Wienstr. 7 Herzog-Ernst-Gasse. 8 Bismarckstr. 9 Rosegger-Gasse. 10 Grazerstr. 11 Bahnhofstr. 12 Koloman Wallisch-Platz. 13 Minoriten Platz.

and its castle (1580). The road next runs through **Mixnitz** *From here, on foot along the romantic Bärenschützklamm (gorge) with its numerous waterfalls, you can reach the* **Hochlantsch** *(1,772m).*

A little further on are two dams with hydroelectric plants and big paper mills.

A Recommended Hotel

Bruck an der Mur. ★ Hotel Schwarzer Adler.

FROHNLEITEN ★

Medieval town with several forges. Beautiful **frescoes** by the painter von Mölk on ceiling in the parish church (Pfarrkirche).

On left of the road, after Frohnleiten, the ruin of Pfannberg with funeral monument of the troubadour Hugo von Montfort, and, to right of road, **Rabenstein Castle** (12th century), rebuilt in 1680, with two beautiful halls of the

N. 67 25 km

N. 67 8 km

knights. The road runs along the Badlwand, far above the
railway line.

A Recommended Hotel

Frohnleiten: * Hotel Strassburg.

★ PEGGAU

(411m). Town famous for the **Lurgrotte**,
one of the loveliest caves with stalactites
in the world. Entrance to the cave is
immediately on the left, on entering the
town. It is actually a series of caves, 5 km
long, with a giant "dome" in which is
found the biggest stalactite in the world,
measuring 12½ m. *(Visits daily from 8 to 6.)* The "Wall of
Peggau" contains several other caves in which interesting
prehistoric relics have been found.

The road runs through **Gratkorn** (paper mills), near **Grat-
wein** (on the opposite bank) not far from the Cistercian
monastery of **Rein** which has a fine library and a baroque
church.

We are now near Graz. On right, pilgrim Church of
Maria Strassengel, a beautiful Gothic building of the 14th
century, with belfry. A little further south is the old
Weinzödl Bridge, 350 years old, open to pedestrians and
cyclists only.

Further on to left is the Church of Sankt-Veit, and, on
right, ruins of the castle-fortress of Gösting. Cross the Mur
by the new Weinzödl Bridge. Down the Wiener Strasse,
into:

★ GRAZ

(pop. 226,000 - 365m). Capital of Styria,
second largest city in Austria. Founded in
1115 at the fork of the old Bruck-Leibnitz
road *(Flavia Solva)* to Hungary. Fortified
in the 16th century, when Turkish invasion
threatened, Graz did not absorb the surrounding places which had grown up until
the end of the 18th century. Of its fortifications, only the **Burgtor**
and the **Paulustor** remain (Castle Gate and St Paul's Gate). Of
its proud fortress on the Schlossberg, there remains only the

Clock Tower, 28m high, built in 1561, emblem of the city, and the bell-tower dating from 1588 containing the biggest bell in Styria, the *Liesl*, weighing over four tons. Graz has a university and a school for Higher Technical Studies, as well as a public university which organizes international holiday courses. Its main industry is electrical. Graz International Spring Fair (April-May) and Autumn Fair (September-October). In July there are the Graz Festival Weeks: opera, theatre, and music. To tour Graz, cross the Lend Platz with its column commemorating the plague epidemic, follow the Maria-Hilfer-Strasse, in which stands the **Maria Hilfer Church**, built in 1607 by Pietro de Pomis, with a baroque façade dating from 1742. On the high altar (1769) is a painting of the Virgin, *Mariahilf*, by the same Pietro de Pomis, who is buried in the church itself. At the Südtiroler Platz, turn left and cross the main bridge (Hauptbrücke) which leads to the Old Town. Then through the Murgasse to the main square **(Hauptplatz)**, with the Town Hall (1883). In the centre of the square is a statue of Archduke Johann. At No. 14 is the Tourist Information Bureau and Travel Agency (from which passengers leave for Graz airport, 12 km south of the city). Take the **Herrengasse**, the busiest shopping street in the city. At No. 3 is the Painted House **(Gemaltes Haus)**, whose façade frescoes date from 1742. No. 16 is the Federal House **(Landhaus)**, built in the 16th century, former administrative headquarters for the Styrian States. Very beautiful courtyard which is used as a theatre in summer. A plaque here recalls that the astronomer Kepler taught mathematics at Graz from 1594 to 1600. Visit the hall of the Styrian Parliament (1741). Not far away is the Arsenal **(Landeszeughaus)** (1742), built to stave off a subsequent attack by the Turks. It is the biggest arsenal in Europe and the only one which has kept its original form. It contains some 30,000 weapons of all types of the 16th, 17th, and 18th centuries. A little further on, on left, is the parish church (Pfarrkirche), 1515. In a little chapel added later is an Assumption by Tintoretto (1595). At the end of the Herrengasse is the Square of the Iron Gate **(Platz am Eisernen Tor)** with a column **(Mariensäule)** erected in 1665 to commemorate the triumph over the Turks in 1664. On left, the Opernring with the Graz Opera House. On right of the square, the Kaiserfeldgasse. Take the second road

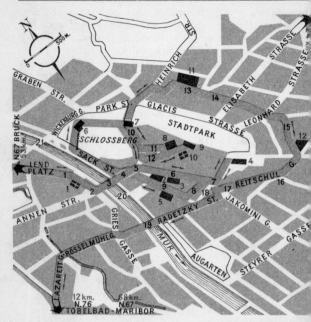

1 Mariahilfer Str. 2 Südtiroler Platz. 3 Hauptbrücke. 4 Murgass
5 Haupt Platz. 6 Herrehgasse. 7 Platz am Eisernen Tor. 8 Kaiserfel
gasse. 9 Raubergasse. 10 Paulustorgasse. 11 Ballhausgasse. 12 Ho
gasse. 13 Halbärth Gasse. 14 Hugo Wolf Gasse. 15 Garten Gass
16 Dietrichstein Pl. 17 Jakomini Pl. 18 Joanneum Pl. 19 Radetzk
Brücke. 20 Tegetthoff Brücke. 21 Kepler Brücke.

1 Maria Hilfer Kirche. 2 Town Hall. 3 Landhaus. 4 Opernring. 5 Joan
neum. 6 Schlossberg Museum. 7 Paulustor. 8 Schauspielhaus. 9 Burg
tor. 10 Domkirche. 11 University. 12 Higher Technical School.

on right, the Raubergasse. At No. 10 is the **Joanneum**, provinci
Museum founded in 1811 by Archduke Johann of Austria, i
a 17th-century building. Natural history, mining, geologica
and technical axhibits; mineralogical, zoological, and botanica
coin collection and collection of prehistoric relics found i
Styria. In the new museum, behind the Joanneum (entrance i
the Neutorgasse), are notable collections of painting on glas

statues and Styrian reredos of the 14th and 15th centuries. These museums are open from April to October daily from 9-1; Sunday 9-12. At 12 Sackstrasse is the *Krebsenkeller*, a restaurant which specializes in Serbian dishes, with two courtyards with arcades (1538). At No. 17 is the Attems Palace (1716), then the Wildenstein Palace now the police headquarters. At end of the Sack Strasse is the Franz Josefs Kai. At No. 38 is the starting point of the cable railway for the **Schlossberg** (15-minute service, trip takes 3 minutes). In addition to the Clock Tower and the belfry mentioned earlier, there is the Schlossberg Museum with a model of the original fortifications on this hill. *(Visits to museum and tower: daily, 9-11 and 2-5.)* Open-air theatre built in the remains of the old fortifications for the annual Graz Festival. Go down to the beautiful **municipal park,** a natural park. Its fountain, illuminated at night, is the work of Durenne; it was bought by the City of Graz at the World Exhibition in Paris in 1875. The Ballhausgasse leads to Graz Theatre and to the castle (Burg) which is the seat of the provincial government. On the same square is the **cathedral** (Domkirche) erected by Emperor Frederick III. Note the Gothic reredos with a Crucifixion by Conrad Laib (1457) in the right side nave, and two marriage coffers executed in 1470 at Mantua, which are used as coffers for relics.

Alongside the cathedral is the *mausoleum* of Emperor Ferdinand II, built by Pietro de Pomis in 1614 (Venetian style). Magnificent interior decoration. High altar from rough plans by Fischer von Erlach (1687). Red marble sarcophagus of Archduke Charles II in the crypt. At the corner of the Sporgasse and the Hofgasse is the House of the Order of German Knights with a beautiful courtyard and arcades dating from the early 16th century. Further on, to left, an old house richly decorated with stucco ornamentation of the 16th century *(Luegg),* with, at ground-level, picturesque shops. The University stands behind the municipal park and the School for Higher Technical Studies in the Copernicus Gasse. There are many good restaurants in Graz. The Hotel Steirerhof (Jakominiplatz), Reif (Am Eisernen Tor), the Elisabethhof (Elisabethstrasse), and the Parkhotel (Leonhardstrasse) merit special mention. The Rosenhain specializes in grills, while the Krebsenkeller serves Serbian specialities. The Keplerkeller, the Stempferg, and the Herzl-Weihstube in the Prokopigasse are taverns where Styrian wine and beer can be drunk to music. The Styrians claim to be able to yodel louder than the Tyroleans, and their "Schuhplattlers", dances with hobnail boots, give a striking impression of strength. The main business streets are the Herrengasse, the Opernring, and the Joanneumring.

Excursions in the neighbourhood: On the right bank of the Mur, **Eggenberg Castle** (17th century) with a beautiful courtyard and arcades; museum inside.

The **Schöckel circuit:** Go as far as Sankt-Radegund, health resort and spa with beautiful walks (50 km) and fine natural park. From there, a cable railway takes you to the Schöckel (1,445m) from which there is a wonderful view.

Visit the **Semriach Caves,** and go from them into the Peggau Caves (see p. 174), from which a motor-coach or the train can be taken to return to Graz.

Northwards to **Maria Trost** with its beautiful baroque pilgrim church.

*The Riesstrasse which, from Bachwirt, runs along the River Raab as far as Gleisdorf, provides a panorama of Styria as a whole. From **Gleisdorf** (365m), a small industrial town of 4,400 inhabitants, a road to the south, via Studenzen and Feldbach (pop. 3,300 - 282m), beautiful holiday resort, leads to **Bad Gleichenberg** (317m), the most famous spa in Styria with a very mild climate. Its springs were known to the Romans. Treatments: respiratory disorders, intestinal and heart troubles. Nearby is Gleichenberg Castle, and the Riegersburg, a powerful 11th-century fortress with 10 gates. The road continues south to **Radkerburg**, on the Yugoslav frontier. From Gleisdorf another road (50 km) leads to Hungary, in the east, via Fürstenfeld, but this road is impracticable because the section between Fürstenfeld and Rudersdorf is in the Soviet zone and banned to foreigners.*

Graz is 67 km from Maribor in Yugoslavia. *Leave the city by the Triesterstrasse and the suburb of Puntigam, with the most famous brewery in Styria, to Kalsdorf and Wildon (315m), on the right bank of the Mur and dominated by the Wildoner Berg. At **Ober-Wildon** is the old castle in which the famous astrologer Tycho Brahé lived. The road runs to the east of **Leibnitz**, dominated by Seckau Castle, crosses the Mur at the approach to Landscha, by-passes Strass, then,*

after re-crossing the Mur, reaches **Spielfeld** *(263m), and the Austrian Customs. Via Sv. Ilj, the old* Sankt-Egidi, *to* **Maribor** *(formerly Marburg), on the Drave, 148 km from Zagreb and 420 km from Belgrade.*
Leave Graz by the Kärntner Strasse (Carinthia road). On right, Sankt-Martin Castle, then **Strassgang** Church. Before Tobelbad, also on the right, is the *Waldschloss* Inn, where the speciality is roast chicken. The road follows the River Kainach fairly closely. Via Lieboch, Krottendorf, and **Krems**, with its massive ruined castle-fortress, to Voitsberg.

Some Recommended Hotels

Bad Gleichenberg: ** Hotel Possenhofen. * Hotel Regina.
Graz: ** Hotel Steirerhof, 12 Jakominiplatz. * Hotel Goldenes Ross, 9 Mariahilfer Strasse.
Radkerburg: * Hotel Österreich.

VOITSBERG *

(394m). Old mining town. Visit ruins of the castle-fortress of Ober Voitsberg. Beside them is a restaurant with a magnificent view, and a camping site. Very old church of Sankt-Michael which has stood unaltered since 1500. Local museum in an old tower. Glassworks. After Voitsberg, on right on a hill, is the little **Church of the Holy Mount**. On left, hydroelectric plant.

A Recommended Hotel

Voitsberg: * Hotel Rathaushof.

KÖFLACH *

(442m). Mining town, centre of a vast lignite field which stretches from Voitsberg to Köflach, in some parts worked by the open-cast system. Site of the biggest glass-blowing factory in Austria and a big shoe factory.

A road to the right at the approach to Köflach leads to **Maria Lankowitz**, *a place of pilgrimage, and, nearby, the* **Piber Stud**, *where the famous Lippizaner horses of the Spanish School of Riding in Vienna are bred. To the north, a small road (13 km) leads to* **Salla** *where, on 12th August each year, the biggest livestock market in the country is held: the Clara Market, which is marked by a great festival with dancing and folklore songs, processions, and a big fair.*

N. 70   34 km

N. 70   6 km

N. 70   20 km

The road now heads towards the south-west. Up to **Edel-schrott**, there is a superb view of the Stub and Glein Alps, to the north, and over the Graz Plain to the east. *At Edelschrott, a fork to the left runs to the lake dam of Hierzmann, in the heart of the forest. After Scherveitl, another road on the left (10 km) leads to Modriach, passing by the lake dam of Pack (Stausee).*

The road climbs with several turnings up to Pack and to the Packsattel.

A Recommended Hotel

Köflach: ★ Hotel Simoni.

★ PACKSATTEL

(1,166m). a pass which forms the frontier between Styria and Carinthia. The road runs down, via Preitenegg and Waldenstein, to **Twimberg** (castle ruins and lime-kilns). *Road No. 78, to the right, rejoins the National Road No. 17 at Judenberg, passing through **Sankt-Leonhard**, an old thermal station with sulphur baths, **Reichenfels** (809m), with its castle-fortress, and the **Obdach Pass** (bad stretches between St Leonhard and Reichenfels).*

★ ST GERTRAUD

Big paper and cellulose mills.

★ WOLFSBERG

(462m), in the Lavanttal. Not far away, on a height, is the castle of Count Henckel-Donnersmark, in Windsor style, and Kirchbichl Castle, which houses a fine collection of pictures.

★ ST ANDRÄ

(433m). Small town, former episcopal see of the Lavant. Nearby is a castle and big 17th-century church.

The road climbs (1 : 7) to the Griffenberg and drops down again to:

★ VÖLKERMARKT

(461m). Little old fortified town and summer resort. *(Camping site.) A straight road to the south leads, via Eisenkappel and Bad Vellach, a hydro-mineral station, to the **Seeberg***

N. 70 26 km
N. 70 5 km
N. 70 9 km
N. 70 20 km

Pass *(1,206m), on the Yugoslav frontier (39 km), in the direction of Ljubljana, which is 56 km from the frontier.*
The road to Klagenfurt crosses the Gurk, runs through St Jakob and across the Glan just before entering, by the Völkermarkter-Strasse, the town of Klagenfurt.

A Recommended Hotel

Völkermarkt: ★ Gasthof Alte Post.

KLAGENFURT ★

N. 70   27 km

SECONDARY ITINERARY:
BRUCK-KLAGENFURT VIA JUDENBERG: 161 KM.

BRUCK AN DER MUR ★

National highway No. 17 leads direct to Klagenfurt, via Niklasdorf.

N. 17   16 km

LEOBEN ★

(pop. 36,000 - 532m). Old mountain town. Centre of Styria's heavy industry and lignite mining. Seat of the College for Higher Montanist Studies, which is situated in the Kaiser-Franz-Josefstrasse. The Erzherzog-Johannstrasse is the "frontier" between the new and the old town. In the latter, visit the **Hauptplatz** with its fountain, the Town Hall, and beautiful private houses. Nearby is the **Old Burg**, which is now a grammar school and municipal museum. Every year, Leoben is the setting for Montanist meetings, folklore festivals, and craftsmanship and industrial exhibitions.

N. 17   9 km

*Excursions to **Donawitz** (3 km), important iron centre with numerous blast furnaces and steelworks, headquarters of the Alpine Montan Gesellschaft, and, to the north, to **Eisenerz**, mining town at the foot of the Erzberg (1,534m), heart of the Styrian iron industry, and biggest source of wealth for this federal country. Here also are the biggest open-cast iron-ore workings in the whole of Europe. Terraces 12 to 36m high run up for 800m on the slopes of the Erzberg. Tourists are allowed to visit these installations, as well as those at the foot of the mountain where the ore extracted is treated. On holidays, the Eisenerz*

*miners still wear the old dress of miners of the Maximilian period.
To be noted, on the road from Leoben to Eisenerz (N. 115 - 29
km), a hill of 1 : 8 climbing to Prebichl (1,220m), ski-lift on
the Polster (1,820m) with a view over the Erzberg, and a steep
drop down to Eisenerz (1 : 4¹/₂)*

Some Recommended Hotels

Leoben: ** Grandhotel. * Hotel Post.

★ ST MICHAEL

(pop. 3,400 - 570m). Old parish church (Gothic). Nearby,
the Walpurgis Chapel (13th century). Fork of the N. 113,
to the right, towards Salzburg *(see itinerary No. 6)*. Via
Kraubarth and Sankt-Lorenzen, to:

★ KNITTELFELD

(pop. 13,000 - 645m). Industrial town (metallurgy, and
production of rolling stock for the Austrian State Railways),
heavily bombed towards the end of the Second World War.
The road runs slightly north of Zeltweg (670m), an industrial town with a big metal works. A little further on,
right fork (2 km) towards Fohnsdorf, a big lignite centre.
These two places were also hard-hit by bombing.

A Recommended Hotel

Knittelfeld: * Hotel Steirerhof.

★ JUDENBURG

(pop. 10,300 - 734m). In a lovely setting
on the right bank of the Mur, at the foot
of the Wenzelalpe (2,153m). Cast-iron
works and scythe-making. On the main
square **(Hauptplatz)** is the Town Tower,
built between 1449 and 1509, and parish
church dating from 1673. Standing on a
window ledge in the south façade of the "Post" hostelry
is a **Jew's Head,** carved in the stonework; it is over 500
years old and the insignia of the town. The name (Judenburg
means Fortress of the Jews), the insignia, and the blazon of
the town recall the big colony of Israelites who lived there
in the 11th century. 13th-century ducal castle and, to the
east of the town, the ruins of the castle-fortress of Liechtenstein (12th century). The cable railway which climbs from

Judenburg to Schmelz (1,600m) in 58 minutes, can be used only by permission of the British Occupation authorities, whose headquarters is in the Burggasse. Via Woll and Sankt-Georgen to Unzmarkt.

A Recommended Hotel

Judenburg: ★ Hotel Post.

UNZMARKT ★

N. 17 12 km

(pop. 870 - 757m). Old market town dominated by the ruins of the old Frauenburg, the fortifications, and the parish church, dating from 1450. Metallurgical plants and saw mills.

Via **Scheifling** and the **Perchauer Sattel** (also known as the Neumarkter Sattel), 1,005m, to:

N. 17 22 km

NEUMARKT ★

(841m). Alpine health resort near the grand castle-fortress of **Forchtenstein,** on the site of the Celtic town of *Noreia* where the Cimbri and the Teutons fought a great battle in the year 113 B.C.

Via Wilbad Einöde (735m), small spa with radio-active sulphur springs (79° F.), to the frontier of Styria and Carinthia and to:

N. 17 15 km

FRIESACH ★

(pop. 3,500 - 637m). Small medieval town, founded in the 9th century. Up to 1805, Friesach belonged to the Prince Archbishops of Salzburg, who chose it as a residence in the Middle Ages. The fortifications, walls, and towers which surround this little town with its narrow lanes have been well preserved. In the main square **(Hauptplatz)** is the Town Hall and a beautiful Renaissance-style fountain dating from 1563. In the Wiener Strasse is the 12th-century parish church with a Gothic choir and a sculpture of the Virgin, in stone (1300). On the other side of the moat is the Dominican abbey, with a little church without a tower dating from the 13th century. In the Petersberg is the little **Church of St Peter's,** 927, with remarkable frescoes, as well as the ruins of the old episcopal castle.

N. 17 45 km

North of the town is the **Geiersberg**, with a 12th-century castle, recently entirely rebuilt. *(To visit it, apply to the Friesach Town Hall.)* To the south-east, the church of the Order of the German Knights, with a magnificent altar with reredos. Via **Hirt** (613m), small town with a big brewery, to Zwischenwässern, then through Mölbling and Sankt-Veit (475m) *(see description in itinerary No. 10)*, to:

★ **KLAGENFURT**

KLAGENFURT AND CARINTHIA
LENGTH OF ITINERARY: 264 KM.

Carinthia is the most southerly federal country in Austria. In the centre, it forms a wide basin surrounded by high mountains, including the Grossglockner (3,797m), the highest mountain in Austria. The Hohe Tauern divide Carinthia from the Salzburg country, while the Gurktal Alps and the Noric Alps, to the east, form the frontier between Carinthia and Styria. To the west stand the Dolomites of Lienz and to the south the Carnic Alps and the Karawankens, natural frontiers between Carinthia and Italy, on the one hand, and Yugoslavia on the other. For the tourist, the main attraction of this province is its great lakes, which are found in the eastern region: the Klagenfurt basin. Their high temperature—sometimes reaching 82° F.— allow for a bathing season from May to October. The itinerary outlined further on covers the six biggest lakes. At the beginning of July, it is possible to drive up the Grossglockner by car to ski on the Pasterze glacier, and then come down in the afternoon for a swim in a lake. Apart from the tourist traffic, the principal resources of this province, are the metal and timber industries; but there are also the chemical plants of Treibach and Weissenstein, as well as the iron ore, lead, zinc, and magnesite mines. The gold and silver mines which formed its wealth in the 16th century are completely exhausted. Two great hydroelectric stations on the Drave, at Reisseck and Sankt-Stefan i. Lungau, supply electric power for the whole province.

Carinthia was inhabited before the Celtic epoch. It became an important centre after the Roman colonization, and during the great invasions of the 6th century it was occupied by the Slavs, who founded an independent state there, which became the core of the Slovene peoples. In struggles with the Avars, this state fell under Bavarian domination and Carinthia formed part of the Roman-German Empire from Charlemagne's time. In the 10th century it was raised to a duchy which, in the 14th century, became the hereditary fief of the House of Habsburg. The arrival of numerous Bavarian colonies gradually changed the ethnical character of the country, which became German-speaking. Even so, in the middle of the 19th century, a third of Carinthia's population was still Slovene. (The Slovenes of Carinthia played a major role in the cultural revival of the Slovene peoples in the 19th century.) Since then, the absorption of the Slovene element has been accentuated and now about 40,000 inhabitants use the Slovene tongue. This is always spoken in the country-districts of the southern part of the country, that is to say in the lower valley of the Gail and in the valley of the Drave below Villach, up to the Wörthersee, and beyond Völkermarkt.

In the southern section of the country, the family names and place-names, and even some signs on the schools, are in Slovenian, and recall the origin of the inhabitants. A country inhabited for so many centuries, whose gold and silver mines and southern climate attracted so many noblemen of the Empire and the Church, naturally possesses an old culture and many art treasures. It is a land rich in tales, in legends and songs, where many old traditions are kept up, like the *Kufenstechen* at Feistritz on the Gail: a Slav dance performed in picturesque local costume, followed by a very old roundelay dating from the Middle Ages; the Whitsun race at Weitensfeld, the miners' festival at Huttenberg, etc. Klagenfurt has been the capital of Carinthia since 1518.

PRINCIPAL SIGHTS

CHURCHES: Klagenfurt, Karnburg, Maria-Saal, Gurk, Villach and Maria-Wörth. ABBEYS of: Mill-statt, Ossiach. CASTLES: Hochosterwitz, Taggen-brunn, Porcia at Spittal, and Archbishop's Palace at Klagenfurt. MUSEUMS of: Rudolfinum at Klagen-furt. VIEWS and MONUMENTS: Landhaus, Gurk's House, Dragon Fountain at Klagenfurt; Town Hall of Sankt-Veit; Seignorial Chair and Ducal Chair, near Annabichl; Relief Map of Carinthia at Villach; the Villacher Alp; the Kanzelhöhe.

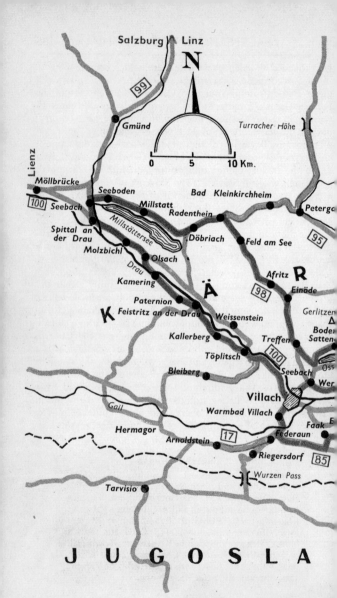

Gastronomy: The two gastronomical specialities of Carinthia are the *Krainerwürste*, a savoury sausage, and the *Kärntner Reindling*, a cake which, in this province, replaces the traditional *Guglhupf* (kind of light bread). The southern position of Carinthia has had its influence on the cooking, and the *Gulyas* there is excellent. Of course, in this land of lakes and rivers, there is a good variety of fish, including pike, the hucho, and the *Schied*, also known as *Rapfen*.

★ KLAGENFURT

 (pop. 65,000 - 444m). At the eastern tip of the Wörther See. Capital, cultural, and industrial centre of Carinthia. Klagenfurt was mentioned as a town for the first time in the will of Duke Philip in 1279. Emperor Maximilian I gave it to the Corporations of Carinthia in 1518. The town at that time had 70 houses and 700 inhabitants.

The town is approached via the Völkermarktstrasse which runs in front of the **Archbishops Palace** (1770) in the north-east of Klagenfurt, and in which is found the diocesan museum of Gurk. By the Priesterhausgasse to the **Old Square** (Alter Platz), centre of the old town which has retained its medieval character despite the great fires of 1519 and 1536. Via the Pfarrkirchgasse to the parish church, rebuilt around 1700, with a tower 91m high. From its gallery 47m up, there is a very fine view. Down the Herrengasse to the Ursulinengasse in which stands the **Landhaus**, a building erected between 1574 and 1590, with a beautiful courtyard with archways. Notable Hall of Blazons, with frescoes by Lobisser (1930). *(Open daily, 8-12 and 2-5.)* A little further on, on right, Holy Trinity Square (1639) and, at No. 3, a niche with the Steinerne Fischer (The Fishing-boat of Peter), carved in 1606, who awaits near his bark to get rid of his catch. Via the Stauderplatz to the Pernhartgasse. On left, Gurk's House, very beautiful, and on right, the main Post Office, with a commemorative plaque to the reputed inventor of the postcard, Emanuel Hermann. A little to the south of the Post Office is the Benediktiner Platz, where the flower market is held. Via the Postgasse to the Neuer Platz with the emblem of the city, the **Dragon Fountain,** which was carved from a huge block of stone in 1584 by Ulrich Vogelsang to ornament the basin placed there in case of fire. The head of the rhinoceros used

95 FELDKIRCHEN 23 km

17 BRUCK 161 km
WIEN 311 km   JUDENBURG 100 km   92 BRÜCKL 26 km

ST VEITER RING   ST VEITER RING

70 VÖLKERMARKT 26 km

BAD VILLACH 40 km
WÖRTHERSEE 4 km

LOIBL   PASS 29 km
LJUBLJANA 84 Km
91

HAUPTBAHNHOF

1 Völkermarkterstr. 2 Priesterhausgasse. 3 Pfarrkirchgasse. 4 Herrengasse. 5 Heiligen-Geist-Platz. 6 Stauder-Platz. 7 Pernhartgasse. 8 Be-
nediktiner-Platz. 9 Postgasse. 10 Neuer-Platz. 11 Lidmansky-Gasse.

1 Alter Platz. 2 Parish Church. 3 Landhaus. 4 Holy Trinity Church.
5 Steinerne Fischer. 6 Gurk's House. 7 Post Office. 8 Dragon Fountain.
9 Town Hall (Rathaus). 10 Travel Agency. 11 Cathedral. 12 Provincial
Government headquarters. 13 Provincial Museum. 14 Botanical Gardens
and Alpine Museum. 15 Landschaftliche Burg. 16 Theatre. 17 Künstlerhaus.

as a model by the sculptor can be seen in Klagenfurt Museum.
In 1636, the sculptor Hönel, creator of the famous high altar of
Gurk, placed Hercules brandishing a club before this dragon,
thus making allusion to the city legend according to which a
dragon is said to have devastated the region and killed the finest
knights who came to do battle with it. A farmer's boy finally
managed to capture the beast, and killed it with a club. As a
reward, the lad married the seigneur's daughter. The Town Hall

is in this square and the provincial travel agency:
the Kärntner Landesreisebüro. Via the Karfreit-
strasse and the Lidmansky-Gasse to the **Cathedral,**
built between 1578 and 1591. The interior is in
rich baroque style, and contains works by
Daniel Gran, Paul Troger, and Luitberg Lobisser.
Via the Bahnhofstrasse to the Landesregierung
(Provincial Government offices), behind which lies the **Provincial
Museum,** Rudolfinum, containing historical, archaeological,
ethnographical, and natural history collections of great importance and a museum of popular art. On the ground floor is a
7 m-high relief of the Grossglockner. Opposite the museum is
the botanical gardens and the Alpine Museum *(open daily from
9-12 and 2-6; Sunday and holidays: 9-12).*

The city having grown rapidly since the second half of the 19th
century, and particularly in recent times, it has the appearance,
apart from some buildings around the Old Square, of a modern
city, well planned, with great squares, straight roads, and many
parks and gardens. There are many fine modern buildings such
as the urban heating plant, Dr Karl Renner's School, the Austrian
State tobacco factory, the Children's Hospital, and the Trade
Union Chamber of Work and Commerce. A big beach which
will hold 10,000 people has been laid out on the banks of the
Wörther See, to which Klagenfurt is linked by a 4 km-long canal.
Camping site on lakeside. The main industries of Klagenfurt are
textiles, leather, and iron. (Provincial industrial fair every August.)
The main shopping streets are the Bahnhofstrasse, the Neuer Platz,
the Burggasse, and the Kramergasse. Beautiful hand-worked
table services can be bought. The cooking has come under the
influence of southern countries, and Hungary. The Rathaus-
stüberl, the Landhauskeller are among the best restaurants in
Klagenfurt.

Apart from the Kärntner Landesreisebüro in the Neuer Platz,
there is another travel agency, the Reisebüro Dossi-Obersteiner,
at the Obstplatz. The Automobile and Touring Club of Carinthia
(KATC) has its headquarters at 5 Domgasse. It lists the service
stations and repair-shops which are open on Sundays and public
holidays. The aerodrome of Klagenfurt lies to the north of the
city, at Annabichl. To obtain a fine panoramic view, climb the
Kreuzberg north-west of Klagenfurt, with viewing tower.
Klagenfurt lies 29 km north of Yugoslavia. A very hilly road (slope.

of 1 : 5 and 1 : 4) leads to the frontier, formed by the Loibl Pass (1,366m), 55 km from Ljubljana.

Leave Klagenfurt in a northerly direction by the Sankt-Veiter Strasse. On right, Annabichl aerodrome; on left, the little **Annabichl** Castle (baroque) and a little further on, Mount Sankt-Ulrich. At the foot of the mountain is the village of **Karnburg**, with the oldest church in Austria (920). North of this church the **Seignorial Chair** (now moved to the Klagenfurt Museum) once stood where, up to the end of the Middle Ages, the first part of the investiture ceremony was held. The future duke, seated on this rock, dressed in peasant costume, received the symbolic assent of the people. This rite, unique in Europe, dated back to the period of Carinthia's independence and, carried out in Slovenian, was a survival of the Slav democracy. The duke then went to Maria-Saal where he changed into his seigneur's dress and from there he moved 2 km north of the town to the **Ducal Chair** (Herzogstuhl), erected in the 9th century with Roman stones. He there took his seat and swore an oath of fidelity to the country nobles, by shaking each of them by the hand. After this ceremony the country nobility recognized the duke's right to dispose of the fiefs.

Some Recommended Hotels

Klagenfurt: ** Hotel Carinthia, 8a Bahnhofstrasse. * Hotel Janach, 5 Bahnhofstrasse.

MARIA-SAAL ★

(473m), on a hill to the right of the road. Famous place of pilgrimage with one of the finest Gothic buildings in Carinthia: the **Cathedral** (15th century), built with stones recovered from the Roman town of *Virunum*, north of Maria-Saal. That is why numerous Roman bas-reliefs of the 2nd century can be seen on the façade of this cathedral, in addition to a Roman ossuary. Inside there are beautiful frescoes of 1491, recently brought to light. On the south-west slope of the hill is the Chapel of St Modeste of Salzburg, who came to Maria-Saal in 767 to preach Christianity.

N. 17 7 km

N. 17 7 km

★ **ST DONAT**

(479m), between the Grazer Kogel, on left, and the
Magdalensberg on right. Recent excavations in the latter
have yielded prehistoric remains of great interest.
Fork to the right (5 km) towards the **Castle-fortress of Hochosterwitz** *(726m), one of the finest in the Alps. It is reached
by a path running through 14 porches. Restaurant in the fortress,
which can be visited. Camping site at foot of the hill. Continuing
along this road, after Gosseling on the right, the remarkable*
Burg Mannsberg.

★ **ST VEIT AN DER GLAN**

(pop. 9,300 - 475m). This market town
was, until 1518, the capital of Carinthia
and the ducal seat. In the main square
(Hauptplatz) is the beautiful *Schlüssel-
brunnen* fountain; **Town Hall,** 15th century,
with a baroque façade and remarkable
stucco decorations in the Hall of Session.
12th-century parish church with ossuary transformed into
a memorial to the dead. The main industry of Sankt-Veit
is the manufacture of wood-fibre plaques (Isorel). In the
neighbourhood of Sankt-Veit there are many castles and
ruins, of which outstanding are the ruined **Castle-fortress
of Taggenbrunn,** 3 km to the east; Frauenstein Castle near
Obermühlbach, and, quite close, the ruins of Freiburg
Castle. The K.A.T.C. (Carinthia Automobile and Touring
Club) has an office at Sankt-Veit. Camping site.
Via Dürnfeld to Mölbling (585m). *Right fork (2 km) towards
Treibach where there are big chemical factories. Slightly before
this fork, another road to the left leads to* **Rastenfeld** *Castle,
the property of Dr Auer, inventor of the famous incandescent
burner. The castle is not open to visitors.*
After Mölbling St Stephen's Church can be seen on left
of the road, then the Siebenbrunnhöhe (970m) **Zwischenwässern** (640m), with the Archbishops Castle of Pockstein.
Here leave the road leading north (8 km) to **Friesach** *(see secondary itinerary No. 9: Bruck-Klagenfurt via Judenburg)*, and
take the road to the left which follows the River Gurk. **Strassburg** (658m), very ancient little town with its ruined castle
(12th century), former residence of the Bishops of Gurk.

N. 17   6 km

N. 17 and N. 93   32 km

Note the numerous Roman-style bas-reliefs on the house façades. Swimming pool.

A Recommended Hotel

St Veit an der Glan: ★ Hotel St Veiter Hof.

GURK ★

(662m). Ancient hamlet famous for its **cathedral,** the most important architectural monument in Carinthia. It is a Roman basilica with three naves and quiet exterior, not very attractive, built between 1140 and 1200. It contains, among other beautiful works, the *Pietà* (1740) one of the master-pieces of the great Austrian sculptor Raphael Donner (at end of the central nave). There are still six beautiful bas-reliefs in lead by the same artist on the pulpit at the third pillar on right. 13th-century frescoes in the vestibule and, above it, the loveliest part of the cathedral, frescoes dating from 1220. Roman-style marble porch, one of the finest in Austria. Below the choir is the famous **Crypt of 100 Pillars,** built in 1174, with the tomb of Countess Hemma, founder-saint of the cathedral, lying in a sarcophagus of 1174. To the north is a marble altar with a wood carving representing the Virgin, which is said to be even older than the cathedral itself. *(Visits to crypt and the frescoes accompanied by guide only; apply at entrance to abbey.)* At Eastertide, the altar is covered with the famous **Sheet of Youth,** of 1458, divided into 100 squares, each portraying a scene from the Old or the New Testament.

Via **Zweinitz** (747m), with its 12th-century church, to **Weitensfeld** (701m). In the little Church of St Magdalene there are very old painted windows (12th century). On Whit-Monday there is a folklore rally of horsemen *(Kranzel-reiten).* Swimming pool, shooting, and fishing.

The road goes through the *Enge Gurk,* a route where the valley narrows almost to the appearance of a gorge. At Klein-Glödnitz, *a road (14 km) towards the north leads via Glödnitz and Weissberg to* **Flattnitz** *(1,390m), alpine health resort and winter-sports centre, at the foot of Mount Eisenhut (2,441m) which provides one of the loveliest views of the Gurktal*

Alps. Shooting. From Flattnitz, a direct road which is poor in parts goes, 35 km, via Metnitz and Grades to **Friesach.**

Via Albeck (795m), with its castle ruins, on left of the road, and Poitschach, where there is an important paper mill, to:

★ FELDKIRCHEN

N. 93 7 km

(pop. 3,200 - 556m). Holiday resort and meeting-place of six roads: from Gurk, Sankt-Veit, Klagenfurt, Turracher Höhe, Villach, and finally Ossiach. K.A.T.C. office. Horse market and timber trade. Baroque churches and houses.

A Recommended Hotel

Feldkirchen: ★ Hotel Germann.

★ STEINDORF

N. 98 4 km

(508m). Holiday resort at the eastern tip of the Ossiacher See which is 11 km long and varies in width from 600 to 1,650m. It is the first of the Carinthian warm lakes on our itinerary, surrounded on all sides by high mountains which shelter it from the wind.

A Recommended Hotel

Steindorf: ★ Gasthof-Pension Hoffmann.

★ BODENSDORF

N. 98 33 km

(509m). Quiet little watering-place opposite **Ossiach** (503 m), well-known resort which is reached by ferry or by the road running round the lake, and with a famous **abbey** founded in 1028, richly decorated with stuccoes. Via Sankt-Urban to the peaceful holiday resorts of Sattendorf (506m) and Annenheim (502m). *Between these two resorts there is a 1,888m cable railway up the* **Kanzelhöhe,** *climbing to 1,500m in ten minutes. Departures every 40 minutes. Beautiful view from the top over the Karawanken massif. Excellent hotel, place for rest and health cure, which enjoys the longest hours of sunshine in Central Europe. The south side of this mountain rises as a steep wall 1,000m high above the lake. From the Kanzelhöhe there is a ski-lift for* **Gerlitzen** *(1,910m, very fine ski-slopes). View over Carinthia, observatory.*

The road leaves the lake and heads north-west. Through

the holiday resort of Treffen (545m) to Einöde (556m) and to **Afritz** (710m), holiday and winter-sports resort (pop. 1,000), near the charming Afritzer See which lies 3 km north of the resort, on left of road. Shooting, fishing, and beach on lakeside. A kilometre past the Afritzer See, on right of road, is another lake, the Brennersee. At northern tip of this lake is Feld am See (743m), small watering-place. Fishing and shooting.

A Recommended Hotel

Kanzelhöhe: ★ Berghotel Kanzelhöhe.

RADENTHEIN ★

(pop. 4,700 - 750m). Only 50 years ago, this town was only a tiny village. In 1907, rich deposits of magnesite were discovered on the heights above Radenthein, 1,700m up. Radex refractory bricks and plaques of Heraklit manufactured at Radenthein are exported all over the world. *The road forks right. Via **Bad Kleinkirchheim**, thermal station with radio-active springs, holiday and winter-sports resort, to Petergassen (14 km), on the Feldkirchen-Turracher Höhe road.* Through Döbriach (606m), with camping site, to the **Millstatt Lake**, 12 km long and 1,000m wide, the second largest lake in Carinthia and the deepest (140m), in a magnificent alpine setting surrounded by the Nock mountains. On the south-western tip is the natural beach of **Döbriach**. The road follows the right shore of the lake. Via **Dellach** (580m), with beach, and Pesenthein (camping site) to:

N. 98 13 km

MILLSTATT AM MILLSTÄTTER SEE ★

(580m), one of the loveliest watering-places in Carinthia. Big modern beach with a high diving-board of 12.5m. Thanks to the high temperature of the waters of the lake, the bathing season extends from May to October. Swimming and diving contests are held in August. From far away can be seen the buildings of the old **Bene-dictine abbey**. This abbey, founded in 1087, has a beautiful portal and interesting frescoes. Notable Roman-style **cloister** with Gothic roof. In centre of the courtyard is

N. 98 11 km

the famous thousand-year-old **lime tree** of Millstatt. The abbey was endowed with towers and ramparts in the 15th century by the Knights of the Order of St George. On the western tip of the lake is **Seeboden** (580 m), alpine watering-place with very modern beaches. Turn left at Seebach to reach Spittal an der Drau.

A Recommended Hotel

Millstatt: ★ Hotel am See.

★ SPITTAL AN DER DRAU

(pop. 9,700 - 554m). Summer resort at the junction of the Lieser and the Drave. Spittal was founded in 1191, a few kilometres east of the old Roman town of *Teurnia*. Right in the centre of Spittal is the fine **Porcia Castle**, erected in 1537 by the Italian architect V. Scamozzi, a masterpiece of the Italian Renaissance. Notable portal and courtyard with arcades. Richly decorated. K.A.T.C. office. Near the castle, national highway No. 99 to the north links Spittal and Salzburg via the Katschberghöhe and the Radstätter Tauern *(see itinerary No. 11)*. To the west, the road leads to Möllbrücke, where it rejoins itinerary No. 4.

Follow the road in an easterly direction beneath a gateway to the town and cross the Lieser. At **Molzbichl**, a left fork of a road leads to Edling Castle and a camping site 800m off the main road. Further on, on a hill to the left, is the Rothenturn Castle. After Olsach (510m), the road crosses the railway line and then the Drave, runs by a great hydroelectric station and through Kamering.

A Recommended Hotel

Spittal an der Drau: ★ Hotel Salzburg.

★ PATERNION

(518m). Old market town with 16th-century castle. The road narrows and climbs steeply to **Nickelsdorf** (552m). (Beware of sharp turn in the centre of this locality.)

To right, a road (20 km) leads to the eastern tip of the **Weissensee,** *a narrow, steep road, to be used only in dry weather. Another mountain road, very hilly (20 km) links up to the south with the national highway No. 111 at Sankt-Stephan and the picturesque Gail Valley.*

N. 100   15 km

N. 100   22 km

After Nickelsdorf, slow down: dangerous turning. At
Feistritz an der Drau (548m), on left, a road (4.5 km)
leads to Fresach from whence a climb up the **Mirnock**
(2,104m) can be made. On right, a road (4 km) leads to a
big hydroelectric station. After Feistritz the road runs by
Kellerberg Castle (16th century) and through the market
town of Kellerberg (574m). Opposite, on the far bank of
the Drave, is **Weissenstein,** with a great chemical plant.
The road becomes narrow in places; poor visibility.
Further on, about 8 km after Töplitsch (571m), *a right fork
of the road leads (11 km) to* **Bleiberg** *(925m), where Austria's
biggest lead mine is found, with its 800 galleries. This mine can
be visited and the whole mountain covered by truck. Above
Bleiberg is the* **Villacher Alpe,** *also known as the* Dobratsch,
renowned for the lovely view obtained from its summit.

VILLACH ★

I Main Square and Holy Trinity
column. 2 Paracelse Court. 3
Parish church of St Jacob. 4 Relief
of Carinthia. 5 Post Office. 6
Castle-fortress.   7 St Nicolai
Church. 8 Church of the Holy
Cross. 9 Station. 10 Protestant
church. 11 Ossiacherzeile. 12
Richard Wagner-str. 13 Tiroler-
str. 14 Hans-Gasser-Platz. 15
Italienerstr. 16 Klagenfurterstr.
17 Bahnhofstr.

(pop. 31,000 - 501m),
which is entered by the
Tiroler Strasse and the
Hans-Gasser-Platz. Second
largest town in Carinthia,
situated on the Drave; big
communications   centre
where five railway lines
and seven roads meet.
Villach is the principal
centre for timber exports
to Italy. Surrounded by
high mountains, this town
is also an excellent base for
climbers   and   skiers.
K.A.T.C. office and travel
agency in the Postgasse,
next to the Park Hotel.
Tourist Inquiry Bureau:
Postgasse 4.
The name of *Uillah* ap-
peared for the first time in
a manuscript of 878 A.D. Earlier it was the Roman colony
of *Santicum.* The site of Villach on the transit-road between

Vienna and Venice gave it great importance in the 16th century up to the time when Venice yielded place to Trieste. Villach again flourished after the building of the Tauern and Karawanken railways. The loveliest part of the town is found around the picturesque **Main Square** (Hauptplatz), with its column of the Holy Trinity (baroque) and several Renaissance period houses. This square is also the business centre of the town. No. 25 was for long the home, in the 16th century, of the great doctor and scientist Theophraste Paracelse. Emperor Charles Quint lived at No. 9 in this square when he fled from Maurice of Saxony. Beautiful 15th-century **parish church** erected on the highest point of the town, in the Kirchenplatz. This church contains a splendid high altar and statue of Christ dating from 1430. Beautiful view from gallery of the tower, 95m high. Opposite the choir is the Town Hall. In the park of the State Grammar School, Street of 10th October, is a remarkable **relief map of Carinthia**, scale 1 : 10,000. *(Visits: 8-12 and 2-4; apply to school porter.)*

Villach lies 17 km from the Yugoslav frontier and 23 km from the Italian frontier.

Leave the town by the Italienerstrasse.

A Recommended Hotel

Villach: ★ Parkhotel, 2 Moritzstrasse.

★ WARMBAD VILLACH

N. 17 and N. 85   16 km

(503m). Thermal station with radio-active springs (86° F.). Thermal establishment and beach; inside the Kurhotel is an indoor thermal swimming pool. Treatments: mild rheumatic troubles, general weakness, and, above all, heart troubles. The curative power of these springs was known to the Romans and the Celts. There are numerous tombs dating from 2,500 to 1,000 B.C. and traces of the old Roman road on the Napoleonwiese (Napoleon's Meadow) behind the Kurpark. Near Warmbad Villach are the limestone Eggerloch Caves, 240m long, which can be visited.

Towards the south the road climbs the foothills of the

Villach Alps (Graschlitzenberg). At the top of the road is a view of the Julian Alps. It then runs through the valley of the Lower Gail and **Federaun** (566m) with ruins of a very old fortress whose tower rises just above the road.

A Recommended Hotel

Warmbad Villach: ★★ Kurhotel Warmbad Villach.

A little further on, at **Riegersdorf,** *the road forms a fork: to the left it leads (6.8 km) to the* **Wurzen Pass** *(1,071m), on the Austro-Yugoslav frontier (steep climbs, up to 1 : 4), 90 km from Ljubljana. Straight on, it leads first to Arnoldstein (581m), the main marshalling yard for the Carinthian timber industry. On left, ruins of fortress and an old tower. On right of road, the plant of the Mining Union of Bleiberg (lead mines). 2 km after Arnoldstein there is a dangerous turning, running beneath the railway line.* **Thörl-Maglern** *(636m), on Austro-Italian frontier, 8 km from Tarvisio. Ö.A.M.T.C. kiosk alongside the Customs post. Currency exchange, petrol pump.*

2 km before Riegersdorf, a road to the east leads via Mallestig to:

FAAK AM SEE ★

(565m). Watering-place opposite an island which is reached by motor-boat, and on which stands the Inselhotel with a beautiful beach on the **Faaker See.** A picturesque setting at the foot of the Mittagskogel (2,143m). This beautiful blue-green lake is 2 km long, 1.7 km wide and surrounded by forests. The temperature of the lake waters sometimes reaches 75° F.

Via **Egg** (565m), watering-place on the north-east shore of the Lake Faak, to Dobrollach (586m). Then turn right towards **Rosegg** (483m), small holiday resort of 650 inhabitants. Not far away is the castle of the Prince of Liechtenstein, a zoo, and the ruins of the Ras fortress (10th century). Follow the road to the north and turn right shortly before rejoining national Highway 17. Through Selpritsch and Augsdorf to the **Wörther See,** the biggest and most popular lake in Carinthia (16.6 km long and 1.6 km wide). Its high temperature (up to 82° F. in summer) allows a bathing season lasting from May to October.

Some Recommended Hotels

Egg am Faaker See: ★ Strandhotel Aschgan.

Faak am See: ** Inselhotel.

★ DELLACH

3 km

(458m). Watering-place opposite Pörtschach, on the other shore of the lake. Here is the finest golf-course in Austria, 2,830m long, nine holes. International tournament in August. Still along the lake shore, past the Island of the Capucines, to:

★ MARIA WÖRTH

N. 100 21 km

(pop. 1,400 - 458m). Picturesque watering-place on a peninsula in the loveliest part of the lake, which here is only 646m wide, with a Gothic-style church built at the end of the 9th century. Also visit the **Rosenkranzkirche**, with its 12th-century Roman frescoes and cemetery surrounding the church. The road climbs steeply and runs through **Reifnitz** (450m), a watering-place in a calm, peaceful setting. *A road to the south leads to Keutschach (508m), on the Keutschacher See; camping site on lakeside.* Through Maria Loretto on the Wörther See, the road reaches the great beach of Klagenfurt after crossing the Glanfurt. This beach is equipped with a water-ski jumping platform and the first water-ski-lift in Europe, in use since 1953. A closed-circuit cable above the water tows the water-skier like a ski-lift, a more economical method than using a motor-boat and one which, in addition, can tow a great number of skiers at a time. The road rejoins the National Highway No. 17 which crosses the canal linking Klagenfurt to the Wörther See. The road runs round the lake and through **Krumpendorf** (474m), watering-place with camping-site, and Pritschitz.

A Recommended Hotel

Maria Wörth: ★ Seehotel Pirker.

★ PÖRTSCHACH AM WÖRTHERSEE

(446m). Famous health resort and watering-place on a wide peninsula, with beautiful grounds. Beautiful view over the lake and the Karawanken mountains. Lake festivals, international regattas, water ski-ing, international tennis and dancing contests. Boat service between Pörtschach and Dellach, with its fine golf-course on the opposite shore. Tourist Information Bureau (Kurdirektion) in the centre of the resort.

The road runs along the northern shore of the lake to Velden am Wörthersee.

N. 17 9 km ★

Some Recommended Hotels

Pörtschach: ⋆⋆ Strandhotel Europa. ⋆ Hotel-Pension Haus Columbia.

VELDEN AM WÖRTHERSEE ★

(470 m). Fashionable international watering-place, the most popular resort in Carinthia. Numerous sporting and public displays throughout the season: international tennis and dance competitions, water-ski contests. At end-July and in early August the Inter-national Sporting Weeks of the Wörther See are held at Velden. Casino (roulette and baccara). Beautiful lake-side promenade. Travel agency and Tourist Information Bureau (Kurdirektion) in the centre of the resort. Camping site.

N. 17 17 km ★

Some Recommended Hotels

Velden am Wörthersee: ⋆⋆ Hotel Excelsior. ⋆ Hotel Bacherlwirt.

The road climbs now through the woods towards **Wernberg** (610 m) with its castle and, in the rear, the Mittagskogel (2,143 m). It runs gently down again towards **Seebach.** To the south is the little Magdalenensee. On right, the road to the Ossiacher See. The road runs through the Seebach-graben and runs beneath the railway line before coming, down the Klagenfurter Strasse, into

VILLACH ★

VILLACH-SALZBURG

LENGTH OF ITINERARY: 201 KM.

The Tauern road linking Spittal in Carinthia to Radstadt in Salzburg is not recommended for motorists who dislike mountain roads and mountain passes. Those who do, however, will find

this picturesque road very charming. It is rather wide (5m), and has been used by traders since pre-Roman times. The Romans widened the existing path which became one of the major commercial highways of the Middle Ages. It is the most direct route between Villach and Salzburg (200 km), the road through the Gastein Valley necessitating transhipment of the car by railway through the Tauern Tunnel, and the Grossglockner road being impassable for a great part of the year.

On leaving Spittal for the north, the Tauern road first takes the Liesertal, then part of the Pöllatal, before arriving at the Katschberg, boundary between Carinthia and Salzburg province. Once the Katschberg is passed, the road runs through the Lungau, a kind of high plateau with a wealth of larch forests, between the Niedere Tauern and the Gurktal Alps. Then comes the Radstädter Tauern. At Radstadt the motorist will find roads leading in all directions: north-west to Salzburg and the Salzkammergut; west to Zell-am-See and Innsbruck; east, through the Enns Valley, to Linz and Vienna.

PRINCIPAL SIGHTS

CHURCHES: St Egide at St Michael im Lungau; St Leonhard at Tamsweg. CASTLES of: Gmünd; Moosham. MUSEUM of Lungau in Moosham Castle. VIEW: Alpenfriedhof der Namenlosen.

VILLACH ★

Leave this town by the Tiroler Strasse, following in the reverse direction the Spittal-Villach route described in *itinerary No. 10*. At Spittal, take the road running northwards, opposite Porcia Castle, which runs through the romantic valley of the Lieser. Via Seebach, Lieserhofen, and the little hydro-mineral resort of Trebesing to

N. 120 and N. 99   52 km

GMÜND ★

(pop. 1,900 - 742m). Small town of medieval appearance in a picturesque setting surrounded by a fortified enclosure with four town gates. Camping site. South-west of Gmünd is the old castle, almost entirely in ruins, which belonged to Leonhard of Keutschach. A new castle was built in the

N. 99   22 km

northern part of the town by Count Lodron
in the 17th century. At the approach to
Gmünd the road forks towards Maltatal
(12 km), narrow and difficult, but very
picturesque. After 4 km, **Dornbach** with it
castle and ruined Gothic church; then **Malta**
(838m) with the ruined Kronegg Castle
View of the Hochalpenspitze (3,355m). At the end of the
road, along which can be seen more than 30 waterfalls,
is the **Pflüglhof,** centre for climbs and walks, including
that of the Blauer Trumpf which is rated one of the most
beautiful to be made in the Alps. Camping site at Pflüglhof
Through Eisentratten (802m) and Leoben (862m) to
Kremsbrücke (952m). Fork to the right of a narrow road
(12 km) towards **Innerkrems** (1,467m) in one of the loveliest
winter-sports regions in Carinthia, and base for climbs of
the Königstuhl (2,331m). The road climbs even more
steeply (1 : 5), passing by the Church of Sankt-Nikolai
on left, and runs through the gateway of the ruined fortress
of Rauchenkatsch (12th century). Through **Rennweg**
(1,140m), holiday resort and winter-sports centre, to the
Katschberghöhe.

A Recommended Hotel

Gmünd: ⋆ Gasthof Sorgo.

⋆ KATSCHBERGHÖHE

(1,641m). Winter-sports centre, boundary between Carinthia and the country of Salzburg. Camping site. In the
local inn is an interesting Golden Book which also contains
invaluable hints concerning the road of the Tauern. The
northern slope of the Katschberg, which had gradients of
1 : 4, now follows a new path which never exceeds 1 : 7
and by which descent is made to the Mur Valley, to
Sankt-Michael im Lungau (1,068m), little old town of
2,300 inhabitants. On the slopes is the very ancient **Church
of St Egide,** which is mentioned in MSS dating from 1278.
On right, 6 km further on, is **Moosham Castle** with the
magnificent art collection of Count Wilczek and in which
is also housed the **Museum of Lungau,** the name of the region
lying between the Gurktal Alps (to the south) and the
Niedere Tauern (to the north).

N. 99 39 km

A Recommended Hotel

Katschberghöhe: ★ Alpengasthof Katschberghöhe.

MAUTERNDORF ★

(1,110m). Holiday resort and winter-sports
resort with picturesque old houses and a
restored castle. Thermal Institute of Kelchs-
brunn, radio-active sulphur spring. Shooting. By Road No. 96 to the right, 12 km,
to **Tamsweg** (1,021m). **St Leonard's Church**
with ten famous stained-glass windows,
dating from 1400. In this little-known region, old customs
are retained in the pure original form. The best-known are:
the Procession of Samson, the Unifying, and the popular
shoots of Preber (north-east of Tamsweg). A little road
to the north, 7 km, leads to **Lessach**, a hamlet where several
of Napoleon's guards, having lost contact with the army,
stopped in 1808 and decided to settle down. Their des-
cendants piously preserve the uniforms and banners of
their ancestors.

*Road No. 96 continues in an easterly direction and rejoins, after
54 km, Scheifling on the No. 9 secondary itinerary. Via* **Predlitz,**
from which a good road runs south to **Turracher Höhe,** *holiday
resort and winter-sports centre. After Predlitz, the road becomes
poor and motorists are advised not to use it. After 25 km,* **Murau**
*(819m), holiday resort and winter-sports centre on the Mur,
dominated by the Stolzalpe. 13th-century church and Obermurau
Castle (17th century).*

At **Tweng** (1,235m) beginning of the steep climb (1 : 5)
up to the pass of the Radstädter Tauern (1,738m), where
there are several up-to-date mountain
hotels. Well-equipped winter-sports and
holiday resort near several little mountain
lakes: Grünwaldsee, Krummschnabelsee,
Hundsfeldsee, and Wildsee. Steep descent
(1 : 5) to the "Alpine Cemetery of the
Unknown Dead" (**Alpenfriedhof der Namenlosen). Obertauern** (1,649m), holiday and winter-
sports resort, and through a wooded gorge along traces of
the old Roman road, to Untertauern (1,009m) and to
Radstadt.

A Recommended Hotel

Turracher Höhe: ★★ Hotel Hochschober.

★ **RADSTADT**

(pop. 3,600 – 856m), old town at the junction of the Taurach and the Enns, standing on a rock surrounded by a fortified enclosure. Shooting and fishing. Högger ski-lift (856m) up the Königslehen (1,300m) The Tauern road ends at Radstadt, where it rejoins the road through the Enns Valley Towards the right, the latter road reaches (56 km) **Steinach** *(see itinerary No. 6),* via **Schladming** (745m), old mining town, holiday resort and winter-sports centre which is very popular.

A Recommended Hotel

Radstadt: ★ Gasthof Haberstatter.

Leave Radstadt in a westerly direction. Via **Hüttau,** to rejoin national highway No. 159, between Bischofshofen and Werfen. Follow the final stage of *secondary itinerary No. 3:* Wörgl–Salzburg, as far as:

★ **SALZBURG**

N. 112 and N. 159   73 km

FRONTIER POSTS

(All open 24 hours a day)

BETWEEN AUSTRIA AND GERMANY

Place of Departure	Austrian Customs	German customs	Destination
Schärding	Mariahilf	Passau	Passau
Schärding	Schärding	Neuhaus	Neuhaus
Braunau	Simbach-Innsbrücke	Simbach	Simbach
Salzburg	Saalbrücke	Freilassing	Freilassing
Salzburg	Walserberg–Bundesstrasse	Schwarzbachstrasse	Bad Reichenhall
Salzburg	Walserberg–Autobahn	Schwarzbachstrasse	Bad Reichenhall
Salzburg	Hangendenstein	Schellenberg	Berchtesgaden
Lofer	Steinpass	Steinpass	Bad Reichenhall
Kufstein	Kiefersfelden	Kiefersfelden	Kiefersfelden
Thiersee	Ursprung	Schöffau	Bayrisch-Zell
Jenbach	Achental	Stuben	Tegernsee
Seefeld	Scharnitz	Mittenwald	Mittenwald
Ehrwald	Ehrwald	Griessen	Garmisch
Reutte	Pinswang	Füssen	Füssen
Reutte	Vilsrain	Pfronten-Steinach	Kempten
Tannheim	Schattwald	Oberjoch	Sonthofen
Bregenz	Unterhochsteg	Lindau	Lindau

BETWEEN AUSTRIA AND SWITZERLAND

Place of Departure	Austrian Customs	Swiss Customs	Destination
Bregenz	Gaissau	Rheineck	Rorschach
Bregenz	Höchst	St Margrethen	St Gallen
Feldkirch	Tisis	Buchs (S.G.)	Buchs
Landeck	Schalklhof	Martina	Schuls

BETWEEN AUSTRIA AND ITALY

Place of Departure	Austrian Customs	Italian Customs	Destination
Landeck	Nauders	Resia	Merano
Innsbruck	Brenner	Brennero	Sterzing
Sillian	Arnbach	San Candido	Innichen
Kötschach Mauthen	Plöckenpass	Monte Croce Carnico	Tolmezzo
Villach	Thörl-Maglern	Cocau	Tarvisio

BETWEEN AUSTRIA AND YUGOSLAVIA

Place of Departure	Austrian Customs	Yugoslavian Customs	Destination
Riegersdorf	Wurzenpass	Jezersko	Krainburg
Klagenfurt	Loiblpass	Ljubelj	Ljubljana
Bad Vellach	Seeberg	Podkoren	Ljubljana
Völkermarkt	Lavamünd	Dravograd	Unter Drauburg
Graz	Spielfeld	Sentilj	Marburg

CELEBRITIES OF YESTERDAY

EARLY AND MIDDLE AGES

After the Roman era and the period of the great invasions, the history of Austria begins in the 9th century. **Charlemagne,** by founding in 803 the Ostmark (Eastern Marches), in fact gave birth to Austria. Its conversion to Christianity dates approximately from this period. **Othon II,** king of Germany, presented the Ostmark in 976 to the margrave **Leopold I** (976-994), founder of the House of Babenberg. In 996 we first find mention of "Ostarrichi", from which Oesterreich is derived. **Leopold III,** the Holy (1095-1136), became the patron saint of Austria; his reign saw the first crusade to liberate the Holy Land. In 1262 the King of Germany made a gift of the Babenberg provinces to King **Ottokar II** of Bohemia; but in 1273 **Rudolph I** of the House of Habsburg became Emperor of Germany, and soon afterwards began a mortal struggle with King Ottokar, who was vanquished in 1278. **Albert I,** son of Rudolph I, became Duke of Austria (1283-1298), and in 1298 he became Emperor of Germany.

Architecture. In 690, **St Rupert** founded the Benedictine St Peter's Abbey at Salzburg. **Jacobus Parisiensis** (14th century), architect and sculptor, helped to reconstruct the Franciscan brothers' church in Vienna.

Literature. Othon of Babenberg, Bishop of Freising, wrote in 1158 his *Universal History*. The greatest poet of the German tongue was **Walter von der Vogelweide** (1176-1230 approx.).

THE RENAISSANCE (1400-1600)

At the death of **Sigismond of Luxemburg** (1437) the crown of the Holy Roman German Empire passed to his son-in-law **Albert V** of Habsburg, Duke of Austria (1398-1439). **Frederick III,** Duke of Austria (1415-1493) was elected Roman Emperor and strove to reinforce the power of Austria. **Maximilian I** (1459-1519), son of Frederick, strengthened the power and fortunes of the House of Habsburg, into whose patrimony fell the thrones of Spain,

Rudolph I

Maximilian I

Hungary, and Bohemia. In 1517 the German Martin Luther nailed his declaration to the doorway of the church of Wittenberg, signalling the start of the Reformation.

Charles V (1500-1558), grandson of Maximilian I, inherited Austria on the death of the latter in 1519. By the Treaty of Brussels he ceded Austria in 1522 to his brother Ferdinand, who also inherited Hungarian and Bohemian lands on the death of Louis II of Hungary and Bohemia (1526). The Order of Jesuits, founded in 1540, was established in Austria in 1551 and gave the signal for the counter-Reformation.

Art, Culture. Michael Pacher, painter and sculptor (1440-1498), created in the Salzkammergut, at St Wolfgang's church, the best-known Austrian altar triptych. Other notable artists were **Johannes von Villach, Jakob Kaschauer,** and **Jorg Külderer.** Emperor Maximilian I, a generous patron of the arts, wrote works in verse and prose, and lent his collection of manuscripts to **Konrad Celtis** (1459-1508) and **Cuspinian** (Johann Speishammer, 1473-1529), of Vienna University.

17th CENTURY

Mathias I (1612-1619) died at the beginning of the Thirty Years War. **Ferdinand II** (1619-1637) was a militant Catholic and protector of the order of Jesuits. **Albrecht von Wallenstein** (1583-1634), nominated chief general of the imperial army in 1625, undertook also the creation of an imperial fleet. **Ferdinand III** (1608-1657), more tolerant than his father, concluded the Peace of Westphalia which ended the Thirty Years War with considerable gains for the Protestant powers. In the reign of **Leopold I** (1640-1705) the Turkish empire undertook, as in 1529, the siege of Vienna in 1683. Count **Starhemberg** (1638-1701) and Andreas Liebenberg, burgomaster of Vienna, defended the city and secured its

Albrecht von Wallenstein

liberation after the Battle of Kahlenberg (12th September, 1683). Prince **Charles V of Lorraine** (1643-1690) turned defence into attack, and after 150 years of Turkish domination Hungary was also liberated. Victory against the Turks was sealed in 1699 by the Peace of Carlowitz.

Charles VI

Literature. Wolf Helmhard von Hohberg (1612-1688) was the leading poet; and **Abraham a Santa-Clara** (Hans Ulrich Megerle, 1644-1709), Augustine monk, was the most famous preacher of his epoch.

Fine Arts. The Schwanthaler and **Lederwasch** families formed dynasties of artists for nearly 200 years. **Bassi Santino** (1663-1736) and **André Pozzo** (1642-1709) also were notable painters.

Science. Johannes Kepler (1571-1630), astronomer, discovered the laws of planetary motion.

Theatre. Nicolaus Avancinus (1612-1686) was the greatest Jesuit dramatic author. **Simon Rettenbacher** (1634-1706) founded the Austrian Benedictine Theatre.

18th CENTURY

In 1700 the Spanish branch of the House of Habsburg died out. Neither the Emperor **Joseph I** (1678-1711) nor the **Emperor Charles VI** (1685-1740) had a male heir, and in 1713 the succession fell to the female Austrian branch. Prince **Francis I of Lorraine** (1708-1765), by his marriage in 1736, became the prince consort of **Maria-Theresia** (1717-1780), who ascended the throne

Joseph Haydn

in 1740. She instituted important reforms and stamped her personality on a whole epoch. Vencel Anton, Count **Kaunitz-Rittberg** (1711-1794) was the greatest Austrian statesman of his century. Emperor **Joseph II** (1741-1790), son and successor of Maria-Theresia, was the first reigning prince from the House of Habsburg-Lorraine. He was succeeded by **Francis II** (1768-1835).

Literature. Leading authors were **Michael**

Metternich

Denis (1729-1800) and **Aloïs Blumauer** (1755-1798), poets; **Cornelius Hermann von Ayrenhoff** (1733-1819), and **Paul Weidmann** (1744-1810), dramatists.

Painting. Noteworthy painters of frescoes in churches and castles were **Daniel Gran** (1694-1754), **Johann Michael Rottmayr** (1654-1730), and **Anton Franz Maulpertsch** (1724-1786). Many religious pictures were painted by Martin Johann Schmidt (**Kremser-Schmidt,** 1718-1801).

Sculpture. **Raphael Donner** (1693-1741); **Balthasar Moll** (1717-1785).

Architecture. **Johann Bernhard Fischer von Erlach** (1656-1723), **Lucas von Hildebrandt** (1668-1745), **Jacob Prandtauer** (1660-1720), and **Nicolaus Pacassi** (1716-1796).

Music. **Christoph Willibald Gluck** (1714-1787) began his career in Vienna, by now the centre of musical art. **Joseph Haydn** (1732-1809), prolific composer of symphonies, was also the author of the Austrian national anthem. **Wolfgang Amadeus Mozart** (1756-1792) was born in Salzburg. His symphonies and chamber music are of unforgettable beauty; the operas and the magnificent *Requiem* always attract audiences.

Science. **Joseph Sonnenfels** (1732-1801), juridical and political science; **Gerhard van Svieten** (1700-1772), public hygiene and teaching reform; **Nikolaus Joseph von Jacquin** (1727-1817), great botanist.

19th CENTURY

Francis II (1768-1835) took the title of Emperor of Austria. He gave his daughter Marie-Louise in marriage to Napoleon I, and later declared war on him. Prince Clement Lothaire **Metternich** (1773-1859) brought about the European coalition against Napoleon which defeated the Grand Army. Emperor **Francis-Joseph I** (1830-1916) came to the throne in 1848 and, with the aid of Hungarian statesmen, he created in

Francis-Joseph I

1867 the Austro-Hungarian Empire, over which he ruled as constitutional monarch.

Literature. **Franz Grillparzer** (1791-1872), dramatist, is considered the greatest Austrian author. Other writers of the period included **Ferdinand Raimund** (1790-1836) and **Johann Nestroy** (1801-1862), playwrights; **Nikolaus Lenau** (1802-1850), **Anastasius Grün** (real name, Alexander Count Auersperg, 1806-1876), **Ferdinand von**

Franz Schubert

Saar (1833-1906), **Peter Rosegger** (1843-1918), and **Mary, Baroness Ebner-Eschenbach** (1830-1916), poets and novelists.

Fine Arts. Leading painters were **Peter Fendi** (1776-1842), **Joseph Danhauser** (1805-1845), **Friedrich Amerling** (1803-1887), **Ferdinand Georg Waldmüller** (1793-1865), **Moritz von Schwind** (1804-1871), **Rudolf von Alt** (1812-1905), **Franz von Defregger** (1835-1921), and **Hans Makart** (1840-1884). The sculptors included **Anton Fernkorn** (1813-1878), **Caspar Zumbusch** (1830-1915), and **Victor Tilgner** (1844-1896). Leading architects were **Heinrich Ferstel** (1828-1883), and **Eduard Hasenauer** (1833-1894).

Music. **Ludwig van Beethoven.** (1770-1827) was born in Germany but lived in Vienna from the age of 18. His nine great symphonies, the concertos and chamber music, and other works figure among the cultural treasures of mankind. **Franz Schubert** (1797-1828) enchants music-lovers with his *Lieder*. Mention must also be made of **Johannes Brahms** (b. 1833 in Germany; d. 1897 in Vienna) and **Anton Bruckner** (1824-1896); and of the charming waltzes

of **Joseph Lanner** (1802-1843) and of the two **Johann Strausses** (1804-1849; 1825-1899). **Hans Richter** (1843-1916), distinguished interpreter of Wagner, conducted many times at Bayreuth.

Science. *Medicine.* **Karl Rokitanszky** (1804-1878), pathologist; **Joseph Skoda** (1805-1881), internal maladies; **Joseph Hyrtl** (1811-1894), anatomist; **Theodor Billroth** (1829-1894), surgeon; **Philipp Semmelweis** (1818-1865), pioneer of antiseptic methods. **Gregor Mendel**

Gregor Mendel

(1822-1894), botanist, discovered the laws of heredity. *Economics*. **Popper-Lynkaeus** (1838-1931), **Adolf Menger** (1841-1905), and **Böhm Bawerk** (1851-1914). Inventors included **Madersperger** (sewing-machine, 1815); **Joseph Ressel** (screw-steamer, 1829); **Mitterhofer** (typewriter, 1864).

CELEBRITIES OF TODAY

At the beginning of the century, Archduke **Francis Ferdinand** (1863-1914), heir-apparent to the throne, opposed the traditional policy of his uncle, especially on the question of the nationalities, in which his federalist sympathies were averse to the rigid centralism of Francis-Joseph. In 1914, the Archduke and his wife were assassinated at Sarajevo, in Bosnia, this being the spark that lit the flames of the First World War. Coming to the throne in 1916, Emperor **Charles I** (1887-1922) would have liked to conclude a separate peace and to achive a happy solution of the nationalities problem; but only after the 1918 *débacle* was this problem resolved.

After the collapse of the Austro-Hungarian Empire, nine provinces were united in a democratic republic. From 1919, two political parties dominated the situation: Christian Socialists and Social Democrats. **Karl Seitz** (1869-1950), Social Democrat M.P., was the first President of the Republic; **Karl Renner** (1870-1950), also a Social Democrat, the first federal Chancellor.

The early Social Democrat era gave way to that of the Christian Socialists, and three great political leaders emerged: **Ignaz Seipel** (1876-1932) was, except for a brief interval, Chancellor of Austria from 1922 until his death. **Engelbert Dollfuss** (1892-1934), became Chancellor at a time when party antagonisms had reached an acute phase, and fell victim to an assassination plotted by the Nazis at the Vienna Chancellery. **Kurt von Schuschnigg** (b. 1897) tried to settle the dispute with the Reich by the treaty of July 1936. This, however only delayed, but could not avoid, the *Anschluss* carried out in March 1938. Austria was thus annexed by the Reich until the liberation of April 1945.

The Socialist and Popular parties formed   *Kurt von Schuschnigg*

and maintain a coalition government. Since the spring of 1945, Austria has been occupied by the four Powers—France, Britain, the U.S.A., and Soviet Russia. Re-adopting the 1920 Constitution, Austria remained a republic, Karl Renner occupying the Presidential chair (1945-1950). He was succeeded by **Theodor Körner**. Leopold Figl was Chancellor from 1945 to March 1953, when he was replaced by **Julius Raab**.

Theodor Körner

Literature. **Rainer Maria Rilke** (1875-1926), born in Prague, became one of the greatest poets of the German language *(Book of Images* etc.). Other leading authors of poems, plays, and novels were **Hugo von Hofmannsthal** (1874-1929), **Hermann Bahr** (1863-1934), **Anton Wildgans** (1881-1932), **Arthur Schnitzler** (1862-1931), **Franz Werfel** (1890-1945) *(The Song of Bernadette)*, **Stefan Zweig** (1881-1942), **Jakob Wassermann** (1873-1933), **Georg Trakl** (1887-1914), **Rudolf Brunngraber**, **Hermann Broch** (1886-1951), **Ernst Lothar**, **Karl-Heinrich Waggerl**, **Fritz Habeck**, **Max Brod**, **Enrica Handel Mazetti**, **Egon Caesar Count Corti**, **Frank Thiess**, **Max Mell**, **Richard Billinger**, **Ferdinand Bruckner**, **Franz Theodor Csokor**, **Alexander Lernet-Holenia**, **Fritz Hochwälder**, **Paula Preradovic** (1887-1951), **Josef Weinheber** (1892-1945), **Rudolf Henz**, and **Felix Braun**. **Franz Kafka** (1883-1924) has greatly influenced modern literature by his novels, tales, and *Diary*.

Painting. **Gustav Klimt** (1862-1918) was, with his brother, the decorative artist of Vienna theatres, and also painted landscapes

and portraits. **Albin Egger-Lienz** (1868-1925) depicted the daily life of Tyrolean peasants. Other notable painters are **Alfred Kubin**, **Ludwig Heinrich Jungnickel**, **Anton Feistauer**, **Egon Schiele** (1890-1918), **Oskar Kokoschka**, **Herbert Boeckl**, **Albert Paris Gütersloh**.

Sculpture. **Josef Hanak** (1875-1934), **Augustin Ambrosi**, and **Josef Thorak** (1889-1952) rank among the leading sculptors. **Fritz Wotruba** directs the

Rainer Maria Rilke

Professional School of Sculpture and

Gustav Klimt

the "Wuerthle" Gallery in Vienna; his *Young Giant* is famous.

Architecture. Otto Wagner (1841-1918), **Adolf Loos** (1870-1933), **Josef Hoffmann, Clemens Holzmeister, Aloïs Welzenbacher,** amd **Siegfried Theiss** have been responsible for many important buildings.

Music. Gustav Mahler (1860-1911), an outstanding conductor, is best known for his symphonies and *The Song of the Earth*. **Richard Strauss** (1864-1949) was also director of the Vienna Opera, and composed some of his masterpieces at Salzburg; his most popular works now are the symphonic poems. Other important composers are **Franz Schmidt** (1874-1939), **Arnold Schönberg** (1874-1951), **Alban Berg** and **Gottfried von Einem**; also **Ernest Krenek,** composer and professor at Los Angeles. **Franz Lehar** (1870-1951) and **Oscar Strauss** wrote charming light operas. **Ralph Benatzky** composed the famous operetta *White Horse Inn*.

Two remarkable orchestras are the Philharmonic Orchestra of Vienna and the Vienna Symphony Orchestra. Several conductors, Austrian born or Austrian by adoption, have won international fame. They include **Franz Schalk** (1863-1931), **Clemens Krauss** (1893-1954), **Bruno Walter, Herbert Karajan, Karl Böhm, Bernhard Paumgartner, Josef Krips,** and **Rudolf Moralt.**

Science. The Nobel Prize has been awarded to many Austrian scientists. *Physics:* **Erwin Schrödinger,** contributor to the development of the atomic theory; **Viktor Franz Hess,** investigator of cosmic rays; **Hans Thirring,** famous atomic research worker; **Wolfgang Pauli,** research into the characteristics of the electron. *Chemistry:* **Fritz Pregl** (1869-1930), micro-chemical analysis; **Richard Kuhn,** biochemist. *Medicine:* **Julius Wagner-Jauregg** (1857-1940), study of cerebral paralysis; **Karl Landsteiner** (1868-1943), discoverer of the blood groups; **Otto Löwi,** treatment of nervous

Oskar Kokoschka

diseases; **Lauda,** internal medicine; also the surgeons **Eiselsberg,** (1860-1939), **Hochenegg, Schrönbauer,** and **Böhler.** It was in Vienna that **Sigmund Freud** (1856-1939) probed the mysteries of the human mind and of the forces directing it. *Economics:* **Friedrich von Wieser** (1851-1926); **Gottfried Haberler,** professor at Harvard University; **Friedrich August Hayek,** who teaches at the London School of Economics.

Gustav Mahler

Technology. Robert Lieben (1878-1913) cathode ray tubes; **Kaplan,** the turbine; **Auer-Welsbach** (1858-1929), the incandescent gas mantle and Osram electric bulb; **Ferdinand Porsche,** car builder; **Franz Wallack,** builder of the highest motor-road in Europe, the Grossglockner.

Theatre. Max Reinhardt (1873-1943), one of the greatest stage managers of the century, also founded a theatrical school that bears his name. Other well known producers are **Josef Gielen, Berthold Viertel, Ernst Lothar, Oscar Fritz Schuh, Adolf Rott, Rudolf Steinböck, Leon Epp,** and **Hubert Marischka.**

Founder of the Thimig dynasty of actors was **Hugo Thimig,** whose successors were **Helena Thimig,** widow of Reinhardt, and his two sons **Hermann** and **Hans. Hedwig Bleitbreu** and **Maria Eis** were outstanding actresses; also worthy of mention are **Käthe Dorsch, Adrienne Gessner, Else Wohlgemuth, Hilde Mikulicz, Judith Holzmeister, Käthe Gold, Anne-Marie Düringer, Inge Konradi, Suzanne Almassy, Erna Mangold, Lotte Lang,** and **Johanna Matz.** Actors include **Raoul Aslan, Edwald Basler, Otto**

Sigmund Freud

Tressler, Werner Krauss, Ernst Deutsch, Albin Skoda, Fred Hennings, Gustav Waldau, Oskar Werner, Curd Jürgens, Fred Liewehr, O. W. Fischer, Karl Skraup, Hans Jaray, Erik Frey, and **Hans Holt.**

Cinema. Among the best-known producers are: **Georg Wilhelm Pabst, Willy Forst, Hubert** and **Ernst Marischka.** Actresses: **Paula Wessely,** best known abroad; **Marte Harell, Maria Andergast, Elfie Mayerhofer, Hilde Krahl.** Actors:

Hans Moser

The two **Hörbiger** brothers, **Attila** and **Paul**; the comedians **Hans Moser, Theo Lingen, Rudolf Carl** and **Fritz Imhoff**; the singer **Johannes Heesters**.

Dancing. Stars of the Vienna Opera are **Tony Birkmayer, Willy Fraenzel,** and **Julia Drapal. Grete Wiesenthal, Erika Hanka, Rosalia Chladek,** and **Cilly Wang** (who plays real pantomime) are also eminent.

Singing. Everyone remembers **Maria Jeritza, Lotte Lehmann, Richard Tauber**; and the Vienna Opera maintains its reputation with artistes of equal fame. Sopranos: **Sena Jurinac, Maria Reining, Ezther Rethy, Elisabeth Schwarzkopf, Irmgard Seefried,** and **Ljuba Welitsch.** Contraltos: **Elisabeth Höngen** and **Judith Hellwig.** Tenors: **Anton Dermota, Max Lorenz, Julius Patzak, Helge Roswaenge.** Baritones: **Erik Kunz, Paul Schoeffler.** Bass: **Herbert Alsen, Ludwig Weber.**

Sport. *Football:* The leading Austrian teams: Austria, Rapid, and Vienna. *Tennis:* **Fred Huber, Hans Redl, Gustav Specht** (men); **Hella Strecker, Liesl Broz-Fischer** (women). *Swimming:* **Koppelstädter, Steinwender** (men); **Ali Pascher-Staudinger** (woman). *Javelin:* **Herma Bauma** (Olympic Gold Medal, 1948). *Motorcycling* (speedway): the brothers **Killmayer, Fritz Dirtl.** *Table Tennis:* **Wertl** and **Pritzi.** *Skating:* **Helmuth Seibt.** *Foils* (women **Ellen Müller-Preiss.** *Horse-riding:* Colonel **Podhajsky** head of the famous "Spanische Reitschule" (Spanish School of Riding). *Ski-ing:* **Sepp Bradl** (world ski-jumping champion), **Othmar Schneider, Toni Spiess, Egon Schöpf. Christl Pravda, Andreas Molterer, Walter Schuster,** and **Martin Strolz** (men). **Trude Jochum-Beiser, Dagmar Rom, Erika Mahringer, Trude Klecker,** and **Rosl Seiler** (women).

Erika Mahringer

AUSTRIA IN FIGURES

POPULATION

Austria, with 6,934,000 inhabitants (density: 83 to the sq. km.), is the least populated of the Danubian States.

Vienna has 1,766,000 inhabitants (over 2 million in 1934), or 25 % of the total population; 4 other cities have over 100,000, and 13 cities have between 20,000 and 50,000. Communes of fewer than 2,000 inhabitants make up 34 % of the population. About 60,000 Slovenes live in Carinthia and 38,000 Croats in Burgenland.

There are 1,160 women per 1,000 men (in Vienna, 1,300).

Variation of the population

 1913: 6.76 million

 1937: 6.75 million

 1952: 6.9 million

Analysis by Sex and Age *(in thousands):*

Age	Men	Women	Total	Percentage
0-17	938	905	1,843	26.5
18-59	1,822	2,181	4,003	58
over 60	455	628	1,083	15.5

Marriage.— *Legal Age,* 21; *average age,* 25 for women, 28 for men. 1 divorce per 6 marriages.

Births and Deaths *(per 1,000 inhabitants):* Births, 14.8 (31.4 in 1901); deaths, 12.7 (22.2 in 1901); excess of births over deaths, 2.1 (9.2 in 1901).

18 % of births are illegitimate.

If the birth-rate has seriously declined (it is the lowest in the world), the death rate has also shown a reduction. Infant mortality : 61 per 1,000 (104 in 1930).

Losses and results of war (1939-1945) — Military : 150,000 dead and 117,000 missing. Civilian victims : 24,000. Injured : 120,000. Displaced persons, 313,000, mostly German-speaking.

White: 0 to 50 inhabitants to sq. km.
Light grey: 50 to 100 inhabitants to sq. km.
Dark grey: over 100 inhabitants to sq. km.

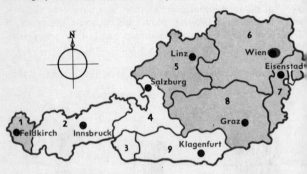

DENSITY OF POPULATION, BY REGIONS

1 Vorarlberg: 75 inhabitants per sq. km.   2 Tyrol and   3 East Tyrol: 34. 4 Salzburg: 46.   5 Upper Austria: 93.   6 Lower Austria: 68.   7 Burgenland: 70.   8 Styria: 68.   9 Carinthia: 50.   10 Vienna: 1,453.

MAJOR LOCALITIES OF AUSTRIA

Vienna: 1,760,784 inhabitants — Graz: 226,271 — Linz: 182,177 — Salzburg: 100,096 — Innsbruck: 95,000 — Klagenfurt: 65,800 — Sankt Pölten: 40,700 — Wels: 37,000 — Steyr: 39,000 — Leoben: 36,000 — Wiener Neustadt: 31,800 — Villach: 31,000 — Baden: 23,400 — Bregenz: 22,000 — Bad Ischl: 10,450 — Gmunden: 12,900 — Hall (Tyrol): 10,030 — Kitzbühel: 7,120 — Zell am See: 6,724 — Eisenstadt: 5,388 — Badgastein: 5,051.

AUSTRIA — PHYSICAL

Passes: 1 Hochtor (Grossglockner road): 2,505 m. 2 Arlberg: 1,802 m. 3 Reschenscheideck: 1,500 m. 4 Brenner: 1,371 m. 5 Loiblpass: 1,369 m. 6 Seeberg: 1,218 m. 7 Packsattel: 1,166 m. 8 Wurzenpass: 1,073 m. 9 Semmering: 985 m.

ČESKOSLOVENSKO

MAGYARORSZÁG

JUGOSLAVIJA

ITALIA

SUISSE

N

BODENSEE

ZUGSPITZE 2968 m.

WILDSPITZE 3774 m.

Inn

HOCHKÖNIG 2941 m.

HOHE TAUERN

GROSSGLOCKNER 3797 m.

NIEDERE TAUERN

Drau

Mur

DACHSTEIN 2995 m.

HALLSTÄTTERSEE

WOLFGANGSEE

MONDSEE

ZELLERSEE

ATTERSEE

TRAUNSEE

Enns

Salza

DONAU

350 km.

NEUSIEDLERSEE

SCHNEEBERG 2075 m.

MILLSTÄTTERSEE

OSSIACHERSEE

WÖRTHERSEE

WEISSENSEE

HOCHSTUHL 2238 m.

AGRICULTURE

Agricultural production on an average reaches only 75 % of the pre-war level, except for wine (115 %). Agriculture covered in 1950, 78 % of national food supplies (82 % in 1937). One person working in agriculture nourishes 5.

Division of land: Agricultural land, 50 %; Woods and forests, 37 %; Uncultivated, 13 %.

DIVISION OF AGRICULTURAL AREA

Arable	Orchards Vineyards Gardens	Grassland	Pasture and Mountain slopes

42 %   2 %   25 %   31 %

PRINCIPAL CROPS

Percentages of total production

Wheat, 2.7; rye, 2.6; barley, 2.0; oats, 2.4; maize, 1.1; potatoes, 17.3; sugar beet, 8.5; clover and hay, 57.4; fruit, 6.0. (Total production, 125 M.q.)

Rye is much-used for bread-making, while potatoes form the staple diet of the country population.

Wine production: 1.2 M hectolitres. White wine, 92 % of production. Wine areas, mainly lower Austria and Burgenland.

Cider: production of cider apples and pears, 3.54 M q.

MECHANIZATION OF AGRICULTURE (1949)

Tractors: 14,000 (1,780)
Sowers: 60,000 (40,700)
Mowers: 70,000 (41,500)

Austria ranks 10th in Europe for arable land available to tractors and 11th for consumption of fertilizer per ha.

LIVESTOCK *(in thousand head)*

Horses	276 (247)	Pigs........... 2,448 (2,868)
Cattle.........	2,284 (2,579)	Sheep 332 (315)
(inc. milking		Goats 310 (349)
cows)	1,129 —	

PRODUCTION FROM LIVESTOCK *(in 1,000 t)*

Meat..... 260 (276)	Butter	Cheese	Eggs	Milk (M hl)
	17.5	10.8	30	20.85
	(22)	(17)	(40)	(25.14)

DIVISION OF AGRICULTURAL PROPERTIES

Farmers		%	Area		%
Less than 5 ha.	213,000	49	476,000 ha.		6
5 — 20 ha.	158,000	36	1,692,000 ha.		22
20 — 100 ha.	158,000	14	2,070,000 ha.		27
over 100 ha.	6,300	1	3,515,000 ha.		45

95 % own their own farms. Salaried workers in agriculture total 206,000.

FORESTS

After Finland and Sweden, Austria is the most densely wooded country in Europe. Forests cover about 37 % of the total area (49 % in Styria and 44 % in Carinthia).

Wood output: 10.2 M st, including 3.1 of firewood; 106,000 quintals of tanning bark.

Commercial production: 7.4 M st (including 1.1 M st of firewood; 4.4 M st of workable timber; 1.4 M st of newsprint wood; 0.2 M st of pit-props, 80,000 st of cross-bars and 76,000 st of posts).

Export: 0.35 M st of rough timber; 2.46 M st of sawn wood (53,000 st of prefabricated houses, 66,000 st of pit timber, 3.17 sq. m. of plywood). There has been a steady increase in the export of Austrian transformed wood: 87 % (against 55 % pre-war). Wood and wood products represent 18 % (35 % if cellulose and paper are added) of the total exports of Austria. Timber is, in fact, a mainstay of the national economy.

Principal customers: Italy, Western Germany, France.

INDUSTRY

The major coal mines and metallurgical industries are nationalized. The index of total industrial output stands at 166.

Austria is the world's leading producer of magnesite and third European producer of petrol (after Soviet Russia and Rumania). The Austrian oilfields are now exploited by the Soviet authorities.

495,000 people are engaged in industry, including 70,700 employers.

MINERAL PRODUCTION

(Percentages of total weight)

Coal, 2.1; lignite, 56.7; iron ore 29.0; lead and zinc ore, 1.7; copper ore, 1.5; magnesite, 8.1; salt, 0.90.

In addition, petrol (estimated): 3 M t.

Austria relies on imports for almost all her coal requirements: 3.7 M t (2.66) and 0.98 M t of lignite. Her resources furnish only about 36 % of her solid fuel requirements. The mining industry employs 32,000 workers.

ELECTRIC POWER

Production: 7.38 Md of KwH for a power installation of 2.2 million KW.

About 75 % of production is of hydraulic origin; hydraulic resources (35 Md KWH per year) are, however, only slightly exploited.

Index of output (1938 = 100) is 312.

Annual consumption per inhabitant: 945 KWH.

METALLURGICAL PRODUCTION

Cast iron........... 1.17 M t (0.39)
Raw steel.......... 1.06 M t (0.65)
Other metal industries (in th t): aluminium: 26 (4.4); lead: 11.1 (12); copper: 6.4 (2.1). Index of metallurgical production (1938 = 100) is 195.

MECHANICAL INDUSTRIES

Buses and lorries: 2,795 (1,194) — Tractors: 7,063 (110) — Motor-cycles: 28,367 (7,564) — Trucks: 279 (345) — Cycles: 175,100 (149,300) — Agricultural machines: 20.4 th t (8.4).
Electrical industry. Bulbs: 31.8 million (11.5) — Radio Sets: 244,400 (127,500) — motors: 5,500 (2,300).

BUILDING MATERIALS

Cement, 1,47 M T (0.43); lime, 0.3 M T (0.07); bricks, 628 M (290 M); tiles, 101 M (60 M).
162,000 dwellings built since 1945.

CHEMICAL INDUSTRIES

Fertilizer 436 th t; soap and washing powders 40 th t (33); matches (boxes) 521 (200 M); rubber products: 20.4 th t.
Paper industry. Cellulose 273 th t (268); paper 261 th t (232); cardboard 68 th t (64).

TEXTILE INDUSTRIES

Cotton: Thread 21.8 th t (32.5); cloth 14.4 th t (13.0).
Wool: Thread 11.5 th t (13.5); cloth 7.6 th t (10.8).
Rayon: cloth 980 t.
Jute: thread 8.9 th t; cloth 7.0 th t.

Boots and shoes: Leather footwear, 4.98 M pairs (5.5); rubber, 2.5 M; others, 1.9 M.

FOOD INDUSTRIES AND TOBACCO

Food products: Flour 340 th t (650); farinaceous foods 22.1 th t (10); chocolate 11 th t (6.5); margarine, oil 32.4 th t (24.3); beer 3.05 M hl (2.7).

Tobacco: cigarettes 6.711 million (4,149); cigars 69 million (92); pipe tobacco 1.3 th t (3.0).

COMMERCE

INTERNAL TRADE

Trade is the realm of private enterprise. The co-operatives account for about 5 % of total business turnover.

Total expenditure on advertising is about 400 Md S.

Total turnover, 28 Md S., as follows *(percentage)*:

Foodstuffs, 54; Clothing, leather, 21; Furniture, 6; Household utensils, glassware, 4; Cosmetics, etc., 2; Tobacco, 7; Miscellaneous 6.

Number of commercial enterprises: about 100,000, employing 145,000 workers.

Index of price increases (1938 = 100):

> *Wholesale prices* 790
> (foodstuffs: 748, industrial products: 867)
> *Retail prices* 670

FOREIGN TRADE

Austrian exports cover only 69 % of imports (against 84 % prewar); the adverse trade balance is made up by Marshall Aid.

Development of Foreign Trade

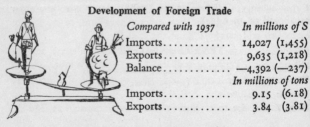

	Compared with 1937	In millions of S
Imports	14,027	(1,455)
Exports	9,635	(1,218)
Balance	—4,392	(—237)
		In millions of tons
Imports	9.15	(6.18)
Exports	3.84	(3.81)

Composition of imports and exports

Percentages of values	Imports	Exports
Raw materials	40 (36)	35 (26)
Foodstuffs	27 (29)	1 (4)
Semi-finished products	15 (15)	18 (24)
Finished products	18 (20)	46 (45)

Main suppliers: United States 22 % (wheat, fuel, machinery); Germany 18 % (fuel, machinery, finished products); Great Britain 12 % (raw materials, finished products); France 5 % (wheat, chemical products, finished products); Belgium-Luxemburg 5 % (finished products).

Main customers: Germany 15 % (finished products, wood, electric power); Italy 11 % (wood, finished products, newsprint); United States 6 % (finished products, chemical products); Holland 5 % (wood finished products).

Since the war, Austria has been cut off from the Danubian countries which were both her natural source of supply for food and raw materials and her customers. The Western countries, particularly the U.S.A. with Marshall Aid, have become Austria's principal suppliers.

TRANSPORT

As the Danube river highway has lost some of its importance, the railways and roads remain the major means of transport restricted only by geography and climate.

RAILWAYS. Length of rail network, 3,770 miles (6,026 km) including 1,000 miles (1,599 km) double-tracked and 315 miles (505 km) narrow-gauge. 750 miles (1,200 km) or 20 %, are electrified and carry 34 % of the traffic.

Equipment: 2,250 locomotives, including 296 electric and 80 self-propelled. Passenger coaches, 3,494; goods wagons 28,110.

Traffic: passengers, 123,716,000; freight, 39.1 M t. *Employees:* 75,800.

Budget. Receipts: 22 Md S; total expenditure: 23 Md S.

ROADS. Length of road network: national, 5,020 miles (8,035 km); provincial, 8,690 miles (13,906 km).

Traffic: private cars 59,400 (32,400); coaches 3,500 (2,400); lorries, 46,300 (13,800); total 109,200 (48,600); motor-cycles 152,900.

Motor-coach services: major lines, 10.09 M people; total carried, 135 M people.

RIVER TRANSPORT. Danubian traffic was reduced to a minimum following the new political situation created since the war in the Danube Valley, but now there is a daily service between Passau, Linz, and Vienna. Length of Danube in Austria: 350 km.

Fleet: 258 vessels, including 31 tugs (1936: 482 vessels, of which 65 were river boats).

Traffic: passengers: 370,000; freight: 15,000 t.

AIR TRANSPORT. Austria has no air fleet. There are 8 aerodromes which handle some 2,000 foreign civilian planes.

WORKING LIFE

The working week in principle is 48 hours, with a maximum of 44 hours for minors. Overtime is rated 25 % above ordinary rates.

Employees have the right to a paid holiday of 12 working days annually (minors, 24 days), and may get as much as 30 days according to length of service.

Trades Unions: Austria has one overall Trade Union with a membership of about 1,300,000, including 536,000 salaried employees and 755,000 wage-earners. Almost two-thirds of salaried people belong to the Trade Union, including about three-quarters of the men and more than 50 per cent of the women. At elections to the Chamber of Labour parties represented are: the Socialists, the Popular Party, the Independents (pro-German tendency), and the Communists.

DISTRIBUTION OF THE ACTIVE POPULATION

Total: 3,347,000 people, including 2,048,000 men and 1,299,000 women.

Division according to Situation

Employers and members of family working with them 35 %. *Workers* 65 %. Among the women who work there are 150,000 employers and 722,000 salaried workers, the remainder being members of the employers' family, for whom they work.

WAGES AND SALARIES

There is no legal minimum, but minimum rates can be established by collective bargaining.

Average weekly wage: Workman 272 S; woman worker 215 S; labourer 241 S.

Earnings of industrial employees in Vienna per month: Executives 3,000 to 4,400 S; middle standard 2,000 to 2,500 S; lower categories 1,500–1,600 S; typist (woman) 1,250 S.

SOCIAL SECURITY

Insured against sickness, 1,956,000; against accident, 1,468,000. Total cost of Social Security scheme (in one recent year): 4.4 Md S.

Health insurance: The insured person has the right to choose his own doctor from a list approved by the Fund (78 % of practitioners). Repayment of medical charges is 100 % for the insured person and his wife; for prescriptions and hospital charges, 100 % for the insured person and about 50 % for his wife. In the event of incapacitation, the allocation is 50 % of his salary.

Old age pensions: Retiring age is 65 for men and 60 for women. Pension is 544 S per month.

Family allowances: Allowances for children and tax relief.

Maternity Insurance: Medical care, benefits for insured women and wives of insured persons.

Insurance cost: for workers, 19 % to 21 % of salary, of which 8.5 % to 9.5 % is paid by the worker and 10.5 % to 11.5 % by the employer.

For employees, payments amount to only 16.7 % to 18.7 % of salary; they are contributed at a rate of about half each by employee and employer.

Unemployment. 117,300 workless assisted, but 177,000 seeking work, or 10 % of the wage-earning population. Unemployment benefit is, according to the category of worker, from 82 to 115 S a week, plus 30 S for the first dependant person and 11 S for the others. After a period of 12 to 30 weeks, the assistance granted varies from 87 % to 100 % of unemployment benefit.

STANDARD OF LIVING

After a heavy fall following the war, the standard of living has now reached the pre-war level.

AVERAGE FAMILY BUDGET

Food	Misc.	Clothing	Rent, Furniture, Heating
47 %	27 %	14 %	12 %

Amenities. There is: 1 motor-cycle, power-bicycle, scooter per 45 people; 1 car for every 63 people; 1 telephone for 16 people; 1 wireless set per 4.8 people.

COST OF LIVING INDEX (above 1938)

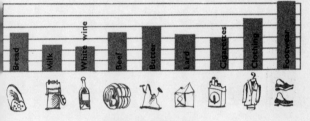

PUBLIC HEALTH

In Austria there are 147 public hospitals and 90 private hospitals, totalling together 51,000 beds (39,300 in 1936); 793,000 sick people were admitted (536,600 in 1936).

Anti-tuberculosis campaign. 28 sanatoria (5,400 beds) to which 27,100 patients were admitted. In addition, 122 dispensaries received 583,000 visits. Deaths from tuberculosis per 100,000 inhab.: 54.5 in one recent year. (1950.)

Mental and Nervous disorders: 17 centres (10,100 beds) admitted 46,420 persons.

Maternal and Child Care: There are 1,500 maternity and nursing centres for consultation; 292 children's and youth homes can cater for 22,240 children. Infant mortality rate per 1,000 children below one year of age: 61 (104 in 1930; 92 in 1937).

Medical corps: 12,000 doctors, including 2,230 specialists (or 1 for every 578 inhabitants); 2,200 dental surgeons (or 1 per 3,150 inhabitants); 1,600 chemists (or 1 per 4,300 inhabitants); 2,370 midwives.

Red Cross: 5,670 posts and 283,000 people treated.

Principal causes of death: circulatory diseases 23 %; cancer 17 %; nervous troubles 13 %; tuberculosis 4; accident 4.4 %.

RELIGION

Strength of the different religions

Catholics 6,170,000	89%
Protestants ... 429,000	6.2%
Freethinkers .. 264,000	3.8%
Old-Catholics 33,000	0.5%
Other sects... 22,600	0.3%
Jews 11,200	0.2%

The Churches of the different faiths are financed by a special tax (about 10 % of the total tax), paid by all the faithful.

CATHOLICS:

Ecclesiastical organization: 6 dioceses, including 2 archbishoprics, 1 Papal administration, 1 episcopacy, 1 abbey, 238 deaneries, 2,841 parishes. There are about 4,000 churches.

Clergy: 4,531 priests, including 14 bishops, among them 1 cardinal. 2,531 regular priests; 3,000 nuns; 300 convents. Great seminaries: 8.

Teaching: 4 State faculties of theology with 675 pupils.

Private secondary teaching: 35 schools with 7,800 pupils.

Private primary teaching: 27,200.

Religious teaching is a charge on the State.

Press: 3 principal weeklies with a total circulation of 120,000 copies. Total circulation of small weeklies: 1,550,000.

Principal pilgrimage: Mariazell, in Styria (500,000 pilgrims).

PROTESTANTS: Members of the Lutheran church in the proportion of 96 %, grouped in 143 parishes. The number of clergymen is 243, and that of the places of worship about 1,500.

Teaching: 1 State faculty of theology with 30 pupils. Primary teaching: 500 pupils.

OLD CATHOLICS: sect of German origin which refused to recognize the infallibility of the Pope in 1870: they number 17 priests and 12 parishes.

JEWS: 5 rabbis and 5 synagogues.

CULTURAL LIFE

EDUCATION

School attendance is compulsory from 6 to 14.

Public and private education include the *Gymnasium*, the *Realgymnasium* and the *Realschule*.

PRIMARY EDUCATION

Number of public schools ...	5,153
,, ,, teachers	35,629
,, ,, boy pupils	430,000
,, ,, girl pupils	427,000

SECONDARY EDUCATION

Number of schools	175
,, ,, teachers	2,033
,, ,, boy pupils	39,000
,, ,, girl ,, ...	22,000

HIGHER EDUCATION

This is shared between the Universities and the big Technical Schools.

Number of students
,, boys .... 15,500 } 19,663
,, girls 4,163

This total includes 1,000 foreign students.

Universities

There are 4 universities in Austria.

Number of professors	3,288
,, ,, male students	10,678
,, ,, girl students	4,012

Fine-Arts:

Academy of Painting 414 pupils
Other arts 316 pupils
The 6 principal Austrian museums are visited by about 366,000 annually.
Music: Academy of Music 1,037 pupils.

Big Technical Schools

Number of professors 2,595.

	Boys	Girls
Total number of pupils ...	4,822	151
Building	1,363	9
Architecture	626	67
Mechanics	2,020	5
Science and mathematics...	587	50
Natural Science	226	20

PUBLISHING

Press. 36 daily newspapers (of 6 to 8 pages), with a total circulation of about 1,800,000 copies (or 254 copies per 1,000 inhabitants). More than half the output is sold in Vienna.

Periodicals. 114 newspapers, including 47 weeklies.

Newsprint: annual consumption is 23,000 t. Two-thirds of newsprint production is for export.

Books. In one recent year, compared with 1937,

total number of titles published	3,962	(1,489)
Division by types:		
Belles-lettres.	1,468	(1,104)
Arts	208	(1,026)
Technical, Science	1,050	(587)
Economics, history	1,236	(1,071)
Translations	1,003	(—)

LIBRARIES

	Number	Volumes	No. of readers
National libraries	1	1,409,000	76,000
University libraries ...	3	2,157,000	114,000
Higher Study libs.....	11	1,091,000	196,000
Public Lending libs. ..	1,600	1,200,000	—
Specialized libraries ...	780	8,000,000	—

LEISURE AND PLEASURE
THEATRE

Plays performed in one recent season:
lyric theatre, 80; comedy drama, 31;
Akademietheater, 21. The most-acted
authors were Verdi, Strauss, Wagner,
Suppé, Shakespeare, Grillparzer.

MUSIC

During a recent season, the Society of the
Friends of Music (Gesellschaft der Musikfreunde) gave 282 concerts.

Salzburg Festival: In July and August, Salzburg
receives about 48,800 visitors, of whom two-
thirds come from abroad. The number of
tickets sold reaches 84,000 (76,600 in 1951). During the Festival
there are: 24 Opera performances, 11 theatrical performances,
8 symphony concerts, 2 ballets, 6 chamber music concerts,
2 soloist recitals, 6 Mozart serenades. 4 Mozart matinees, 6 concerts
at the cathedral. The total number of seats available in the
different concert halls is about 6,500.

CINEMA

Fifteen companies produced 25 full-length
films in one recent year. One news-reel a week
is shown in 250 cinemas; also 1 reel imported
from each of the Occupying Powers. 180
imported full-length films came from: U.S.A.
30 %; France 25 %; Soviet Russia 20 %;
United Kingdom 10 %.

Silent educational films are numerous; more than 2,000 schools
possess projection equipment.

Number of cinemas, 790; number of seats, 240,000.

Audiences: 90 M (an annual attendance per head of 13 times).

Austria as yet has no television transmitting station.

RADIO

The State holds a monopoly of broadcasting, under the control
of the four Occupying Powers. Transmitting stations: 16
(power, 191.2 kw).

Number of receiving sets: 1,260,000. There are daily programmes
for schools; 1,500 schools (out of 5,000) have receiving sets.

SPORT

The most popular sports are football, ski-ing, mountaineering, and gymnastics. Highest speed attained on skis was 136 km by L. Gasperl (1932). The Austrian jumping record, held by Bradl is 130m.

In recent international contests, Anderl Molterer came first in the Gornergrat Derby, the Kandahar, the slalom at Chamonix, the slalom and team race at Sestrières. Other Austrians (Walter, Schuster, Huber, Strolz, etc.) also scored brilliant victories.

In addition to about 1,280 football clubs with a membership exceeding 117,000, 1,785 clubs for other sports (ski-ing, cycling, etc.) have more than 440,000 members. Total number of sports clubs is 5,500.

Shooting. Rights, except for owners of more than 117 ha, are leased by the communes.

Fishing. There are 18,500 km of rivers and streams and 40,000 ha of lakes and ponds; about 400 professional fishermen, 18,800 amateur anglers.

TOURIST TRAFFIC

Austria receives about 1,200,000 foreign visitors annually. Analysed by nationality, they comprise:

Germans	Various	British	Dutch	French	Italians	Americans	Swiss
51%	16.5%	9%	6.5%	5.5%	4%	4%	3.5%

Average length of stay for foreigners was 5.2 days. Foreign visitors brought in 621 M S in currency; Austrian visitors abroad spent 156 M S.

Hotel amenities: 10,320 hotels, inns, and boarding houses, providing 152,000 beds, plus 63,500 beds in private houses.

Principal holiday districts: the Tyrol, Vorarlberg, Salzburg-town, Salzkammergut lakes, and the lakes of Carinthia.

Spas: Austria has 28 thermal stations, including 8 of the first importance (see chapter on *Practical Information*).

Winter Sports: There are 254 winter-sports resorts, of which 92 are above 1,000 m. The Vorarlberg has 72, the Tyrol 64, Salzburg 43 and Carinthia 20.

Facilities: 8 mountain railways, 36 cable railways, 245 ski-lifts, 152 ski-jumps; 102 skating rinks. (See also our chapter *Practical Information.*

POLITICAL ORGANIZATION

Austria is a parliamentary democratic Republic. A federative State, it is made up of 9 autonomous "countries", which correspond to the 8 provinces, plus Vienna. After the break-up of the Austro-Hungarian Empire in 1918, the present Austria adopted in 1920 the Republican Constitution, which was restored after the war in May 1945.

The Federation and the "Countries": The Federation is responsible for foreign affairs, maintenance of public order (except local police), civil, penal, and labour laws, the federal finances with monopolies and Customs, the currency, credit, industrial affairs, transport, mines, forests, health services, and cultural affairs. All other business comes under the autonomous administration of the "Countries".

Legislative power is exercised by the National Council, jointly with the Council of the Countries.

The National Council, comprising 165 members, is elected for four years by universal suffrage, on the proportional system, by Austrians of both sexes over 21 years of age.

The Council of the Countries has 50 members, elected by proportional representation, by the Diets of the Countries for the duration of their own term of office.

The initiative of legislation belongs to the Federal Government and members of the National Council. The texts voted by the National Council are promulgated, if the Council of the Countries has not put forward strongly grounded opposition. If the National Council stands by its early decision, then this is promulgated.

The Federal President is elected for ten years by the nation by direct vote.

The Government is nominated by the Federal President. If the National Council witholds its confidence, the Government is relieved of its functions.

The Countries: each country has a Diet and a government, with a president of the Country who exercises the Federal executive power in his country.

• OCCUPATION

Austria, still without a peace treaty, is divided into four Occupation zones: the French (Vorarlberg and Tyrol); the British (Styria, Carinthia, and East Tyrol); the American (Salzburg and Upper Austria south of the Danube); the Russian (Lower Austria, Upper Austria north of the Danube, Burgenland). The territory of Vienna, federal capital, is shared between the four occupying powers and is quite international, though there are no barriers, visible or invisible.

The Austrian authorities are obliged to carry out the directives of the Allied Occupation authorities, whose supreme body is the Allied Commission, made up of the High Commissioners of the U.S.A., Great Britain, France, and Russia, and their staffs.

FORCES

By agreement among the four Occupying Powers, Austria is demilitarized.

The proposed peace treaty provides for the authorization of an armed force of 58,000, including the gendarmerie and frontier guard. She would be allowed 90 military planes.

Police. *Gendarmerie* effectives: 10,700 (See sketches of uniforms page 12).

Police effectives: 15,218 (Reserve: 1,407).

JUSTICE

Penal Jurisdiction. About 100,000 cases annually are tried by the local tribunals, and about 30,000 by the Courts of Justice. Convictions in one recent year numbered 92,416: crime, 18,948; misdemeanour, 3,492; minor offences, 69,976. One criminal was condemned to death and executed.

Civil Jurisdiction. Cases heard in one recent year: 134,471 by local tribunals; 44,061 by Civil Courts. Also, **Labour Tribunals** dealt with 10,139 cases.

In Austria there are some 2,000 barristers and 300 notaries.

ENGLISH	GERMAN
good morning, good afternoon	Guten Tag
good evening	Guten Abend
good night	Gute Nacht
good-bye	Auf Wiedersehen
yes	ja
no	nein
thank you	danke
please	bitte
sorry	Verzeihung
excuse me	entschuldigen Sie bitte
how do you do?	es freut mich, Sie kennen z lernen
Mr., Mrs., Miss	Herr, Frau, Fräulein
I am English	ich bin Engländer (f. En länderin)
I do not speak French, German, Italian	ich spreche nicht Deutsch (Fra zösisch, Italienisch)
you speak too quickly	Sie sprechen zu schnell
I know	ich weiss
I don't know	ich weiss nicht
I can	ich kann
I cannot	ich kann nicht
I understand	ich verstehe
I don't understand	ich verstehe nicht
give me	geben Sie mir bitte
how much?	wieviel?
when?	wann?
what time is it?	wie spät ist es?
at what time?	um welche Zeit?
noon	zwölf Uhr
afternoon	Nachmittag
midnight	Mitternacht
half an hour	eine halbe Stunde
quarter of an hour	eine Viertelstunde
the days of the week:	die Wochentage:
Monday, Tuesday, Wednesday, Thursday, Friday, Saturday, Sunday	Montag, Dienstag, Mittwoch Donnerstag, Freitag, Samstag Sonntag
months of the year:	die Monate des Jahres:
January, February, March, April, May, June, July, August, September, October, November, December	Januar, Februar, März, April, Ma Juni, Juli, August, September Oktober, November, Dezemb

DICTIONARY

ITALIAN	FRENCH
buon mattino, buon giorno	bonjour
buona sera	bonsoir
buona notte	bonne nuit
arrivederci	au revoir
sì	oui
no	non
grazie	merci
per favore	s'il vous plaît
con permesso	pardon
scusate	excusez-moi
come sta?	comment allez-vous?
Signore, Signora, Signorina	monsieur, madame, mademoiselle
io sono Inglese	je suis Anglais
io non parlo Italiano, il Francese, il Tedesco	je ne parle pas français (allemand, italien)
lei parlate troppo presto	vous parlez trop vite
io so	je sais
io non so	je ne sais pas
io posso	je peux
io non posso	je ne peux pas
io comprendo	je comprends
io non comprendo	je ne comprends pas
datemi	donnez-moi
quanto?	combien?
quando?	quand?
che ora è?	quelle heure est-il?
a che ora?	à quelle heure?
mezzogiorno	midi
dopo mezzogiorno	après-midi
mezzanotte	minuit
mezz'ora	demi-heure
un quarto d'ora	quart d'heure
i giorni della settimana:	les jours de la semaine:
Lunedì, Martedì, Mercoledì, Giovedì, Venerdì, Sabato, Domenica	lundi, mardi, mercredi, jeudi, vendredi, samedi, dimanche
i mesi dell'anno:	les mois de l'année:
Gennaio, Febbraio, Marzo, Aprile, Maggio, Giugno, Luglio, Agosto, Settembre, Ottobre, Novembre, Dicembre	janvier, février, mars, avril, mai, juin, juillet, août, septembre, octobre, novembre, décembre

ENGLISH	GERMAN
the seasons:	die Jahreszeiten:
spring, summer, autumn, winter	Frühling, Sommer, Herbst, Winter
today	heute
tomorrow	morgen
day after tomorrow	übermorgen

PUBLIC SIGNS

entrance, way in	Eingang
exit, way out	Ausgang
stairs	Treppe
lift	Fahrstuhl
free	frei
engaged	besetzt
no smoking	Nichtraucher
beware	Achtung
danger	Gefahr

GOING BY TRAIN — EISENBAHN FAHREN

where is the station?	wo ist der Bahnhof?
the waiting room	der Wartesaal
the refreshment room	das Buffet
the cloakroom	die Gepäckaufbewahrung
the Information (Enquiry) Office	die Auskunft
I want a time-table	einen Fahrplan bitte *or* ich bitte um einen Fahrplan
at what time is there a train to X. . . . ?	wann geht ein Zug nach X. . . .
from which platform?	von welchem Bahnsteig?
what time does it get to X. . . . ?	wann kommt der Zug in X. . . an?
where shall I change?	wo muss ich umsteigen?
where is the booking-office for X. . . . ?	wo ist der Schalter für X. . . .
a single ticket	eine einfache Fahrkarte
a return ticket	ein Rückfahrkarte
I want to reserve a seat	ich möchte einen Platz reservieren
is this seat taken?	ist dieser Platz besetzt?
may I smoke?	gestatten Sie, dass ich rauche?
may I open, close, the window?	erlauben Sie, dass ich das Fenster öffne, schliesse?
is there a dining-car?	

ITALIAN	FRENCH
le stagioni:	les saisons:
la primavera, l'estate, l'autunno, l'inverno	le printemps, l'été, l'automne, l'hiver
oggi	aujourd'hui
domani	demain
dopo domani	après-demain
ingresso	entrée
uscita	sortie
scala	escalier
ascensore	ascenseur
libero	libre
occupato	occupé
vietato fumare	défense de fumer
attenti	prenez garde, attention
pericolo	danger

VIAGGIARE COL TRENO	EN CHEMIN DE FER
Dove è la stazione?	où est la gare?
la sala d'aspetto	la salle d'attente
il buffet	le buffet
il deposito bagagli	la consigne
l'ufficio d'informazione	le bureau de renseignements
desidero un orario	je voudrais un indicateur
a che ora c'è un treno per X?	à quelle heure y a-t-il un train pour X....?
Da quale banchina?	sur quel quai?
a che ora arriva a X...?	à quelle heure arrive-t-il à X...?
dove devo cambiare?	où dois-je changer?
dove lo sportello per i biglietti?	où est le guichet pour X....?
biglietto semplice	un billet simple
biglietto di andata e ritorno	un aller et retour
desidero riservare un posto	je désire retenir une place
è preso questo posto?	cette place est-elle occupée?
posso fumare?	puis-je fumer?
posso aprire, chiudere, la finestra?	puis-je ouvrir, fermer, la fenêtre?
c'è un vagone restorante?	y a-t-il un wagon-restaurant?

ENGLISH	GERMAN
IDENTITY PAPERS, LUGGAGE, CUSTOMS	**PÄSSE, GEPÄCK, ZOLL**
passport	Pass
triptyque	Triptyk
driving licence	Führerschein
identity documents	Personalausweise
health certificate	ärztliche Bescheinigung
to report to the police	sich bei der Polizei melden
porter	Gepäckträger
take my luggage	nehmen Sie mein Gepäck
suitcases	Koffer
parcels	Pakete
call me a taxi	besorgen Sie mir ein Taxi
nothing to declare	nichts zu verzollen
only things for personal use	nur persönliche Gebrauchsgegenstände

HOTEL	**HOTEL**
I desire	Ich möchte (or Bitte)
a single bedroom	ein Einbettzimmer
a double-bedded room	ein Doppelzimmer
with, without, a bathroom	mit, ohne, Bad
send me the . . . . page-boy, valet, chambermaid, porter	schicken Sie mir bitte. . . . den Hausdiener, das Zimmermädchen, den Gepäckträger
come in	herein
wait a moment	einen Augenblick
we leave to-morrow morning	wir reisen morgen früh ab
please get my bill ready	machen Sie bitte die Rechnung fertig

PLEASE, COULD YOU. . . .?	**WÜRDEN SIE, BITTE**
call me at	wecken Sie mich um . . . . uhr
bring me breakfast	bringen Sie mir das Frühstück
send for a doctor	schicken Sie mir einen Arzt
clean this	reinigen Sie dies
iron this	bügeln Sie dies
sew on this button	nähen Sie diesen Knopf an
polish my shoes	putzen Sie meine Schuhe
send my linen to the laundry	geben Sie meine Wäsche zur Waschen
get me some cigarettes	besorgen Sie mir Zigaretten

ITALIAN	FRENCH
CARTE D'IDENTITA, BAGAGLIO, DOGANA	PAPIERS D'IDENTITÉ, BAGAGES, DOUANE
passaporto	passeport
trittico	triptyque
licenza di guida	permis de conduire
documenti d'identita	pièces d'identité
certificato medico	certificat médical
presentarsi al Commissariato	se présenter au commissariat
portabagagli	porteur
prendete i miei bagagli	prenez mes bagages
valigie	valises
pacchi	paquets
chiamatemi un *taxi*	appelez-moi un taxi
niente da dichiarare	rien à déclarer
solo oggetti per uso personale	seulement des objets personnels

ALBERGO	HOTEL
desidero	je désire
una camera ad un letto	une chambre à un lit
una camera a due letti	une chambre à deux lits
con, senza, un bagno	avec, sans, salle de bain
mandatemi... il fattorino, il cameriere, la cameriera, il portiere	Envoyez-moi le chasseur, le valet de chambre, la femme de chambre, le porteur
entrate	entrez
aspettate un momento	attendez un instant
partiamo domattina	nous partons demain matin
preparatemi il conto	préparez la note, s'il vous plaît

PER FAVORE, POTRESTE..	POURRIEZ-VOUS, S'IL VOUS PLAIT?....
svegliarme alle...	me réveiller á .... heures
portatemi la colazione	m'apporter le petit déjeuner
mandarmi il medico	m'envoyer le docteur
pulire questo	nettoyer ceci
stirare questo	repasser ceci
cucire questo bottone	recoudre ce bouton
pulire le mie scarpe	cirer mes chaussures
mandate la mia biancheria alla lavanderia	donner mon linge à laver
andarmi a cercar sigarette	aller me chercher des cigarettes

ENGLISH	GERMAN
IN THE STREET	**AUF DER STRASSE**
please can you tell me the way to . . . . ?	Bitte, wie kommt man nach . . ?
this way	hierhin, *or* hierher
straight on	geradeaus
a taxi-stand	Taxistand-haltestelle
a bus stop	Autobus-haltestelle
I want a guide-book, a map	ich möchte einen Reiseführer, einen Stadtplan
where is the travel-office?	wo ist ein Verkehrsbüro?
SHOPPING	**LADENBESUCH**
do you speak English?	sprechen Sie Englisch?
have you got . . . . ?	haben Sie . . . . ?
will you show me . . . . ?	bitte zeigen Sie mir . . . . ?
I will take this one	ich nehme dies
may I try it on?	kann ich das anprobieren?
I don't like it	das gefällt mir nicht
what is the price?	was kostet das?
it is too expensive	das ist zu teuer
something cheaper?	haben Sie etwas Billigeres?
no, thank you, I am sorry	nein, danke, ich bedauere
would you accept a cheque?	nehmen Sie einen Scheck an?
send it to this address	schicken Sie mir das bitte an diese Adresse
give me invoices for the customs	bitte geben Sie mir Rechnungen für den Zoll
AT THE POST OFFICE	**AUF DEM POSTAMT**
I want stamps for	bitte Briefmarken für . . . .
letters	Briefe
postcards	Postkarten
air mail	Flugpost
registered	eingeschrieben
send a telegram	ein Telegram aufgeben
reply paid	mit bezahlter Antwort
poste restante	Postlagernd
TELEPHONING	**AM TELEPHON**
please, operator	Fräulein bitte
trunk call	Ferngespräch
don't cut off	unterbrechen Sie nicht
number engaged	die Linie is nicht frei
wrong number	falsche Nummer

ITALIAN	FRENCH
PER LA STRADA	DANS LA RUE
per favore per andar a . . . ?	s'il vous plaît, pour aller à . . . . ?
per di qua	par ici
sempre dritto	tout droit
una stazione di taxi	un station de taxis
una fermata dell'autobus	un arrêt d'autobus
desidero una guida, una pianta	je voudrais un guide, un plan
dove e l'ufficio del turismo?	où est le bureau du tourisme?
COMPRE	ACHATS
parlate l'Inglese?	parlez-vous anglais?
avete . . . ?	avez-vous . . . . ?
volete mostrarmi?	voulez-vous me montrer . . . . ?
prendero questo	je prendrai celui-ci
posso provarmelo?	puis-je l'essayer?
non mi piace	cela ne me plaît pas
quanto costa?	quel est le prix?
e troppo caro	c'est trop cher
qualche cosa piu a buon mercato?	quelque chose de meilleur marché?
no, grazie, mi rincresce	non, merci, je regrette
accettate un assegno?	acceptez-vous un chèque?
mandatelo a questo indirizzo	envoyez-le moi à cette adresse
datemi la fatture per la Dogana	donnez-moi la facture pour la douane
ALL'UFFICIO POSTALE	AU BUREAU DE POSTE
desidero francobolli per . . .	je voudrais des timbres pour
lettere	lettres
partoline	cartes-postales
costa aerea	par avion
raccomandata	recommandé
mandare un telegramma	envoyer un télégramme
risposta pagata	réponse payée
ermo in posta	poste restante
AL TELEFONO	AU TELEPHONE
ignorina, per favore	mademoiselle, s'il vous plaît
chiamata interurbana	appel interurbain
on tagliate	ne coupez pas
umero occupato	ligne pas libre
umero sbagliato	faux numéro

ENGLISH	GERMAN
PHOTOGRAPHY	**PHOTOGRAPHIE**
I want a roll of film .... of this size	bitte einen Rollfilm.... dieses Format
will you develop this?	bitte würden Sie diesen Film entwickeln
a print of each	einen Abzug pro Aufnahme
will you enlarge this snapshot?	bitte würden Sie dieses Photo vergrössern
AT THE HAIRDRESSER'S	**BEIM FRISÖR**
I have very little time	ich habe sehr wenig Zeit
I must be ready by	ich muss um .... fertig sein
I want to have	ich möchte ....
a shave	rasiert werden
a hair-cut	mir die Haar schneiden lassen
my hair washed	mir die Haar waschen lassen
a rinse	mir eine Pakkung machen lasse
a wave-set	mir eine Wasserwelle machen lassen
a permanent wave	mir eine Dauerwelle machen lassen
an iron wave	mir die Haare ondulieren lassen
my hair bleached	bleichen lassen
dyed	färben lassen
THEATRE, CINEMA, etc.	**THEATER, KINO**
where can I book seats?	wo gibt es Eintrittskarten?
for the performance on	für die Vorstellung um ....
orchestra stall	Parkettplatz
dress circle	erster Rang
news reel	Wochenschau
original version dubbed	Originalfassung synchronisiert
sub-title	Untertitel
	GASTRONOMIC
WHERE TO GO?	**WOHIN GEHT MAN?**
inn	Gasthaus
café	Café
hotel	Hotel
can you direct me to a good restaurant?	können Sie mir ein gutes Restaurant empfehlen?
waiter	Herr Ober
head waiter	Herr Oberkellner
waitress	Fräulein

ITALIAN	FRENCH
FOTOGRAFIA	**PHOTOGRAPHIE**
desidero una pellicola... di questo misura	je voudrais un rouleau de pellicule .... de ce format
volete sviluppare questo?	voulez-vous développer ceci
stampate una copia di ciascuna	une épreuve de chaque
vogliete ingrandire questa istantanea?	voulez-vous agrandir cette photo?
DAL BARBIERE, DAL PARRUCCHIERE	**CHEZ LE COIFFEUR**
ho poco tempo	j'ai très peu de temps
devo essere pronto alle...	je dois être prêt à .... heures
vorrei farmi...	je voudrais me faire ....
radere	raser
tagliare i capelli	couper les cheveux
lavare i capelli	laver les cheveux
una sciacquatura	un rinçage
un'ondulatura dei capelli	une mise en plis
ondulatura permanante	une permanente
arricciare col ferro	un coup de fer
scolorare	décolorer
tingere	teindre
TEATRO, CINEMA, ecc.	**THEATRE, CINEMA**
dove posso prenotare posti?	où puis-je louer des places?
per la rappresentazione di...	pour le séance de ....
poltroncina	fauteuil d'orchestre
prima galleria	balcon
attualita	actualités
versione originale doppiata	version originale doublé
sotto-titolo	sous-titre
DICTIONARY	
DOVE ANDARE?	**OÙ ALLER?**
trattoria	auberge
caffe	café
albergo	hôtel
potete indicarmi un buon ristorante?	pouvez-vous m'indiquer un bon restaurant?
cameriere	garçon
primo cameriere	maître d'hôtel
cameriera	serveuse

ENGLISH	GERMAN
MEALS	DIE MAHLZEITEN
breakfast	Frühstück
luncheon	Mittagessen
tea	Tee
dinner	Abendessen
à la carte	à la Karte
fixed price meal	Menu
the menu	die Speisekarte
the bill, please (check, U.S.A.)	die Rechnung bitte
the change	das Kleingeld
the tip	das Trinkgeld
AT TABLE	BEI TISCH
bottle	Flasche
chair	Stuhl
corkscrew	Korkenzieher
cup	Tasse
decanter	Karaffe
dish	Schüssel
fork	Gabel
glass	Glas
knife	Messer
napkin	Serviette
plate	Teller
salt-cellar	Salzfass
saucer	Untertasse
spoon	Löffel
tablecloth	Tischtuch
DRINKS	GETRAENKE
ale	helles Bier
beer	Bier
brandy	Branntwein
chocolate	Schokolade
cider	Apfelwein
coffee	Kaffee,
(white)	Milchkaffee
fruit juice (see *Fruits*)	Obstsaft
ice	Eis
liqueur	Likör
milk	Milch
mineral water	Mineralwasser
soda water	Sodawasser
stout	dunkles Bier
tea	Tee
water	Wasser

TALIAN	FRENCH
'ASTI	LES REPAS
affe-latte (prima colazione)	petit déjeuner
olazione	déjeuner
e (merenda)	thé, goûter
ranzo	dîner
la carta	à la carte
prezzo fisso	à prix fixe
lista	le menu
er piacere, il conto	l'addition, s'il vous plaît
cambio	la monnaie
a mancia	le pourboire
TAVOLA	A TABLE
ottiglia	bouteille
edia	chaise
avatappi	tire-bouchon
azza	tasse
araffa	carafe
iatto	plat
rchetta	fourchette
icchiere	verre
oltello	couteau
lvietta	serviette
iatto	assiette
liera	salière
ottotazza	soucoupe
ucchiaio	cuiller
ovaglia	nappe
EVANDE	BOISSONS
irra chiara	bière blonde
irra	bière
cquavite	eau-de-vie
occolata	chocolat
dro	cidre
affè	café
caffe con latte	(au lait)
ago di frutta	jus de fruit
elato	glace
quore	liqueur
tte	lait
cqua minerale	eau minérale
cqua gassosa	eau gazeuse
irra scura	bière brune
è	thé
cqua	eau

ENGLISH	GERMAN
WINES	**WEINE**
burgundy	Burgunder
claret	Bordeaux
hock	Rheinwein
port	Portwein
red	Rotwein
rosé	Rosa
Sherry	Südwein, Sherry
white	Weiss
CONDIMENTS, etc.	**ZUTATEN**
butter	Butter
fat	Fett
garlic	Knoblauch
gherkins	Gurken
lard	Schmalz
mustard	Senf
oil	Oel
pepper	Pfeffer
salt	Salz
sugar	Zucker
lumps	Würfelzucker
granulated	feiner Zucker
vinegar	Essig
BREAD	**BROT**
white bread	Weissbrot
brown bread	Schwarzbrot
roll	Brötchen, Semmel
rusk	Zwieback
HORS D'ŒUVRE	**VORSPEISEN**
anchovy	Anchovis
beetroot	rote Rüben
celery	Sellerie
cucumber	grüne Gurke
cured meat	Aufschnitt, Wurstwaren
ham	Schinken
olives	Oliven
oysters	Austern
pickled herrings	Heringe
prawn	Rosa Krebse
radishes	Radieschen
salads (see *Vegetables*)	Salate
sardines	Sardinen
sausage	Wurst

ITALIAN	FRENCH
VINI	**VINS**
Borgogna	Bourgogne
Bordeaux	Bordeaux
del Reno	du Rhin
Porto	Porto
rosso	rouge
rosato	rosé
Xeres	Xérès
bianco	blanc
CONDIMENTI	**CONDIMENTS**
burro	beurre
grasso	graisse
aglio	ail
cetriolini	cornichons
lardo	saindoux
mostarda	moutarde
olio	huile
pepe	poivre
sale	sel
zucchero	sucre
a quadretti	en morceaux
cristallizzato	cristallisé
aceto	vinaigre
PANE	**PAIN**
pane bianco	pain blanc
pane bruno	pain bis
pannino	petit pain
biscottato	biscotte
ANTI PASTI	**HORS D'ŒUVRE**
acciuge	anchois
barbabietola	betterave
sedano	céleri
cetriolo	concombre
salumeria	charcuterie
prosciutto	jambon
olive	olives
ostriche	huîtres
aringe marinata	harengs marinés
gamberetto di mare	bouquet
ravanelli	radis
insalate	salades
sardine	sardines
salsiccia	saucisson

ENGLISH	GERMAN
shell-fish	Muscheln
shrimps	Garnelen
smoked salmon	geräucherter Lachs
stuffed eggs	gefüllte Eier
tomatoes	Tomaten
tunny-fish in oil	Thunfisch in Oel
vegetable salad	gemischtes Gemüse

SOUPS	SUPPEN
broth	Kraftbrühe
clear (meat) soup	Fleischbrühe
fish soup	Fischsuppe
thick soup	gebundene Suppe
vegetable	Gemüsesuppe

EGGS	EIER
boiled	gekochtes Ei
fried	gebackene Eier
hard-boiled	harte Eier
omelette	Omelette
poached	verlorene Eier
scrambled	Rührei
sunny-side up (U.S.)	Spiegelei

FISH	FISCHE
bass	Wolfsbarsch
carp	Karpfen
coalfish	Kohlfisch
cod, fresh	Kabeljau
cured	Kabeljau
crab	Seestern
crayfish	Krebs
eel	Aal
gilthead	Goldkarpfen
herring	Hering
lobster	Hummer
mackerel	Mackreele
mussel	Muscheln
pike	Hecht
red-mullet	Rötling
salmon	Lachs, Salm
sardine	Sardine
scallop	Muscheln St-Jacques
sea-crawfish	Languste
shad	Maifisch

ITALIAN	FRENCH
ostacei	coquillages
ranchiolini	crevettes
lmone affumicato	saumon fumé
ova imbottite	œufs farcis
omodori	tomates
onno sott'olio	thon à l'huile
salata di verdure	macédoine de légumes
MINESTRE	**POTAGES**
rodo	bouillon
rodo concentrato	consommé
uppa di pesce	soupe au poisson
uppa crema	crème (de . . . .)
uppa di legumi	soupe aux légumes
OVA	**ŒUFS**
ova al guscio	à la coque
ova fritte	frits
ova sode	durs
ittata	omelette
ova affogate	pochés
ova strapazzate	brouillés
ova nel tegame	au plat
ESCE	**POISSON**
nbrina	bar
rpione	carpe
erluzzo	colin
erluzzo	cabillaud
baccala	morue
anchio	crabe
mbero	écrevisse
guilla	anguille
ata	dorade
inga	hareng
mbero	homard
ombro	maquereau
sella	moule
ccio	brochet
glia	rouget
lmone	saumon
rdina	sardine
tonchio	coquille St-Jacques
mbero di mare	langouste
eppia	alose

ENGLISH	GERMAN
skate	Rochen
sole	Seezunge
trout	Forelle
turbot	Steinbutt
whiting	Merlan

MEATS	FLEISCH
beef	Rind
lamb	Lamm
mutton	Hammel
pork	Schweinefleisch
veal	Kalbfleisch
bacon	Speck
chop	Kotelett
fat	Fett
fillet	Filet
gravy	Saft
ham	Schinken
head	Kopf
kidneys	Nieren
liver	Leber
rib	Rippe
roast, joint	Braten
sausage	Wurst
steak	Rumsteack
sweetbreads	Bröschen
tongue	Zunge
just right	gerade richtig
underdone	halb roh
well done	gut durchgebraten

POULTRY	GEFLÜGEL
chicken	Huhn
duck	Ente
goose	Gans
pigeon	Taube
turkey	Truthahn

GAME	WILD
hare	Hase
partridge	Rebhuhn
pheasant	Fasan
rabbit	Kaninchen
venison	Wildbret

ITALIAN	FRENCH
azza	raie
ogliola	sole
rota	truite
ombo	turbot
merlano	merlan

CARNI	VIANDES
manzo	bœuf
gnello	agneau
montone	mouton
maiale	porc
itello	veau
ardo	lard
ostoletta	côtelette
rasso	graisse
iletto	filet
ugo	jus
rosciutto	jambon
esta	tête
ognone	rognons
egato	foie
ostola	côte
rrosto	rôti
alsiccia	saucisse
istecca	entrecôte, bifteck
nimella	ris
ingua	langue
l punto	à point
l sangue	saignant
en cotta	bien cuit

POLLAME	VOLAILLE
ollo	poulet
nitra	canard
ca	oie
iccione	pigeon
acchino	dinde

CACCIAGIONE	GIBIER
epre	lièvre
ernice	perdreau
agiano	faisan
oniglio	lapin
elvaggina	venaison

ENGLISH	GERMAN
VEGETABLES	GEMÜSE
artichoke	Artischocke
asparagus	Spargel
beans	weisse Bohnen
Brussels sprouts	Rosenkohl
cabbage	Kohl
carrot	Karotte
cauliflower	Blumenkohl
celery	Sellerie
cress	Kresse
egg-plant	Melanzane
endive	Chicoree
French beans	grüne Bohnen
green peas	grüne Erbsen
leek	Lauch
lentils	Linsen
lettuce	grüner Salat
macaroni	Makaroni
marrow	Schmorgurke
mushroom	Pilz
onions	Zwiebeln
pumpkin	Kürbis
red cabbage	Rotkohl
rice	Reis
salsify	Schwarzwurzel
sorrel	Sauerampfer
spinach	Spinat
split peas	getrocknete Erbsen
tomato	Tomate
truffle	Trüffel
turnip	Rüben
SWEETS	NACHSPEISEN
biscuits	Biskuits
cake	Kuchen
cream	Sahne
fritters	Krapfen
ice-cream	Eis:
flavours: caramel, chocolate, cinnamon, coffee, fruit (see *Fruits*), mixed flavours, pistachio, vanilla	Karamel, Schokolade, Zimn Kaffee, Früchte gemischt, P tazie, Vanille
jam	Marmelade
jelly	Gelee
marmalade	Orangenmarmelade
pancake	Palatschinken

ITALIAN	FRENCH
LEGUMI	LÉGUMES
arciofo	artichaut
asparagio	asperge
fagioli bianchi	haricots blancs
cavoli di Bruselles	choux de Bruxelles
cavolo	chou
carota	carotte
cavolfiore	chou-fleur
sedano	céleri
crescione	cresson
melanzana	aubergine
indivia	chicorée
fagioli verdi	haricots verts
piselli	petits pois
porro	poireau
lenticchie	lentilles
lattuga	laitue
maccheroni	macaroni
zucchino	courgette
fungo	champignon
cipolle	oignons
zucca gialla	potiron
cavolo rosso	chou rouge
riso	riz
scorzonera	salsifis
acetosa	oseille
spinacci	épinards
piselli seccki	pois casses
pomodoro	tomate
tartuffo	truffe
rapa	navet
DOLCI	DESSERTS
biscotti	biscuits
torta	gâteau
crema	crème
fritella	beignets
gelato	glace
sapori: caramella, cioccolata, cannella, caffe, frutta misto, pistacchio, vaniglia	parfums: caramel, chocolat, canelle, café, fruit, panaché, pistache, vanille
confettura	confiture
gelatina	gelée
marmellata d'arancia	confiture d'oranges
fritella	crêpe

ENGLISH	GERMAN
pastry	Gebäck
pie, tart	Torte
pudding (sweet)	Pudding (Nachspeise)
stewed fruit	Kompott
whipped cream	Schlagsahne

FRUIT	FRÜCHTE
almond	Mandel
apple	Apfel
apricot	Aprikose
banana	Banane
blackberry	Brombeere
cherry	Kirsche
chestnut	Kastanie
coconut	Kokosnuss
date	Dattel
fig	Feige
grape	Weintraube
grapefruit	Grapefruit, Pampelmuse
lemon	Zitrone
melon	Melone
nut	Nuss
orange	Orange, Apfelsine
peach	Pfirsich
pear	Birne
pineapple	Ananas
plum	Pflaume
prune	Backpflaume
raspberry	Himbeere
strawberry	Erdbeere
tangerine	Mandarine
walnut	Walnuss

CHEESE	KÄSE
cream cheese	Weisskäse
hard cheese	Hartkäse
soft cheese	Weichkäse

MOTORIN

ON THE ROAD	AUF DER LANDSTRASSE
The road to X..., please?	Die Strasse nach X...., bitt
How many kilometres am I from X....?	Wieviel Kilometer sind es na X....?

ITALIAN	FRENCH
pasticceria	pâtisserie
torta	tarte
budino	entremets
frutta composta	compote
panna montata	crème chantilly (fouettée)

FRUTTI	FRUITS
mandorla	amande
mela	pomme
albicocca	abricot
banana	banane
mora	mûre
ciliegia	cerise
castagna	châtaigne
noce di cocco	noix de coco
dattero	datte
fico	figue
uva	raisin
pompelmo	pamplemousse
limone	citron
melone	melon
noce	noisette
arancia	orange
pesca	pêche
pera	poire
ananasso	ananas
prugna	prune
prugna secca	pruneau
lampone	framboise
fragola	fraise
manderino	mandarine
noce	noix

FORMAGGIO	FROMAGE
formaggio bianco	fromage blanc
formaggio duro	fromage sec
formaggio fresco	fromage frais

DICTIONARY

SULLA STRADA	SUR LA ROUTE
Per piacere, la strada per X?	La route de X...., s'il vous plaît?
Aquanti chilometri sono da X?	A combien de kilometres suis-je de X....?

ENGLISH	*GERMAN
Is the road good? bad?	Ist die Strasse gut? schlecht?
Where is there a filling station?	Wo ist eine Tankstelle?
Can you help me?	Können Sie mir helfen?
I have got to be taken in tow	Ich muss abgeschleppt werden

ROAD SIGNS	VERKEHRSSCHILDER
dead slow	langsam fahren
diversion	Umleitung
road clear	Freie Fahrt
road works ahead	Strassenarbeiten
school	Schule
single-line traffic	Nicht Überholen

INCIDENTS OF TRAVEL	REISE VORKOMMNISSE
bends	Kurven
crossroads	Strassenkreuzung
level crossing	Bahnübergang
pass	Pass
to skid	ins Schleudern geraten
to run into	einen Zusammenstoss haben
to damage	beschädigen
to run over	überfahren
to knock down	umwerfen
insurance	Versicherung
police station	Polizeiamt
report	Tatbestandsaufnahme
fine (n.)	Strafe
Your identity papers	Ihre Papiere

AT THE GARAGE	IN DER GARAGE
WILL YOU PLEASE	WOLLEN SIE, BITTE ....
give me X litres of	X Liter
petrol	Benzin
best quality	beste Qualität
with lubricant	mit Schmieröl
check the oil level	prüfen Sie den Oelstand
give me X litres of	X liter
light oil	dünnflüssiges Oel
heavy oil	dickflüssiges Oel

ITALIAN	FRENCH
La strada è buona? Cattiva?	La route est-elle bonne? mauvaise?
C'è un posto rifornimento di benzina?	Où y a-t-il un poste à essence?
Potete aiutarmi?	Pouvez-vous m'aider?
Bisognerebbe rimorchiarmi	Il faudrait me remorquer
SEGNALAZIONI STRADALI	SIGNALISATION ROUTIÈRE
rallentare	ralentir
deviazione	déviation
strada libera	route libre
lavori in corso	travaux
scuola	école
fila unica	ne pas doubler
INCIDENTI DI PERCORSO	INCIDENTS DE PARCOURS
curve	virages
crocevia	carrefour
passaggio a livello	passage à niveau
passo	col
slittare	déraper
scontrarsi con	entrer en collision avec
danneggiare	endommager
schiacciare	écraser
travolgere	renverser
assicurazione	assurance
posta di polizia	poste de police
verbale	constat
multa	amende
le vostre carte d'identita	vos papiers d'identité
NELL'AUTORIMESSA	AU GARAGE
PER FAVORE.	VOULEZ-VOUS, S.V.P. . . .
volete darmi X litri di benzina	me donner X litres d'essence
di super	de super
con lubrificante	avec lubrifiant
verificare il livello dell'olio	vérifier le niveau d'huile
darmi X litri	me donner X litres
d'olio fluido	d'huile fluide
denso	d'huile épaisse

ENGLISH	GERMAN
fill up the radiator	füllen Sie den Kühler
drain the radiator	leeren Sie das Kühlwasser ab
grease the chassis	schmieren Sie den Wagen durch
check the gear-box and rear-axle oil levels	prüfen Sie das Getriebe und das Differential
charge the battery	laden Sie die Batterie
top-up the battery (with distilled water)	füllen Sie die Batterie mit distilliertem Wasser
clean, change, the sparking plugs	reinigen, wechseln, Sie die Kerzen
clean the carburettor, the jets	reinigen Sie den Vergaser, die Düsen
wash my car	waschen Sie den Wagen
How long will it take?	Wie lange dauert das?
How much do you charge?	Was wird das kosten?

TYRES AND WHEELS	REIFEN UND RÄDER
Will you, please . . . . ?	Wollen Sie, bitte . . . . ?
inflate the tyres	prüfen Sie die Reifen
the spare wheel	der Ersatzreifen
repair the flat tyre	reparieren Sie den Reifen
put on chains	montieren Sie die Schneeketten
have you got new tyres?	haben Sie neue Reifen?
inner tubes?	Schläuche?
second-hand	gebrauchte?

MOTORING

A	A
accelerate (to)	Gas geben
accelerator	Gaspedal
airtight	luftdicht
axle	Achse

B	B
back-axle	Rück-Achse
back seat	Rücksitz
battery	Batterie
(for torch)	Taschenlampen-batterie
belt	Antriebriemen
bonnet	Kühlerhaube
brake	Bremse
bulb (electric)	Birne
bumper	Stosstange

ITALIAN	FRENCH
riempire il radiatore	remplir le radiateur
caricare il radiatore	vidanger le radiateur
lubrificare lo chassis	faire un graissage complet
verificare la scatola del cambio ed il ponte	vérifier la boîte de vitesse et le pont
ricaricate la batteria	recharger la batterie
metter acqua distillata nella batteria	mettre de l'eau distillée dans la batterie
pulire, cambiate, le candele	nettoyer, remplacer, les bougies
pulire il carburatore gli spruzzatore	nettoyer le carburateur, les gicleurs
lavar la vettura	laver ma voiture
Quanto tempo ci vorra?	Combien de temps cela prendra-t-il?
Qual è il prezzo?	Combien demandez-vous?

PNEUMATICI E RUOTE

PNEUS ET ROUES

volete, per piacere...?	Voulez-vous, s'il vous plaît....?
gonfiare i pneumatici	gonfier les pneus
la ruota di ricambio	la roue de secours
riparare il pneumatico forato	réparer le pneu crevé
metter le catene	poser les chaînes
avete nuovi pneumatici?	avez-vous de pneus neufs?
camere d'aria?	chambres à air?
d'occasione?	d'occasion?

WORD LIST

A

A

accelerare	accélérer
acceleratore	accélérateur
impermeabile all'aria	imperméable à l'air
asse	essieu

B

B

asse posteriore	pont-arrière
sedile posteriore	siège arrière
batteria	batterie
pila	pile
cinghia	courroie
mantice	capot
freno	frein
lampadina	ampoule
para-urti	pare-choc

ENGLISH	GERMAN
C	**C**
can	Kanister
car-licence	Führerschein
change gear (to)	den Gang wechseln
chassis	Fahrgestell
clutch	Kuppelung
consumption	Verbrauch
D	**D**
dashboard	Armaturenbrett
declutch	Entkupplung
defroster	Enteisen
disconnect (to)	Entkuppelung
door	Tür
draining	Entleerung
driver	Fahrer
driving-licence	Führerschein
dynamo	Stromerzeuger
E-F	**E-F**
engine	Motor
exhaust-tube	Auspuffrohr
fan	Ventilator
fan-belt	Ventilator Riemen
filter	Filter
first gear	erster Gang
fit (to)	ein-, anpassen
fitting up	Montage
front seat	Vordersitz
fuel	Treibstoff
fuel-pump	Benzinpumpe
fuel-tank	Treibstoffbehälter
fuses	Sicherung
G	**G**
gasoline (petrol)	Benzin
gauge (petrol)	Benzinstandmesser
gear	Räderwerk
gearbox	Getriebe
go backward (to)	rückwärts fahren
go forward (to)	vorwärts fahren
grease	Schmierfett

ITALIAN	FRENCH
C	**C**
bidone	bidon
bollo (di circolazione)	permis de circulation (carte grise)
cambio di velocita	changer de vitesse
telaio	châssis
frizione	embrayage
consumo	consommation
D	**D**
cruscotto	planche, tableau de bord
disinnesto	débrayage
sbrinatore	dégivreur
sconnettere	déconnecter
porta	portière
scarico	vidange
conduttore, chauffeur	chauffeur, conducteur
patente	permis de conduire
dinamo	dynamo
E-F	**E-F**
motore	moteur
tubo di scappamento	tuyau d'échappement
ventilatore	ventilateur
cinghia per ventilatore	courroie de ventilateur
filtro	filtre
prima velocita	première vitesse
aggiustare	ajuster
montaggio	montage
sedile anteriore	siège avant
carburante	carburant
pompa di carburante	pompe à essence
serbatoio	réservoir d'essence
fusi	plombs
G	**G**
benzina	essence
tazza (di benzina)	jauge (d'essence)
granaggio	engrenage
scatola del cambio di velocita	boîte de vitesses
retrocedere	marche arrière (faire)
avvanzare	marche avant (faire)
ingrassare, lubrificare	graisse

ENGLISH	GERMAN
H-I-J-K	**H-I-J-K**
head-lights	Scheinwerfer
heating	Heizung
hinge	Scharnier
hood	Kühlerhaube
horn	Hupe
hub	Radnarbe
inflate (to)	aufpumpen
inner tube	Schlauch
jack	Wagenheber
jet	Düse
keep to the left (to)	links halten
keep to the right (to)	rechts halten
key	Schlüssel
L-M	**L-M**
leak (to)	es rinnt
light (to)	Lichter anzünden
lock	Schloss
lorry	Lastwagen
lubrication	Abschmierung
luggage-rack	Gepäckträger
magneto	Magnet
misfire	Fehlzündung
motor-car	Auto
mudguard	Kotflügel
N-O	**N-O**
needle	Zeiger
non-skid	Gleitschutz
number-plate	Nummerntafel
oil (to)	ölen
oil	Oel
oil-can	Oelkännchen
oil-pump	Oelpumpe
overtake (to)	überholen
P	**P**
parking	Parken
parking-light	Parkenlampe
pedal	Pedal
pedestrian crossing	Strassenübergang
petrol	Benzin
petrol-pump	Benzinpumpe

ITALIAN	FRENCH
H-I-J-K	**H-I-J-K**
fari	phares
riscaldamento	chauffage
cardine	charnière
mantice	capote
tromba	klaxon
mozzo	moyeu
gonfiare	gonfler
camera d'aria	chambre à air
cricco	cric
spruzzatore	gicleur
tener a sinistra	tenir sa gauche
tener a destra	tenir sa droite
chiave	clé
L-M	**L-M**
colare	fuir
accendere	allumer
serratura	serrure
autocarro	camion
ingrassatura	graissage
porta bagagli	porte-bagage
magnete	magnéto
battuta irregolari	raté
automobile	automobile
ala	aile
N-O	**N-O**
ago	aiguille
anti-slittante	anti-dérapant
targa	plaque réglementaire
oliare	huiler
olio	huile
oliatore	burette à huile
pompa d'olio	pompe à huile
sorpassare una vettura	dépasser
P	**P**
posteggio	stationnement
fanalino di posteggio	feu de position
pedale	pédale
passaggio per pedoni	passage clouté
benzina	essence
pompa per benzina	pompe à essence

ENGLISH	GERMAN
piston-ring	Kolbenring
piston-rod	Achse
plug	Kerze
pump (air)	Luftpumpe

R	R
rack	Gepäcknetz
rackjack	Wagenheber mit Zahnstange
radiator	Kühler
radiator-cap	Kühlerverschlag
rag	Putzlappen
rear-axle	Hinterradachse
rear-mirror	Rückspiegel
repair-shop	Werkstatt
rear seat	Rücksitz
right of way (to have)	Vorfahrtsrecht
rim	Felge
roof	Dach

S	S
saloon car	Limousine
screw-driver	Schraubenzieher
seat	Sitz
front	Vordersitz
rear	Rücksitz
folding	Klappsitz
second gear	zweiter Gang
shock-absorbers	Stossdämpfer
sliding roof	Schiebedach
slowing down	bremsen
spanner	Universalschlüssel
spare wheel	Ersatzrad
speed	Geschwindigkeit
speedometer	Kilometerzähler
sponge	Schwamm
spring	Feder
start (to)	starten
starting	Start, Abfahrt
steam	Dampf
steering gear	Steuerung
steering-wheel	Steuerrad
stop (to)	halten
switch	Umschalten
switch off (to)	Zündung ausschalten
switch on (to)	Zündung einschalten

ITALIAN	FRENCH
segmento di stantuffo	segment de piston
asse di stantuffo	axe de piston
candela	bougie
gonfiatore, pompa d'aria	gonfleur

R

porta-bagagli	porte-bagage
cricco a dentiera	cric à crémaillère
radiatore	radiateur
tappo del radiatore	bouchon de radiateur
straccio	chiffon
ponte posteriore	pont-arrière
specchio retroscopico	rétroviseur
officina per riparazioni	atelier de réparation
sedile posteriore	siège arrière
precedenza (aver la)	priorité (avoir la)
cerchione	jante
tetto	toit

S

limousine	conduite intérieure
cacciaviti	tournevis
sedile	siège
anteriore	avant
posteriore	arrière
seggiolino	strapontin
seconda velocita	deuxième vitesse
ammortizzatori	amortisseurs
tetto-apribile	toit ouvrant
rallentare	ralentissement
chiave inglese	clé-anglaise
ruota di ricambio	roue de secours
velocita	vitesse
contatore	compteur
spugna	éponge
molla	ressort
avviare	démarrer
avviamento	départ, démarrage
vapore	vapeur
direzione	direction
volante, sterzo	volant
fermarsi	arrêter (s')
interruttore	interrupteur
tagliare il contatto	couper le contact
metter il contatto	mettre le contact

ENGLISH	GERMAN
T	**T**
tail-light	Rücklicht
tank (fuel)	Treibstoffbehälter
tap	Hahn
test	Versuch
third gear	dritter Gang
tighten the brakes (to)	die Bremsen ziehen
tool-bag	Werkzeugtasche
tow (to)	abschleppen
tow-rope	Schleppseil
traffic lights	Verkehrslicht
trailer	Anhänger
turn (to)	umwenden, umdrehen
turn round (to)	wenden
tyre	Reifen
V-W	**V-W**
valve	Ventil
water-pump	Wasserpumpe
wheel	Rad
window	Fensterscheibe
windscreen	Windschutzscheibe
windscreen-wipers	Scheibenwischer

SOME US[

A	**A**
after	nach
again	noch
all	alle, alle
already	schon
also	auch
always	immer
around	um
as	wie
ask (to)	bitten
avenue	Allee
B	**B**
bad	schlecht
bank	Bank
bank-note	Banknote
be (to)	sein
been	gewesen
behind	hinter

ITALIAN	FRENCH
T	**T**
fanalino posteriore	feu arrière
serbatoio di benzina	réservoir d'essence
rubinetto	robinet
prova	essai
terza velocita	troisième vitesse
stringere i freni	serrer les freins
astuccio da utensili	trousse à outils
rimorchiare	remorquer
fune per rimorchio	câble de remorque
fari di movimento	feux de circulation
rimorchio	remorque
girare	tourner
fronte indietro	demi-tour (faire)
pneumatico	pneu
V-W	**V-W**
valvola di sicurezza	soupape
pompa d'acqua	pompe à eau
ruota	roue
finestrino	glace
frangi-vento	pare-brise
tergi-cristallo	essuie-glace

USEFUL WORDS

A	**A**
dopo	après
ancora	encore
tutto, tutti	tout, toute, tous
gia	déjà
anche	aussi
sempre	toujours
intorno	autour
come	comme
domandare	demander
viale	avenue
B	**B**
male, cattivo	mal, mauvais
banca	banque
biglietto di banca	billet
essere	être
stato	été
dietro	derrière

ENGLISH	GERMAN
because	weil
before	vor
best	beste
better	besser
break (to)	zerbrechen
bring (to)	bringen
bus	Autobus
buy (to)	kaufen

C	C
carry (to)	tragen
call (to)	rufen
cash	bar
cashier	Kassierer
cheque	Scheck
cigar	Zigarre
cigarette	Zigarette
clean (to)	reinigen
cold	kalt
come in (to)	eintreten
constable	Polizist
cook (to)	kochen
correct	richtig, genau
credit	Kredit
cross (to)	überqueren
cut (to)	schneiden

D	D
dear	lieb, teuer
decide (to)	entscheiden
difficult	schwer
dining-room	Esszimmer, Speisezimmer
direct	direkt
distance	Entfernung
do (to)	machen, tun
double	doppelt
drink (to)	trinken

E	E
each, every	jedermann, jeder, e, es
easy	leicht
eat (to)	essen
end	Ende

ALIAN	FRENCH
rche	parce que
ima, avanti	avant
meglio	le meilleur, la meilleure
eglio, migliore	meilleur, meilleure
mpere	casser
rtare	apporter
tobus	autobus
mprare	acheter

C

rtare	porter
iamare	appeler
contanti	comptant
ssiere	caissier
egno	chèque
garo	cigare
garetta	cigarette
lire, nettare	nettoyer
ddo	froid
trare	entrer
lizotto	gendarme
cinare, cuocere	cuire
rretto, esatto	exact
dito	crédit
versare	traverser
gliare	couper

D

ro	cher
cidere	décider
fficile	difficile
a da pranzo	salle à manger
retto	direct, directe
stanza	distance
e	faire
ppio	double
re	boire

E

scuno, tutti	chaque, tout, toute
cile	facile
angiare	manger
e	fin

ENGLISH	GERMAN
enough	genug
equal	gleich
explain (to)	erklären
F	**F**
far	weit, fern
find (to)	finden
fish (to)	fischen
follow (to)	folgen
food	Nahrung
for	für
forget (to)	vergessen
fresh	frisch
full	voll
G	**G**
give (to)	geben
given	gegeben
go (to)	gehen
good	gut
H	**H**
hear (to)	verstehen
help (to)	helfen
here	hier
high	gross, hoch
his, her	sein, seine, seines; ihr, ihre, ihr
holiday	Feiertag
holidays	Ferien, Urlaub
hot	heiss
house	Haus
how	wie
hurry (to)	eilen, sich beeilen
I-J-K	**I-J-K**
if	wenn, ob
information	Auskunft
in	in
journey	Reise
know (to)	wissen
known	gewusst
L	**L**
late	spät
left	links

ITALIAN	FRENCH
abbastanza	assez
eguale	égal
spiegare	expliquer

F	**F**
lontano	loin, lointain
trovare	trouver
pescare	pêcher
seguire	suivre
cibo	nourriture
per	pour
dimenticare	oublier
fresco	frais
pieno	plein

G	**G**
dare	donner
dato	donné
andare	aller
buono	bon

H	**H**
udire, sentire	entendre
aiutare	aider
qui	ici
grande, alto	grand, haut
il suo, la sua	son, sa, ses
festa, vacanza	fête
vacanze	vacances
caldo	chaud
casa	maison
come	comment
spicciare	se dépêcher

I-J-K	**I-J-K**
se	si
informazione	renseignement
in	dans
viaggio	voyage
sapere	savoir
saputo	su

L	**L**
tardi	tard
sinistra	gauche

ENGLISH	GERMAN
less	weniger
let (to)	vermieten
letter	Brief
listen (to)	hören
live (to)	wohnen, leben
lose (to)	verlieren
lost	verloren
M	**M**
man	Mann, Mensch
manager	Direktor
map	Landkarte
me	mich
more	mehr
morning	Morgen
much	viel
my	mein, meine, meines
N-O	**N-O**
near	neben
new	neu
next	nächster
not	nicht
now	jetzt
of	von
on	auf
or	oder
order (to)	bestellen
other	anderer, e, es
our	unser, unsere
P	**P**
parcel	Paket
pay (to)	bezahlen
perhaps	vielleicht
piece	Stück
place	Ort, Platz
price	Preis
put (to)	setzen, stellen, legen
Q-R	**Q-R**
quick	schnell
rain	Regen
read (to)	lesen

ITALIAN	FRENCH
meno	moins
affitare	louer
lettera	lettre
ascoltare	écouter
abitare	habiter
perdere	perdre
perduto	perdu

M	**M**
uomo	homme
direttore	directeur
carta	carte
me	moi
piu	plus, davantage (de)
mattino	matin
molto	beaucoup
il mio, la mia, i miei, le mie	mon, ma, mes

N-O	**N-O**
presso, vicino	près
nuovo	neuf, nouveau
prossimo	prochain
non	pas
ora	maintenant
di	de
su, sopra	sur
o, oppure	ou
ordinare	commander
altro, altra	autre
il nostro	nôtre, nos

P	**P**
pacco, pacchetto	paquet
pagare	payer
forse	peut-être
pezzo	morceau
posto, luogo, piazza	endroit, place
prezzo	prix
mettere	mettre

Q-R	**Q-R**
presto	vite
pioggia	pluie
leggere	lire

ENGLISH	GERMAN
remove (to)	mitnehmen
return (to)	zurückkehren
right	Recht
run (to)	laufen

S	**S**
same (the)	dasselbe, dieselben
say (to)	sagen
said	gesagt
see (to)	sehen
seen	gesehen
send (to)	schicken
shop	Laden, Geschäft
short	kurz
shut (to)	schliessen
size	Grösse, Mass
sleep (to)	schlafen
slow	langsam
small	klein
something	etwas
sometimes	manchmal
soon	bald
speak (to)	sprechen
spend (to)	ausgeben
stop (to)	anhalten
straight	rechts
strong	stark
suit	Kostüm, Anzug
swim (to)	schwimmen

T	**T**
table	Tisch
take (to)	nehmen
that	das
the	der, die, dás
their	ihr
then	dann
thing	Sache, Ding
this	dies
time	Zeit
too	zuviel
together	zusammen
town	Stadt

ITALIAN	FRENCH
togliere	enlever
ritornare	retourner
diritto	droit
correre	courir

S	S
lo stesso, la stessa	même (le, la)
dire	dire
detto	dit
vedere	voir
visto	vu
mandare	envoyer
bottega	boutique
corto	court
chiudere	fermer
misura, statura	taille
dormire	dormir
lento	lent
piccolo	petit
qualche cosa	quelque chose
qualche volta	parfois
ben presto	bientôt
parlare	parler
spendere	dépenser
fermare	arrêter
diritto	droit
forte	fort
costume	costume
nuotare	nager

T	T
tavola	table
prendere	prendre
quello	cela
il, lo, la	le, la, les
loro	leur, leurs
poi, quindi	ensuite
cosa	chose
questo	ceci
tempo	temps
troppo	trop
assieme, insieme	ensemble
citta	ville

ENGLISH	GERMAN
U-V	U-V
under	unter
understand (to)	verstehen
understood	verstanden
very	sehr
W-Y	W-Y
walk (to)	gehen
warm	warm
well	gut
what	was
when	wann
where	wo
who	wer
why	warum
with	mit
without	ohne
woman	Frau
write (to)	schreiben
you	Sie, ihr
your	euer, eure, Ihr

ALIAN	FRENCH
-V	U-V
tto	sous
mprendere	comprendre
ito	compris
olto	très
-Y	W-Y
mminare	marcher
ldo	chaud
ene	bien
e	quoi
ando	quand
ove	où
i	qui
erche	pourquoi
n	avec
nza	sans
nna	femme
rivere	écrire
i	vous
vostro, i vostri	votre, vos

INDEX

Drukkerij Holland N.V. — Senefelder
Amsterdam

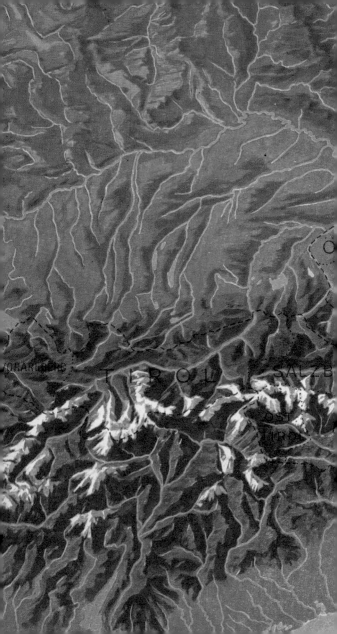